PRAISE FOR *DATA-DRIVEN*

A must-read for professionals and practitioners alike. Unlock your organization's potential and drive real organizational outcomes with this essential guide. All the considerations are here, simplified into a streamlined toolkit, to help you achieve your vision!
Rachel Kuhr Conn, innovation thought leader and Founder of Productable

This book serves as an indispensable guide for the 21st-century landscape of talent management. It's the blueprint organizations need for unlocking the extraordinary capabilities of both individuals and teams, setting them on a trajectory toward unparalleled achievement. If you're looking to transform your talent management capabilities with the right insights and tools necessary for fostering an environment of growth, innovation, and resilience—this is the book for you!
Mika Cross, Workplace Transformation Strategist and Leading Expert on Future of Work

Kris is a shining light. She brings her all to everything she does, inspiring others to excel alongside her. Her diverse background and fearlessness in asking tough questions, coupled with her ability to find even tougher answers, have fostered an environment of innovation in the Army data space and has challenged all of us to lean forward. Kris's legacy will undoubtedly endure for years to come.
Joyce L. Myers, Chief Data Officer, Modern Technology Solutions

When it comes to data and people management, anyone looking to reach the leading edge and incorporate data and AI should study the words and thoughts of Kris Saling. People looking for a resource to get into data-driven talent management must buy this book and get nerdy with Saling.
Jordan Morrow, author of *Be Data Literate* and Chief AI Officer for AgileOne

Kris Saling's book is a brilliant resource for talent management activists and the ways they are enhancing organizations with community heroes. This book is essential reading for anyone who wants to leverage data to optimize their talent management strategies.

Chandra Donelson, United States defense data professional and author of the *Data Detective* series

An absolute masterpiece on how to combine data and 21s-century talent management. Kris is an expert in both disciplines, which she demonstrates brilliantly in this modern approach to solving an age-old problem: recruiting and retaining your most talented employees. Every C-suite officer should read this book.

Major General Tom Drew, Commanding General, US Army Human Resources Command, and former Director, Army Talent Management

Data-Driven Talent Management

Using Analytics to Improve Employee Experience

Kristin Saling

KoganPage

First published in Great Britain and the United States in 2024 by Kogan Page Limited

2nd Floor, 45 Gee Street   8 W 38th Street, Suite 902
London   New York, NY 10018
EC1V 3RS   USA
United Kingdom

www.koganpage.com

Kogan Page books are printed on paper from sustainable forests.

ISBNs
Hardback   978 1 3986 1629 5
Paperback   978 1 3986 1578 6
Ebook   978 1 3986 1630 1

British Library Cataloguing-in-Publication Data
A CIP record for this book is available from the British Library.

Library of Congress Cataloging-in-Publication Data
Names: Saling, Kristin, author.
Title: Data-driven talent management : using analytics to improve employee experience / Kristin Saling.
Description: London, United Kingdom ; New York, NY : Kogan Page, 2024. |
   Includes bibliographical references and index.
Identifiers: LCCN 2024023088 | ISBN 9781398615786 (paperback) | ISBN
   9781398616295 (hardback) | ISBN 9781398616301 (ebook)
Subjects: LCSH: Personnel management–Data processing. | Personnel
   management–Information technology.
Classification: LCC HF5549.5.D37 S35 2024 | DDC
   658.300285–dc23/eng/20240605
LC record available at https://lccn.loc.gov/2024023088

Typeset by Integra Software Services, Pondicherry
Print production managed by Jellyfish
Printed and bound by CPI Group (UK) Ltd, Croydon, CR0 4YY

This book is for my family.

*For my husband and son who supported me by finding
ways to keep themselves and our energetic 80 lb golden retriever
entertained while I wrote.*

*For my parents and sisters who are all authors and creators of much more
lengthy volumes than mine, being academics and such.*

*And for my found family, leaders, and friends, who have talked me out of
retirement from the Army more times than I can count and pushed me to
achieve more than I ever thought possible.*

Thank you for giving me a chance to test my theories, fail, and win.

CONTENTS

PREFACE

Talent management is a strategy, a philosophy, and an approach to creating and managing amazing teams that doesn't just determine an organization's success or failure, but can drive your entire culture and mindset. Understanding the strategy of identifying, hiring, onboarding, developing, employing, promoting, and retaining exceptional talent is essential for any business, both in the public and private sectors, but there's more to this business than just strategy, or even analytics or data.

This goes beyond a human resources function. It fundamentally changes the way you see people. It goes from cataloging your workforce as "how many of what type" to looking deeply into the person, the data, and the potential of "who."

Understanding how we move from "how many" to "who" is at the core of this book, both technically and philosophically. Technically, we'll talk about how data, analytics, assessment, and analyses contribute to how we can understand the "who," but we're very much going to take a philosophical bent through these chapters. We're going to talk about why it's important to understand each and every teammate's knowledge, skills, behaviors, abilities, and other attributes not just from a data perspective, but to understand that human beings are not interchangeable, not when there are so many specific and emerging talents in demand.

We'll talk about how talent management—the strategic identification, acquisition, onboarding, development, employment and utilization, promotion, incentivization, retention, and eventual offboarding—are not just essential functions for businesses and institutions, both in the public and private sectors, to thrive and innovate, but how layering in a data-driven approach, including advanced analytics, automation, and artificial intelligence, is essential for the personalization we've talked about here. It's beyond just a human resources function; it's a core driver of business effectiveness, growth, adaptability, and sustainability.

If I sound like I'm passionate about the concepts and the data, I am, even though my journey into the world of talent management was very much an accident. After serving as an engineer for my first 10 years of commissioned service in the United States Army, I discovered a love for complexity science and data science, particularly in support of work we were doing for theater security cooperation and building ally and partner capacity in the Indo-Pacific. I spent the majority of my time in that field working in highly secure spaces and doing analysis that supported counter-terrorism and counter-threat-finance operations. The only time I encountered anything involving personnel was filling out my own information on manifests.

Doesn't sound like talent management, does it?

Then, as happens with us, after three years at that assignment, around 2016, my career manager reviewed my file as we discussed my next move. I had been working hard to line up a position where I could continue the work I'd been doing, highly secure work informing an important mission, and had spoken with several offices on the Joint Staff who were interested in my skill set. Everything was lining up... until my career manager told me there was no way I was going to back-to-back joint jobs. Instead, I was going to the Headquarters Department of the Army G-1 office to work for the Army Chief of Personnel.

Personnel? I didn't know anything about personnel management.

I began my journey in the G-1 looking to do the kind of work I'd done previously, and to build and support data lakes and analytic platforms. This led me to work with the Assistant Secretary of the Army for Manpower and Reserve Affairs (ASA (M&RA)) on the Human Capital Big Data program, collecting all of our personnel data in a massive data lake underneath an analytic platform that we could use—and still use—to work with this data, create analytic models, and solve leader problems. Additionally, my ideas on how to use data to improve our human systems led me to work with, and set up analytics capabilities for, the Army Talent Management Task Force, U.S. Army Human Resources Command, and U.S. Army Recruiting Command.

While this data and analytics capability is incredibly important, the philosophies I helped develop about talent management were even more critical to changing how the U.S. Army looks at and takes care of people. Moving from assumptions into understanding, from treating people as interchangeable to capitalizing on their unique talents, from one-size-fits-all to tailored development and employment, all of this takes data, but it also takes commitment to the basic philosophy that people are as unique as their fingerprints, and by understanding this uniqueness, we truly understand the depth and breadth of talent in our organizations, and how to acquire, develop, employ, and retain them.

This is the story of how my accidental foray into talent management became a transformative experience, not only for my career but also for my understanding of the critical role that talent plays in driving innovation and growth. I'm hopeful that my discoveries as I stumbled upon a profession that would allow me to unlock the hidden potential within individuals, teams, and organizations, will ultimately help you help your teams reach new heights of success.

Introduction

In today's fast-paced and ever-changing world, organizations have an unprecedented amount of data available to help manage their workforce. However, so many default to a one-size-fits-all standard workplace model, without considering the different ways creative and disparate talent sets need to work, learn, and grow. The more we learn about the various knowledge, skills, and attributes of our workforce, the more we realize that this workforce won't all work the same way.

Data has fundamentally changed the way we conduct business—hyper-accelerating transactions, communication, analysis of markets and environment, and informing decisions. But beyond just harnessing talent data, we must use what we learn in cohesive systems to gain insights into the individuals in our workforce, into their experience and journeys. Through this, we can learn what motivates and engages our employees, what they need to feel productive and valued, and where and how they work best.

To fully leverage the potential of all your workforce talent, it's critical to reshape the way we think about work and the way we think about our personnel. We should not only accommodate but develop methods to understand and maximize different thinking styles, work habits, productivity peaks, talents, and behaviors to enable the creativity that is so crucial in today's environments. We must also balance the different needs of a unique and independently talented and multidisciplinary workforce that still must work together.

By rethinking work from individual to team to organization, moving beyond the industrial one-size-fits-all work environment, employers can create an inclusive workplace where employees, businesses, and new ideas can thrive.

1

Leading Talented Teams in the Age of Data and AI

Teamwork is the ability to work together toward a common vision.
The ability to direct individual accomplishments toward organizational
objectives. It is the fuel that allows common people to attain uncommon
results.

ANDREW CARNEGIE, INDUSTRIALIST AND PHILANTHROPIST[1]

Designing That Winning Team

 When you're told you need to design a winning team, what do you immediately think of?

Maybe you picture a football quarterback dodging back from the line of scrimmage and then spinning away both from the original play and from a defensive lineman before he sprints five yards ahead and fires a hard pass to the wide receiver no one noticed break away. Perhaps you see James Bond, clipping on the latest elegant watch that Q designed for him with a hidden radiation detector as he confers with M and the rest of the MI6 staff on his latest mission, where stealth, agility, and specially engineered gadgets will save the day.

Or you might see the Avengers clustered around a glowing screen as Nick Fury points out the amount of devastation an alien threat has created in a major metropolitan area, a force that only their combined powers can combat.

We're getting fanciful here, but I'm fairly sure you're not picturing an office environment with cubicles, bad lighting, a water cooler, and a whole lot of mind-numbing beige.

I'm pretty sure if you continue to think about that office environment, you're going to start picturing the movie *Office Space*.[2] People come in, they clock in, they're given roughly the same treatment and same assignments, they don't have any upward mobility or motivation, and creativity is stifled in favor of top-down driven direction.

It's no different in the United States Army. I do this same exercise with many Army groups I speak to about using talent management to build winning teams. And when we talk about winning teams, almost everyone describes a Special Forces unit, a team of experts in various fields who come together to leverage their different talents to complete a challenging and dangerous mission. Their realities are often very different, especially outside company-level operations. Cubicles, copiers, routines, endless meetings and calls, lots of slide decks, briefing rehearsals, and not the kind of work that makes them feel empowered to do what many of us joined the military to do: Make a difference.

While a number of organizations, both military and corporate, have invested large amounts of money in things that make their workspace feel more elite—bright colors, white boards and design spaces, technology, and all the various caffeine and snack perks we tend to associate with design spaces—many people don't think about why these things help. And they aren't enough to truly get after what teams need to be effective—the space to be creative, to stretch their full potential individually and together, and the space to innovate.

The foundational understanding of what makes these kinds of teams successful is essential. Let's talk about that.

Your Team Is Not One Size, and Your Structure Does Not Fit All

Success and winning in today's rapidly evolving world starts with the WHY behind the success of the teams we talked about.

That American football team is successful because of the quarterback and the wide receiver, but also because of the coaching team, the medical staff, the general managers, the talent scouts, the marketers, and everyone else who has a hand in making them succeed.

James Bond would be a brawler (albeit an intelligent and creative one) if not for all the scientific work Q does to outfit him behind the scenes, the guidance and mentorship he receives from M, and the intelligence and prep teams that do all the groundwork before he gets launched. And he often ends up with a glamorous, capable, and talented partner along the way.

The Avengers? You get the point. Nick Fury and the S.H.I.E.L.D. team provide direction, intelligence, and boost to the unique capabilities of the superpowered team. And everyone comes to the table with a unique set of talents, experiences, perspectives, needs, and wants.

If a football team were made up of all quarterbacks, it would be far less effective. Even if the team were made up of talented football players at all positions, it's not as effective as the team that takes into account the entire team, and the entire ecosystem.

Inclusive and cohesive teams of multidisciplinary talent are ultimately far more effective than homogenous teams. Organizations that embrace workforces with varied knowledge, skills, and attributes are the ones who win—who have teams that generate fresh ideas, gain insightful new perspectives, and find innovative solutions to complex problems.

This kind of thinking fuels a continuous churn of ideas, enabling organizations to gain and maintain a leading edge in the face of increasingly uncertain challenges. For the U.S. Army, those challenges are ambiguous and spread across time, space, and the physical and digital landscape. Private industry faces much the same, and while they face a market threat more than a physical security threat, it's undeniable that failing to surmount those challenges can mean the end of their existence.

To maintain their proficiency, these teams have to train and develop along different and diverse talent paths in the ways in which they work best. And the likelihood that a collection of unique talents like the ones we've discussed will work in exactly the same way is, well, next to none.

When each individual brings unique strengths, experiences, and thinking styles to the team, they also need to work in unique ways. Even if you have successfully recruited a team with exceptional talents, you aren't going to realize their full benefit if your management style has everyone reporting to an office at the same time to sit in the same kind of cubicle and work on the same schedule during normal business hours. You can't grow them all at the same rate, either, thanks to different skill requirements, learning speeds and styles, aptitudes, and interests. And you can't depend on the idea that just because you employ an individual, you're first on their mind at all times. People have competing responsibilities, desires, and needs that, if left unfulfilled or stifled, will find employment elsewhere.

You just can't squash all this into a typical industrial business model—even if it comes with snacks, coffee, bright furniture, and whiteboards.

So what do we do if we want to build winning teams, if we want to understand people's capabilities and motivations, and how those interact with their teams, the mission, and how they work?

We use actionable insights from data-driven talent management.

So… Why Change?

Every change encounters resistance, and undoubtedly if you are the driver behind changing the way people hire, onramp, promote, employ, develop, incentivize, retain, and offramp employees, someone is going to ask you WHY you even feel the need to change.

You'll hear it all:

- "We've always done it this way."
- "What problem are you trying to solve?"
- "We already do this, I don't see why we have to do it a new way."

[margin note: Accusation Audit]

Personally, the last one is my least favorite, but instead of picking apart the arguments, let's talk about the impetus for change.

We'll start with the Army. Why did the Army need to transition from its original personnel management system to a talent management system?

The U.S. Army's Talent Transformation

The United States Army, like many large organizations, rolled into a manufacturing model for personnel during the 1950s and despite reformations, like the Defense Officer Personnel Management Act of 1980,[3] it has stayed with that model. This model, characterized by hierarchy, standardized processes, and a focus on uniformity, was based on the premise that the Army needed to quickly move people into positions and effectively treat them as interchangeable. The sole differentiating factors that were used fell under two categories, and were used to assume a great deal of information about the knowledge, skills, and behaviors of an individual: Grade/rank and branch/specialty.

This system worked when the Army had to consider a very narrow range of skills and specialties. During conflict throughout the 20th century, most engagements needed some combination of fire and maneuver in ground warfare, or supporting activities such as engineering, aviation, and logistics. However, the nature of warfare has evolved significantly since that time.

In the past, warfare was often characterized by conventional, state-to-state conflicts with clearly defined fronts, known capabilities required, and well-understood strategies. However, today's conflicts are marked by ambiguity, hybrid warfare, non-state actors, underground and insurgent movements, as well as digital and unmanned attacks and cyber-attacks, making them significantly more challenging to predict and navigate. Advances in technology mean we no longer focus on physical domains of conflict, but need expertise in the cyber and space domains as well. The changing nature of decisions made in conflict meant that many functions the Army hadn't considered before not only needed to be part of the team, but wearing a uniform. And the ambiguous and ever-changing global landscape also meant that requirements for roles and capabilities emerged in Army structure far faster than the personnel system could fill.[4]

The traditional personnel management system we used, which was designed for conventional warfare, wasn't nearly agile enough to address these new challenges. Unconventional conflicts require expertise in areas like cyber warfare, information warfare, security cooperation, counter-insurgency operations, building coalitions, building partner capacity, and cultural intelligence, just to name a few. Typical skills constructs weren't built to capture this kind of information and often resulted in the Army trying to create whole new branches, rather than doing inventories to see what skills might already be present in the formation, or what skillsets were the closest to the new requirement and could get there with just a little bit of training.

We couldn't rely on the old paradigm. Instead, we had to move away from mere process improvement and totally transform how we do business in the realm of talent management.

> What we're talking about here was captured well in the 10 percent vs 10x change concept popularized by Peter Thiel in *Zero to One: Notes on startups, or how to build the future*. The concept argues that there are two types of process improvement: Incremental (10 percent) and transformative (10x or tenfold). Most organizations focus on making incremental improvement, but sometimes to succeed you need to reframe the problem, take apart the system, change components, or even design something new altogether.[5]

This led us to initial forays into talent management. We experimented with new means of categorizing people's capabilities and aligning those capabilities with the roles we needed them to fill, and developing algorithms that let us use our personnel data to do that. We discovered how we needed to improve our data quality and engineer our data systems to improve model performance. We experimented with assessments and with job analysis to fill in the gaps where we didn't have enough data either on people's capabilities or the needs of the job to create a good match, or figure out how to best train the capability in our force.

A talent-based approach enables the Army to identify individuals with the right attributes and experiences for various roles regardless of whether they serve in a particular grade or role. And a data-driven talent management approach helps us do this quickly, efficiently, and at scale. Data can help us identify trends, emerging threats, and opportunities both for the roles we need people to fill and the capabilities we need to find, and it can help us continuously learn and adapt. It helps us develop programs to upskill and reskill and rapidly evolve to meet new challenges as they emerge. It helps us learn if there is enough of a demand signal for a new type of skill or capability that we need to create a new functional area, train it across the force, or use rapid hiring authorities to bring in advisory expertise. It helps us rapidly meet those emerging requirements with solutions. And, thinking proactively instead of reactively, it helps us personalize and cultivate development plans for our individuals and teams, wherever they are on their career journey.

We are eight years into our transformation and we continue to learn and grow. And while we have not mastered all of the principles, practices, and capabilities I'm going to lay out for you in this book, we have come a long way in improving how we think about people, how we think about talent, and how we manage and use data.

Talent Management Transformation Beyond the U.S. Army

What I hope to share with you in this book is a combination of lessons learned and research I've done in the talent management space. We're all facing the same imperative to change from traditional, industrial-based management models to talent-based data-driven models, whether that's due to the rapid pace of technological advancements, shifting customer and employee expectations, globalization, the increasing understanding of the power of data, the need for innovation, or compliance with new emerging regulations. While we might have very different mission sets, the end result is the same—we want more modern, more personalized, more agile methods for acquiring, developing, employing, and retaining our people.

The competition in this space is getting fierce. My senior leaders and the chief executives of the businesses we partner with have all cited the same issue: When it comes to particular types of talent, particularly technical talent, there just isn't enough of it. We're all in fierce competition for the talent that there is, and in the public sector, we know we can't compete with the raw compensation options that the private sector has. Even large public sector companies like Amazon[6] can't hire enough technical talent, and must grow it from within. Amazon runs a multitude of different training experiences from on-the-job training to an academy/university experience to give their people the skills they need.

This opens a new set of problems for us beyond just how to effectively grow our talent and hire the people we need, but balancing the expectations of our employees and customers against the experiences they have with other organizations. It isn't just the experience with our organization that can change someone's perspective, but the distance between that experience and what they have had with other organizations and expect to have!

Why Experience Matters

Experience matters, and we're not just talking about the kind of experience you want to see on someone's resumé. We're talking about the customer or employee perceptions of value for a delivered product or service.

McKinsey defines customer experience as "everything an organization does to deliver superior experiences, value, and growth for customers."[7] Organizations deploy new capabilities almost daily to try to capture data on this experience, and we've collected a wealth of knowledge on what people need and want in terms of value and experience.

However, expectations for that experience are changing rapidly, driven by technological advancements, changing societal values, and the availability of data on the responses to those experiences. When people engage your personnel services, their expectations will be shaped by these experiences, whether they have to do with human resources or not.

What kind of experiences are we talking about?

The first type we'll talk about is **personalization**. Between Amazon's powerful product recommendation engines showing us exactly what kind of neat gadget to put on our wish-lists, Netflix and other streaming services gaining increased ability to provide us with the content we most want to watch next after that last great show we binge-watched, and other services catered to our specifications, we want our experiences to be fit for us. We don't want to go hunting for the things we might like or the roles we might be good at—we expect our likes and wants to be cataloged and best-fit alternatives to be presented.

For talent management purposes, this translates to personalized and individual career development plans, training and learning programs, and an approach to our needs that takes into account our strengths, growth areas, and preferences. It also translates into the next kind of change we're seeing in experience, which varies widely across generations.

This falls in line with personalization, but the second thing we're seeing increasing is the overall demand for positive and modern **digital experience**. People have far less tolerance for clunky websites or unhelpful customer service call centers than ever before, and in terms of talent management, far less tolerance for job application websites that drop your application after a cursory screening that drops key words, or don't give you feedback about where your application is in the job process. We want our job applications, school and certificate requests, counseling and coaching, and other talent management experiences to be as seamless as a sophisticated virtual agent can make rebooking a canceled flight or hotel room.

Along with modern experiences, we are demanding **transparency** and **ethical standar**ds. Just as we evaluate companies on their clear communication, ethical sourcing, fair labor practices, and openness about how their data is collected and used, we're evaluating our human resources departments and talent management programs the same way. People have much less tolerance than previously for solutions and processes that are "black box" or "proprietary." Trust hinges on clear understanding and communication. This applies for any kind of program, but especially for programs like talent management, where we're asking people to trust how we manage their pay, benefits, development, and other things with the potential to significantly impact their quality of life and quality of work.

Customers and employees both prefer interactions with companies that place **focus on employee well-being and positive corporate culture**. We often prefer to engage with businesses that show a genuine concern for our well-being and offer things like flexible working conditions, mental health support, inclusive practices, and employee benefits that they see as valuable. This kind of value alignment also shows in expectations for corporate social responsibility, or the ability of a business to contribute positively to society. We'll talk about this in future chapters as we talk about creating the culture you need for innovative teams.

As we think about innovation, there's a growing expectation that businesses should offer **innovative solutions and technical proficiency**. With the rapid advancement of technology, we value businesses that invest in building the levels of creativity and expertise to not only keep up with the tech, but to create cutting-edge solutions. This places extra emphasis on the kind of talent management models we want to create, which enable you to create innovative teams.

Finally, let's talk about the broad interconnectedness of our world and markets. **Globalization** has connected the world, affecting both private and public organizations. Geopolitical dynamics and international relations impact business operations and strategies significantly. Agility and data-driven decision making are crucial to adapt to global changes, whether they involve trade policies, security concerns, or market opportunities. Businesses need to remain vigilant, responsive, and well-informed, which a talent based data-driven model facilitates.

So how do we go about getting after these things? The answer, fortunately for us, is **data**.

The ability to collect, analyze, and leverage data is a competitive advantage in any arena, but especially in talent management. Traditional management models often struggle to extract meaningful insights from data, because they often don't collect enough of it or the right kind. Creating an effective data-driven talent management model takes a holistic look at the experience of an employee and uses data both for individual moments and longitudinally, over the course of a career. This takes time and deliberate planning, but the great thing is that you can iterate over time, add more data for more personalization, and promote more flexibility with policy changes.

As a side benefit, data-driven talent management helps promote a culture of data literacy, providing you with more use cases to drive data-informed decisions, make your operations more flexible, and promote both continuous process improvement and innovation!

Innovation is a critical component for businesses to stay competitive, whether they're operating in the public or private sector. The data-driven talent-based approach we're going to lay out in this book can help you promote an environment where individual skills, creativity, and innovation are valued and nurtured. We'll talk about how to use these skills independently and in teams, and how to bridge that gap. Effective collaboration between creative teams can lead to breakthrough solutions in innovation but also supports continuous improvement programs, improving your overall operational efficiency, and the curiosity you generate with these initiatives creates a culture for continuous improvement.

Let's talk about how data plays into the process.

Understanding Uniqueness and Talent Through Data

Information is exploding. In the last 30 years, with the birth of the internet, we have learned, consumed, and shared information at an incredible rate. We have blown past the Buckminster Fuller Knowledge Doubling Curve,[8] which observed that until 1900, human knowledge doubled approximately every century, accelerating to every 25 years by the end of World War II. From the introduction of the internet, human knowledge was estimated to double every 13 months. With the Internet of Things, a report from IBM anecdotally reduced that to about every 12 hours, compounding the problem of finding knowledge with finding *useful* knowledge. One author argues that we "have reached a point where relevant knowledge is increasing faster than we can absorb...[and] while knowledge is increasing, the useful lifespan of knowledge is decreasing."[9]

It's difficult to say where those metrics are now, but with the amount of content being produced on news websites, online journals, blogs, and every social media platform, information available continues to grow. Sifting through this information to separate actual fact from fiction, relevant knowledge from old news, and useful items from misinformation goes far beyond human capability. Just to make sense of the volume of content, we need advanced analytics and AI.

Fortunately, advances in compute power and cloud technology have given us the ability to run the large statistical models needed to condense this information into more palatable bites. We've learned to crunch this information down into useful components and display it in charts, graphs, and dashboards for rapid consumption, or develop it into user interfaces and mobile applications that we can quickly review and use to guide our days.

We've incorporated these into our personal business processes as much as we have into work. We've developed processes that allow a user to summon literally anything to their doorstep. From food and groceries, to a ride, or even a new car, we can order a variety of items using a mobile application, and we capture this data so we can build robust repositories of information on what we consume and get recommendations on what we might need or want to buy next.

Recently, we have seen another explosion of these capabilities in the form of generative AI interfaces. Generative AI "is a type of artificial intelligence technology that broadly describes machine learning systems capable of generating text, images, code, or other types of content, often in response to a prompt entered by a user."[10] The models behind these systems have been around for a while, but the chat interfaces make them truly impressive. Prior to this, we had low-code and no-code software solutions available to help organizations build data-driven solutions to problems, but these solutions utilize AI to take in and interpret a non-technical user request and return an answer. While these answers come with all the caveats we should apply to our Google searches (i.e. does this come from an authoritative source, can I fact check it across several sources, etc.?), they come to us quickly and in a way that is easily actionable.

Both as a capability and as an experience, generative AI has served as a catalyst for organizations to step up their data collection and incorporation of analytics and artificial intelligence. However, no algorithm, predictive model, or generated AI response is truly useful until we've thought through the use case—the story we are trying to understand, the decision we are trying to make, whatever it is we need this information to inform.

So what exactly do we mean by use cases in talent management? When you think through the total experience journey of your individuals or your teams, what are the decisions you need to make about how those journeys unfold? Here are a few things that you'll need to think about and decide on for talent management that make good analytic use cases:

1 **Recruiting.** Analyzing patterns, trends, and correlation in personnel data, economic data, socio-political data, and other regional information, both geographic and internet locale based, we can gain valuable insights into the recruitment channels that yield the highest-quality candidates for particular areas of focus.

2 **Retention.** By understanding employee preference, performance and satisfaction metrics, assessments, market indicators, and employability statistics, we can build predictive models to better anticipate workforce needs, churn rates, and what incentives are likely to make certain employee groups more likely to stay with the organization if needed.

3 **Training.** Data analysis can be used to understand career aspirations, what training events provide the best return on investment, and what sets of skills, attributes, and motivations are best suited to upskill/reskill into an emerging requirement.

4 **Performance.** Personnel data enables organizations to measure performance, evaluate against career aspirations, and both offer and provide targeted interventions. Top-performing employees can be incentivized

and rewarded, and underperforming employees can receive feedback, performance improvement plans, and additional support.

5 **Personalized experience.** Understanding that every employee is unique, with different skills, aspirations, and work preferences, we understand that their personal experience will also be unique. Creative use of personnel data allows organizations to create tailored development plans, flexible work arrangements, and recognition programs that align with each person's strengths, goals, and preferences.

Collected data show the linkages between talent acquisition, performance, and retention. In the past, these fields relied heavily on subjective evaluation and gut instinct. However, analysis of resumés, applications, assessments, and performance evaluations delivers more information on best-fit candidates for different roles and emerging requirements. Matched with preferences, career aspirations, and areas where employees need support, development, and coaching, organizations can develop robust workforce development plans.

As the data picture for the individual grows, we start being able to see just how unique each employee is, with different skills, aspirations, and work preferences. Employee experience data enables organizations to personalize the experience, creating tailored developmental plans, flexible work arrangements, and recognition programs that align with each employee's strengths and goals. This personalized approach, paired with strong leadership skills, fosters high levels of engagement, job satisfaction, and performance among personnel.

As we see this robust data picture developing for each individual, we must look at the data picture we have for the team and the organization as a whole. This data needs to be harnessed and leveraged in cohesive systems that look at the entirety of the lifecycle and ecosystem of each individual to provide insights about these talents in the context of how they work—their experiences, journeys, motivations, and needs.

A Framework for Building Talented Teams

I've started to think about bridging the balance between prioritizing team cohesion and respecting team member individuality as *the Nick Fury model*. Nick Fury, for those who aren't versed in Marvel lore, directs the Avengers Initiative and a band of very unique, individual, and independent superheroes.

While he might not have any extraordinary superpowers himself, he is extraordinary at building superpowered teams.

When you're bringing together a team of independent people and unique talents, it's easy to want to place yourself in the hero seat. We all want to be the stars of our story. By taking a step back into the coordinator role and not the superhero role, it's easier to identify the different talents your team brings to the table, and better appreciate and manage those resources.

Using lessons learned from developing management systems for unique and creative talent and teams, inside one of the world's largest employers and largest bureaucracies, this book will guide you through data-driven talent management practices that will let you create an inclusive, innovative, and thriving workplace.

We'll be discussing a personalized framework for managing talent primarily for interdisciplinary and cross-functional groups and creating a culture in which they will thrive. That framework (and the way this book is organized) largely follows this construct:

1. **Create and foster a creative and innovative culture.** For a team to function, no matter what kind of team it is, team members must feel energized and free to think, create, and take risks, like their contributions are valued, and like they are empowered to take on challenges. This involves communication, trust, and a learning mindset.

2. **Create the data framework for understanding and contextualizing talent.** To give people a clear understanding of their strengths and weaknesses, how to progress best, and what opportunities are available to them, you need a common language of talent.

3. **Recruit and hire for unique capability.** Actively seek out a varied set of skills across technical and non-technical perspectives. You can't create a winning team if you hire all quarterbacks. Consider backgrounds, skills, experiences, and perspectives. Who is on your dream team of superheroes?

4. **Develop a clear vision and goals.** Ensure that team members have a common understanding of purpose, objectives, and outcomes, and how to best align their individual goals with overall team objectives to foster purpose and cohesion.

5. **Provide training and development opportunities.** Offer individual development experiences that cater to the unique needs and talents of your team members, but also provide opportunities for knowledge sharing and cross-functional learning so that your team learns not just how to work, but how to work well together.

6 Encourage collaboration and cross-pollination. Bring together individuals from different disciplines and backgrounds to share ideas and perspectives, and work towards breakthrough thinking.

7 Embrace thinking differently. Encourage unique and novel approaches to problem solving. Create space for structured and unstructured thinking processes.

8 Promote autonomy and provide support. Give team members the room to experiment, take risks, and explore ideas. See failure as a learning opportunity and an important data point. Offer resources, guidance, and mentorship to help team members navigate challenges and overcome obstacles.

9 Foster innovation rituals and processes. These can include regular brainstorming and design sessions, idea-sharing platforms, hackathons, or other places to converge and generate, evaluate, and implement ideas.

10 Recognize and reward innovation. Celebrate successes, big and small, and publicly recognize the efforts of individuals who contribute to the team's initiatives.

11 Continuously learn and improve. Don't let people become complacent when they reach an objective. Encourage team members to reflect on their experiences, share lessons learned, and use their success as momentum for their ongoing trajectory.

The chapters that follow will dig deeper into these topics. We'll explore the power of data in talent management, from understanding team motivations to understanding, leveraging, and developing different thinking styles and work habits. We will also discuss strategies for maximizing different talents and behaviors, balancing the diverse needs of a workforce, and rethinking work from the individual to the team to the organization's perspective, so we see how to build the entire ecosystem to maximize talent, creativity, and innovation.

By adopting the principles and practices outlined in this book, I hope to empower you to reframe your thinking about how we work as individuals, how we work together, and how we can work as cohesive teams that celebrate our differences while working toward a common objective. We'll talk about building a culture of innovation that values and thrives on new and different perspectives and ideas. And we'll develop processes that support organizational agility, trust, a mindset geared toward curiosity and growth, and ultimately create a workplace where employees, businesses, and new ideas can thrive.

If you're ready to build your winning and innovative team, let's go.

How to Use This Book

My goal for this book is not to teach you the math and the analytics behind creating a data-driven talent management program. Technology and techniques advance so quickly, it would be out of date by publication. The use cases, thinking processes, data collection and analysis methods, and recommendations on how and when to incorporate analysis, automation, and artificial intelligence, however, can be used no matter how simple or advanced your analytics are in maturity level.

By offering you this kind of a guide, we can work through not just creating the building blocks for collecting and analyzing the kind of talent data you need to run these kinds of programs, but creating the vision and strategy you need to employ that data across the diversely talented, flexibly thinking, and creative workforce you need to win in today's competitive environment.

We wouldn't try to create a one-size-fits-all talent management method for a workforce who deserve a tailored approach, so let's instead explore how to set up the framework and processes for you to create the system you need to empower your individuals, empower your talent management teams, and empower your business leaders to make data-driven talent management decisions.

Empowering Individuals

One of the central tenets of a data-driven talent management playbook is empowering individuals to take ownership of their professional growth and career development. How can you give your employees opportunities to evaluate their strengths and weaknesses, both in the context of their performance and in their career aspirations? We'll talk about how to employ *self-assessment* and *professional development* to help individuals align their goals with their best potential for performing. We'll also talk about how to use self-assessment and goal-setting for data-driven *workforce development and skill enhancement*. Data can help you know where to best tie in your organization's learning resources and learning management systems, and where to offer self-initiated education opportunities, empowering your employees to come up with actionable plans that not only help them perform for you, but help them meet their individual goals.

When you enable all of these processes through digital applications and learning management systems, you will gain the ability to show people their progress and show them their future opportunities. You'll also gain data to show to your business learning professionals so that they can gauge employee engagement, learning curves, and other offerings they should make available for skill development.

Having these kinds of feedback and learning systems that can contribute to career progression, compensation, and other advancement incentivizes your individuals to provide their data, where they might not otherwise. In my team development efforts, we've called this the Waze[11] model, based on the traffic application. In exchange for providing the application with your data, it brings that data together with data it receives from transportation authorities and other users, and provides you with a better route to get where you want to go. And it incentivizes you to take certain routes by avoiding tolls or gaining time. You can take the same approach to your organizational assessment and development programs if you draw a direct line between having folks submit their data in assessments, surveys, and other instruments and receiving the benefit of better understanding their performance and potential!

Supporting HR Professionals

It's all well and good to say that we can do these wonderful things with data and systems, but someone is going to have to manage and implement all of these things, coordinate how they're going to be used and updated, and figure out the framework that makes them all work. Unless your organization has an office of the chief of talent management, these people are most likely your people analytics professionals and human resource analysts. Let's talk a little about how we can help them exercise their responsibilities.

We'll talk about how to take your talent management use cases and set up your *data collection plans* and *data governance plans*, along with identifying rules, regulations, laws, and statutes you're going to want to have in place for sensitive data. We'll talk about the type of data you want to collect, the analytics you want to use to inform your decisions, and a little about how to construct your analytics teams and decision cycles.

The two major places your human resource professionals will engage, though, are constructing your *competency frameworks* and your *employee engagement and experience*. Competency frameworks help you contextualize self-assessment and assessment data and your job requirement data into comparable sets. You'll need to compare these so that you can align the right talent to the right job, figure out trends that show you when jobs or skills need to be updated, and look at the performance and potential of your workforce. Data collected and evaluated against these competency frameworks at multiple points in the employee journey can show you not just their performance, but growth and development over time, potential learning curves in emerging areas, and goodness of fit for emerging requirements.

Monitoring data on employee engagement helps you improve the overall experience for better attraction and retention. We'll talk about how to create an inclusive, creative, innovative work environment focused on a growth mindset and the flexibility needed to attract diverse talent, how to apply recognition and rewards, how to think about and assess motivation, and other practices that show employees that their efforts are heard and valued by your organization.

Guiding Organizational Leaders

For those of you who lead your organizations, this is a strategic resource to help you craft your strategic vision for how you'll partner with your human resource professionals and analysts to create that winning team. You're the general manager of that star football team, you're Billy Beane in *Moneyball*, you're the one with the vision about how we're going to take what we need to know about our work and our people and align that with organizational goals.

Aligning talent management strategies with your overarching goals and objectives is a critical part of having a successful effort. We don't acquire, develop, employ, and retain talent just for talent's sake, but to help you and your organization develop the best teams possible with the skills to tackle your mission sets, now and in the future. You can use this alignment (and analyze it through data!) to ensure your talent management decisions are in sync with the company mission, and that you're emphasizing the skills, competencies, and incentive programs that will drive success.

But wait... how do we use data to do that? We'll talk about *accountability and measurement*, and how we develop metrics, objectives, and indicators for evaluating your initiatives across the organization. We will work on developing a maturity model for your talent management and employee experience practices and teach you how to use these indicators to hold teams and departments accountable for their talent management efforts.

And we'll talk about both transformation and continuous process improvement. While everyone loves a 10x change, sometimes all you need is that incremental improvement. No project or program is created perfectly at the first shot. Or the second, or the seventh. We'll pick things to transform and things that can just be made better by a few efficiencies.

Chapter Summary

This data-driven talent management playbook isn't going to provide you with a lot of formulas or code, or a rigid step-by-step process, but a framework for you to use to create your vision and your strategy, your data collection and governance plans, and most importantly, the vision, use cases, and concept of a culture focused on creating the best bench of talent and the individuals and teams focused on helping you meet your organizational goals. By following the guidelines and practices in this book, you'll learn new ways to think about harnessing the full potential of your diverse and talented workforce through innovation, creativity, and, of course, data and analytics.

Notes

1 Scott McLean (2015) *Business Communication for Success v. 2.0*, Flatworld

2 Office Space (1999) Written and directed by Mike Judge

3 Bernard D. Rostker, Harry J. Thie, James L. Lacy, Jennifer H. Kawata, and Susanna W. Purnell (1993) *The Defense Officer Personnel Management Act of 1980: A retrospective assessment*, RAND Corporation. www.rand.org/pubs/reports/R4246.html (archived at https://perma.cc/5HCT-YMPN)

4 Peter Zeihan (2022) *The Accidental Superpower: The next generation of American preeminence and the coming global disorder*, Twelve

5 Peter Thiel (2001) *Zero to One: Notes on startups, or how to build the future*, Virgin Books

6 "Our Upskilling 2025 programs," Amazon, www.aboutamazon.com/news/workplace/our-upskilling-2025-programs (archived at https://perma.cc/29N9-NE7B)

7 Rachel Diebner, David Malfara, Kevin Neher, Mike Thompson, and Maxence Vancauwenbergh (2021) "Prediction: The Future of CX," McKinsey, www.mckinsey.com/capabilities/growth-marketing-and-sales/our-insights/prediction-the-future-of-cx (archived at https://perma.cc/R5M6-9GY7)

8 R. Buckminster Fuller (1981) *Critical Path*, St. Martin's Press

9 Paul Chamberlain (2020) "Knowledge is Not Everything," *Design for Health*, 4 (1)

10 Owen Hughes (2023) "Generative AI Defined: How it Works, Benefits, and Dangers," Tech Republic, www.techrepublic.com/article/what-is-generative-ai/ (archived at https://perma.cc/R5M6-9GY7)

11 Scott Orgera (2020) "What is Waze and How Does It Work?" Lifewire, www.lifewire.com/what-is-waze-4153570 (archived at https://perma.cc/WWF9-YFVW)

2

Cultivating Creativity and Innovation to Tackle Complex Problems

Creativity is thinking up new things. Innovation is doing new things.
THEODORE LEVITT, ECONOMIST AND LEGENDARY MARKETING SCHOLAR
AT HARVARD BUSINESS SCHOOL[1]

Seed Your Teams in Fertile Ground for Ideas

We're going to spend a great deal of time here talking about how to understand and contextualize the unique talent we want, how to exercise elements of the Talent Management Model for your best hires and best teams, and how to encourage those teams to work together and apart toward your organizational goals. However, before we get into those elements, I want to talk about how we build the environment those teams need in order to succeed and thrive, and that's one that values and fosters a culture of creativity and innovation.

For a team to function, no matter what kind of team, your team members need to feel energized and free to think, create, and take risks. They need to feel like their contributions and trials are valued and properly incentivized, and like they are empowered to take on challenges. This involves communication, trust, and a learning mindset—and the proper application of data both to facilitate the creative process and to assess the environment.

The right kind of environment for your teams provides the fuel they need to tackle your most complex problems. It's one where they are both aligned on the vision and mission of your organization and propelled toward new ideas and ways of doing business, but where they also have the relaxed constraints they need to bring their very different perspectives, knowledge, skills, and other attributes to bear in solving problems. When you're dealing with complex problems that don't have straightforward solutions, you need enough diversity of perspective to generate novel ideas, and you need innovation to take those ideas and turn them into action, into new ways of doing business.

Let's talk a little bit about the "why" of innovation, how creativity drives innovation, how data and analytics play into the mix, and how you can bring all of these things to bear to create an environment that really unleashes your teams and their creative energy.

The Quest for Innovation

Our world today is characterized by constant change, ambiguous threats, and unprecedented challenges. That has driven all of us to seek creative and innovative solutions for our problems, so much that both words have become buzzwords cheapened by overuse and a lack of common understanding of what they mean. But that doesn't mean the principles aren't still incredibly important for our organizations to understand and foster.

So what exactly *are* creativity and innovation and why should we be so interested in them? And what does that have to do with data-driven talent management?

Innovation and creativity have been explored and defined several different ways, some synonymously, some differently, and sometimes as complementary pairs, with creativity being the first half of the process, where ideas are generated, and innovation being the second half, the implementation. In plain language, *creativity* is defined as "the ability to make or otherwise bring into existence something new, whether a new solution to a problem, a new method or device, or a new artistic object or form"[2] and *innovation* as "the creation of a new way of doing something, whether the enterprise is concrete (e.g. the development of a new product) or abstract (e.g. the development of a new philosophy or theoretical approach)."[3] My team is more in line with the combination of the two terms as parts of the same overall process.

We define creativity as a cognitive attribute we use to generate ideas for innovation, which we define as the methodology for quickly taking a portfolio of novel solutions—products, processes, or practices—from ideation through rapid testing and down-selecting to scaling and implementation.

While a lot of organizations tend to focus on creativity and the disruptive nature of novel solutions, that's only part of the process.

> **Creativity** is the process of generating novel ideas.
>
> **Innovation** is a business process, the application of transforming these novel Ideas to bring about tangible and valuable change in terms of scalable and integrated products, processes, or practices. In other words, creativity is the seed of innovation.

So why is that important again? Novel solutions are great, but why should we be so concerned about them to the point where it becomes a cornerstone in how we think about managing our people and our teams?

We're dealing with a very dynamic global landscape right now, with rapid advancements in technology, changing customer expectations, and evolving trends. We have to have more flexibility built into our strategies than ever before, and we often can't wait to bring a new capability online across the entirety of our organization to figure out whether it does what it's supposed to or not. Innovation gives us the way to rapidly adapt to changes through testing and experimentation on small populations. The portfolio aspect of it is the most important, because if we can rapidly test a small portfolio of solutions rather than hanging everything on one large solution, we not only have a better chance of selecting something that will work, but we also have the ability to forecast return on investment through the results of the experiment.

Innovation often leads to efficiency and productivity. As we examine processes, we don't always find that we need a fully transformative solution, but we get a better understanding of how the system works. That lets us find places where we can integrate automation, streamline workflows, purchase new technologies, or find other ways to improve our operations. Sometimes my team begins just with a process improvement project when we know we are going to need to transform the system. That efficiency project often gives us the evidence we need to prove that the system itself needs to be transformed, and to understand how.

Ironically, I can say that innovation leads to better risk management. Innovation by its nature means there has to be a willingness to resource and accept risk. Because of that, it forces our decision makers to determine how we want to accept that risk in our portfolios. When we're actually evaluating a diverse batch of solutions for testing, we might find that we're not accepting *enough* risk, that we've put everything in safe low-yield bonds, and for actual growth, we need to push the envelope in a few other places.

And finally, collaboration and partnership is a huge reason to take on innovation challenges. You'll be able to take ideas from all throughout your organization and collaborate with other external partners (e.g. startups and research institutions) to bring in even more new perspectives and resources to get after complex problems.

Convinced? Let's dig a little bit deeper into the relationship between creativity and innovation,

How Does Creativity Drive Innovation?

In a corporate context, innovation is the lifeblood of growth. And without creativity, innovation stalls. If you don't have a mechanism for seeing all aspects of a problem set, sometimes ones that you haven't previously considered, you risk turning innovation into a checklist without the perspective and spark needed for truly transformative solutions. A workplace that encourages and rewards creativity is fertile ground for these kinds of solutions to grow and thrive.

Creativity has been the cornerstone of human progress throughout history, driving advancement in art, science, and technology, and, in periods such as the Renaissance, all three at once. Da Vinci and Michaelangelo both famously blended art with scientific inquiry, leading to groundbreaking works like da Vinci's Vitruvian Man and Michaelangelo's David. Sir Isaac Newton blended mathematics and philosophy when formulating the laws of motion and universal gravity. And in the realm of technology, creativity continues to be exceptionally pivotal. Google has famously encouraged creativity through a policy of allowing and encouraging employees to spend 20 percent of their time on side projects, which has led to successful products like Gmail and AdSense.[4]

Giving people not just time but also incentives and resources to think creatively in their workplace lets them adapt to environmental changes, get the freedom to shift their perspective and mindset when dealing with complex problems, and identify opportunities for innovation. We saw a great deal of this during the Covid-19 quarantine, when many businesses had to drastically change their business models.[5] The evidence of innovation became especially clear looking at restaurants that were able to stay open and ones that had to close. The ones that clung fiercely to their old business model failed. However, other food businesses that were able to update their business models creatively did well. Some embraced food delivery services like DoorDash, GrubHub, and Seamless, while others set up takeaway storefronts and separate sub-businesses that cooked out of their same kitchen. Outdoor dining venues and igloo dining increased in demand. And in the middle of all this change, restaurants found additional benefits in all these safety precautions. Menus became digital, and therefore very easy to update for daily specials or when something was out of stock. Some restaurants converted quickly to having all transactions done through phone apps rather than expensive point-of-sale systems. All of these little efficiencies contributed to restaurant business models and customer experience (even if some people still resist the QR-code menu!).

This isn't the first time we've seen dramatic change happen to a business market, and it won't be the last. Let's think back to the failure of Kodak. Kodak built its business direction on film and printers, and even though Kodak *invented* the digital camera, they focused on investing in ways to get more people to print their photos and buy their printers rather than modernizing their business model. Sharing digital photos online became the new normal, not a way to expand the current business model.[6] Unless organizations learn how to better adapt through creativity and innovation, stories like this will increase, especially as the introduction of new technologies continues to rapidly change our experience expectations.

This isn't solely a culture or a social task—it's also a data-driven task. Organizations need to understand the creative strengths, weaknesses, and preferences of their employees to harness their full innovative potential. This is where data and analytics come into play.

Data and analytics play a crucial role in understanding and fostering creativity in your organization. By analyzing data on your employees that contributes to a deeper understanding of every step of the Talent Management Model, you can identify creative strengths and weaknesses across teams and incorporate that into other functions in the model.

Let's talk about how to do that.

The Role of Data and Analytics in Creativity

Data is a tool for enhancing intuition.

HILARY MASON[7]

Data and analytics aren't the first things we think of when we start talking about creativity and innovation, and it's easy to lose the actual story in dry numbers. I've started many of my speaking engagements after my introduction as a data scientist with jokes about promising not to say "percent" too many times, because all that shining I want to see in the audience is from understanding smiles, not eyes that have glazed over. But whether your mind drifts when you hear "percent" said too many times or not, data and analytics are your most powerful allies in fostering creativity and flexibility in the workplace. And that's something you need to keep in mind when creating your talent data collection plan.

Wait, don't most data plans start with rigid collection rules and strict governance? Those are necessary components, but you need to think about what is possible when you truly understand the capability and potential of the people you work with.

Consider Google. My team has had several meetings over the years with Google's talent management team to share best practices and insights, and their people analytics teams do some incredible work analyzing optimal team sizes, meeting frequency, workplace design, and even the design and offerings of their campus in Mountain View. They do a masterful job of understanding and personalizing employee experience, and then tailoring their processes to make sure that their teams operate in an environment conducive to their unique talents.

Similarly, Adobe leverages data to understand how and where its employees work best. They use insights to tailor flexible work arrangements and optimize schedules that align with both the best collaboration times and peak productivity periods of their teams. Figuring out how to create that alignment is always one of my top goals when assembling teams. This can be done with a combination of performance management data, feedback, and calendar data.

Data and analytics help you personalize not only experience and ways of work, but the creative process itself. Not surprisingly, Netflix[8] and Spotify[9] also apply the data-driven approaches they use to present you with the best content to consume on your platform within their own organizations. They collect and analyze information on individual creative strengths and cognitive styles, and can use that to tailor creativity training and problem-solving approaches in a way best suited for consumption by particular employees. You can do this, too, using a combination of feedback data, assessments, and learning and development data analysis.

Wait, did we say creativity training? Yes, even though it sounds counterintuitive, we can measure and manage creativity through data! We can analyze project outcomes, client feedback, and team collaboration patterns to gauge just how effective our creative processes are, and whether or not the solutions we're producing are novel in some unique way. Objective assessments in these spaces can help us better understand where we can further nurture or streamline creativity in our organizations.

A data-driven approach also helps us promote the culture of curiosity and continuous improvement we discussed earlier. Through the creation of feedback loops, we can constantly refine our strategies to enhance creativity and figure out where we don't necessarily need a novel solution to totally change our processes, but where we can still make them more efficient through project management, Lean Six Sigma, or other process efficiency techniques.

All this goes to show that data and analytics are far from rigid tools, but important allies in enhancing creativity, flexibility, and experience in the workplace. By collecting, analyzing, and leveraging data about how people perform and where and when they perform best, you can gain valuable insights into individual and collective creative behaviors.

Unleashing Creativity and Innovation on Complex Problems

In this dynamic world of ours, the journey toward unleashing creativity and innovation on the most difficult problems you face is one where you first have to challenge a lot of the traditional notions of work. We've been challenging traditional notions of how we look at the workforce, as individual people with unique skills and not as a pay grade and job series. To really capitalize on their skills and to utilize the power of their differences, not just catalog them, we have to rethink how we think about work.

That doesn't mean we work without rules. We aren't completely unbounding the feasible region of our solution set, we're just redefining our parameters and making it a little bit bigger.

Let's talk about how.

Breaking Free from the Conventional Work Box

The 9-to-5 in-office setup has been the standard for knowledge work for a long time. However, anyone who has worked in a job that requires novel ideas, brainstorming, and solution generation knows that while there are exercises you can do to stimulate ideas, you can't just put someone in a chair and tell them that it's now 9 am—ready, think, go! Or at least I haven't figured out how to have ideas on demand when someone tells me it's time. We have to rethink that setup in order to get creative.

One of the most obvious ways to get out of this office box is to literally get out of the office. A friend of mine has rejected the traditional office setup from the start. His company, MKS2 Technologies, provides creative technology services and solutions to both the public and private sectors. One of the reasons they're able to do as much as they do is that they've been a distributed and remote team from inception. Employees are given the freedom to work from anywhere, and have flexible hours based on their time zone. Without being restricted to hiring for talent in a particular area or having people relocate, the company was able to pull in an incredible bench of talent and consistently brings in new and unique perspectives on problems. As we've discussed this business model, he and I both agree that remote and distributed work is the antidote to groupthink.

You can also create mental space to think as well as physical space by making creativity and innovation an integral part of the work process. Google, with its famous 20 percent time policy, where employees can spend 20 percent of their time on personal projects, is a testament to this approach. This policy led to the development of some of Google's most successful products, showcasing the power of allowing creative freedom within the workspace.[10]

Even if you don't get out of the office completely, consider ways to get outside of the conventional work box. Not all people think the same or work the same, and a structured one-size-fits-all approach to work is inadequate to meet their needs or foster the kind of motivation and capability we need to tackle modern problems. Flexible work, hybrid models, and other ways of looking at and leveraging different work styles, which we'll discuss later in this book, can help you break up the monotony and capitalize on people's productivity cycles.

The Intersection of Data and Analytics with Creativity

Integrating data and analytics into the creative process might sound counterintuitive, but it's reshaping the way organizations approach innovation. Creativity can lead to many new ways of interpreting data, and analytics can provide insights that fuel creative solutions. Consider a creative take on outliers, for example. Many statisticians will want to exclude or throw them out, but to my team and I, outliers are interesting data points that need to be interrogated for a full understanding. Why is that outlier an outlier? Is it something that the model you're examining interpreted incorrectly, or did your model uncover an error in the system you can fix?

You can also use data and analytics to assess the environment you've created to see if it truly is permissive of creativity and innovation. Creativity thrives when you have psychological safety, freedom to explore, and recognition of creative efforts. Feedback data on employee experience and satisfaction, productivity, and many other metrics can help you see what elements of your work environment might need readdressing.

When it comes to recognition, Adobe is a case study in creating positive reward and recognition programs for employees and customers with creative and innovative ideas. The Adobe Sneaks program is a way of getting employees to show off early tech innovations at their summits,[11] and the Adobe Experience Maker Awards[12] encourage people who are using Adobe products to submit their innovative and impactful developments for recognition and reward.

Let's not forget how analytics can inform creators of what content their audiences might most enjoy and benefit from. Netflix's well-known data-driven approach to content recommendations is one they also apply to content creation. Their understanding of how different customer segments consume content has informed how they've created hit series tailored to viewer preferences, like *Orange is the New Black* and *The Queen's Gambit*. Both of those series might have seemed too risky or too niche without the analytics and customer touchpoints to back them up, and both now shine as terrific examples of how data can inform creative decisions.

A Paradigm Shift: From Conventional to Creative

The future of work is indeed about incorporating technological advancements into your work and how you process the treasure trove of information out there, but it's also about creating an ecosystem where human uniqueness and ingenuity are valued and nurtured by productive and flexible work environments. We should look at this as an opportunity to step out of the confines of traditional work models and lean into personalization and customization, experience, transparency, and well-being, all things our employees and customers are learning to expect from organizations that provide them with services.

To create any kind of a significant cultural change, you need a combination of strategies. In this case, we are trying to change your organization from one where people are expected to perform in a uniform and interchangeable fashion to one where people are not just allowed but encouraged to work and think differently according to their knowledge, skills, and abilities. How do we go about creating that kind of culture?

First off, transparency is key. Communicating the need and the *why* of this kind of change and anchoring that in the mindset and values of your organization is essential to effect this kind of change. Communicate to your employees the value of creativity and innovation in not just achieving business goals and staying competitive, but in becoming the kind of learning and adaptive organization you need to become to flex along with market trends.

As you communicate the creative imperative, look at your internal and external communication plans and processes. This is the best place possible to start moving out of the assembly line and into iterative feedback loops. How is your message being delivered and how is it being received? What kind of functions do you have to assess how people are receiving and actioning your messages? As you are looking at these processes around one simple theme, the creative imperative, you can build yourself the necessary communication pipelines to discuss your organization's vision for its creative and inclusive culture. You'll need to clearly define and communicate a clear vision for your cultural change. How do you envision your organization expressing that culture and what are the associated values? How does this align with the overall mission and vision for the company?

As you do this, it's helpful to look at how your organization will demonstrate those values. A values crosswalk may be helpful for this, so that your employees not only know the values of your organization, but clearly understand how to commit to these and demonstrate them in their daily roles.

As part of your vision, you will want to make sure your values and your value demonstration actions are included in leadership commitment, training and development, and performance management. These three levels of commitment work in concert to ensure that leaders are committed to both fostering creativity and inclusiveness and leading by example. They help your employees grow and develop the necessary skills through training and development to manage or act as part of diverse teams who work differently, and use individual attribute data and team data to manage and develop optimal teams. They also enforce the demonstration of these values through performance management plans, where employees can be rewarded for supporting this change and corrected when they don't.

As you develop your values and supporting actions, you can roll these into your data-driven talent management plan, using data analytics to identify and nurture creative talent within the organization and to identify patterns and trends related to creativity and inclusion. These attributes should be tied to performance metrics and feedback to help individuals and teams grow and improve their performance.

One of the most important tasks, as your organization becomes more mature in terms of creativity, is creating supportive physical and virtual environments. You should design workspaces that facilitate collaboration, creativity, and inclusivity and that also support flexible work arrangements. This will often require updates to business practices and technology to provide necessary collaborative spaces that include all of your teammates regardless of whether or not they are working in person. This allows teams to meet when and where they work best and allows you to support diverse needs and preferences.

Chapter Summary

As we get ready to start digging into the foundations of data and analytics so that we can apply them to our Talent Management Model, think about creative energy we've just talked about and the workplace we want to create. As you bring new personalities into it, you're going to want to make sure the environment is still driving your teams toward creativity and innovation. You're going to need processes to measure and adjust.

Continually measure the effectiveness of your space, the effectiveness of your communication, and everyone's shared understanding of the mission and vision. We'll talk in later chapters about how to make adjustments. The most important piece of this is to start with the vision for what you want to create, a workplace driven toward novel ways of solving complex problems and finding new methods to attack challenges. That culture is the foundation for building a team with the skills, motivation, growth mindset, and collaboration techniques you need.

Notes

1 Editors (2006) "What Business Are You in?: Classic Advice from Theodore Levitt," *Harvard Business Review*, https://hbr.org/2006/10/what-business-are-you-in-classic-advice-from-theodore-levitt (archived at https://perma.cc/8Q39-X9N5)

2 Barbara Kerr (2023) "Creativity," *The Encyclopedia Britannica*, www.britannica.com/topic/creativity (archived at https://perma.cc/GV2J-QTRP)

3 Sarah E. Boslaugh (2023) "Innovation," *The Encyclopedia Britannica*, www.britannica.com/topic/innovation-creativity (archived at https://perma.cc/DUR6-7W2G)

4 Laszlo Bock (2015) *Work Rules! Insights from inside Google that will transform how you live and lead,* Twelve

5 Sean Ludwig (2020) "20 Small Businesses Thriving During Coronavirus," U.S. Chamber of Commerce, www.uschamber.com/co/start/strategy/coronavirus-successful-businesses (archived at https://perma.cc/7EM4-ZR2U)

6 Iulia-Cristina Uta (2019) "Why did Kodak Fail and What You Can Learn From Its Demise," Brand Minds, https://brandminds.ro/why-did-kodak-fail-and-what-you-can-learn-from-its-demise/ (archived at https://perma.cc/YFN5-JK7N)

7 Drake Baer (2013) "Meet the Data Scientist: How Hilary Mason Turns Research into Business Solutions," Fast Company, www.fastcompany.com/1682931/meet-the-data-scientist-how-hilary-mason-turns-research-into-business-solutions (archived at https://perma.cc/A8SM-8AC9)

8 Rachel Meltzer (2020) "How Netflix Uses Data Science," Lighthouse Labs, www.lighthouselabs.ca/en/blog/how-netflix-uses-data-to-optimize-their-product (archived at https://perma.cc/52KG-Z7BB)

9 Hucker Marius (2021) "Uncovering How the Spotify Algorithm Works," Towards Data Science, https://towardsdatascience.com/uncovering-how-the-spotify-algorithm-works-4d3c021ebc0 (archived at https://perma.cc/56HL-4YZJ)

10 Bill Murphy, Jr. (2020) "Google Says it Still Uses the '20-Percent Rule,' and You Should Totally Copy it," Inc.com, www.inc.com/bill-murphy-jr/google-says-it-still-uses-20-percent-rule-you-should-totally-copy-it.html (archived at https://perma.cc/Y5TW-475W)

11 Kristine Hamlett (2022) "How Adobe Sneaks Go from 'onstage' into App," Adobe, https://blog.adobe.com/en/publish/2022/06/01/adobe-sneaks-on-stage-to-app (archived at https://perma.cc/S2B8-A94V)

12 Adobe Communications Team (2023) "Announcing the 2023 Adobe Experience Maker Awards Finalists," Adobe, https://business.adobe.com/blog/the-latest/announcing-the-2023-adobe-experience-maker-awards-finalists (archived at https://perma.cc/9ZGV-RMNW)

3

Data and Analytics
in the World of People

It is a capital mistake to theorize before one has data. Insensibly one begins to twist facts to suit theories instead of theories to suit facts.

SIR ARTHUR CONAN DOYLE, *A SCANDAL IN BOHEMIA*[1]

I Cannot Make Bricks Without Clay

In the world of talent management, and business in general, much as in the adventures of famed detective Sherlock Holmes, the key to unlocking mysteries and making informed decisions lies in the careful analysis of data. Holmes's keen observation and deductive reasoning and Watson's complementary practicality and focus helped the pair unravel complex cases and solve sometimes seemingly impossible problems. We're going to use the same approach to talk through the fundamentals of data and analytics, and the application of these essential tools of the trade, leading up to your data-driven talent management plan.

Let's talk about data.

In Latin, **data** is simply "that which is given."[2] In application, it's much the same—data is facts, information, or statistics from which you can draw conclusions, either through observation or deliberate analysis.[3] For us, data is (and as a Latin scholar, to me, the word "data" is plural but I'll default to common usage) the cornerstone of decision making, much like clues are for Holmes and Watson when solving a case. Data can range from consumer behavior metrics and sales figures to market trends and predictive indicators, and it is immense in volume and complexity.

Analytics, the next piece of our puzzle, involves the systematic computational analysis of data.[4] It's how we take raw data, the clay, and produce insights, the bricks, on which we can build our business foundations. Data can tell you how much of a particular product you sold, but analytics will reveal patterns in sales, like peak buying times or the most popular product features with your customers. Analytics is the magnifying glass that brings the finer details within vast amounts of data into focus and context.

So how does **artificial intelligence (AI)** play into this construct? AI is a field of computer science that enables machines to mimic human intelligence.[5] AI can process and analyze data at a scale and speed beyond human capability, and when you use it to augment your processes, to conduct the practical work of observing, cataloging, and contextualizing data for you into insights, think of it as a Watson to your Holmes (and no, that's not why IBM named their Watson system, but it's a nice coincidence).

This chapter will serve as a mini-reference book for concepts in data and analytics. We'll talk about different types of data and how they can be collected and utilized effectively for your talent management decisions. We'll discuss various analytics techniques and how they can be best applied to draw meaningful insights from your data. We'll also touch on the revolutionary impact of AI in data processing and analysis, and how automated and intelligent tools can help you reshape your business strategy.

Just as Holmes used his observations to piece together the story behind each clue, you'll learn how to use data to build a narrative that can guide business decisions.

Here's what I hope you data detectives get out of this chapter:

- Foundational concepts in data and analytics
- The four types of analytics and practical examples
- The role and importance of artificial intelligence
- Considerations in data protection and privacy
- An introduction to analytics in human resources and talent management

The game's afoot—a game where data, analytics, and AI are all key players, and the contest is mastering this chapter, which will give you the foundations for building your data-driven talent management strategy. Let's go!

Data Foundations

Let's talk about data and analytics. To get started, it's best to have these terms and their characteristics well defined in your mind. Probably first and foremost, since we've talked about data itself, we should differentiate between data and big data.

Big data refers to extremely large data sets. How large are we talking? Well, you typically need a lot of computational power to analyze it, but we describe big data in terms of the four" "Vs": Volume, variety, velocity, and veracity.[6]

Volume: With big data, vast volumes of data are generated every second. From customer transactions to social media posts to sensor networks, the amount of data generated is colossal. Managing the sheer volume of big data poses significant challenges in terms of storage, processing, and analysis.

Variety: Data comes in various forms and types, which we'll go over in more detail shortly. Up until the advent of big data, traditional data types were structured and fit neatly in a database. Today's data includes that still, but it also is made up of unstructured text, video, audio, and other types of content. This adds layers of complexity to the storage and analysis, requiring more advanced techniques and tools.

Velocity: This refers to the speed at which new data gets generated, and this is staggering for big data. Real-time or near-real-time information makes it possible for businesses to make more timely and agile decisions, but it also requires robust systems and analytics that can keep up with the rapid speed of data.

Veracity: A term used for the reliability, accuracy, or truthfulness of your data. When data comes in from numerous sources, ensuring that it's accurate and trustworthy is critical. With analytics, if you put in bad data, you just get bad decisions faster.

There are numerous ways to categorize the **types of data** you'll work with, but the best starting point is to look at how structured it is.

Structured data is highly organized and formatted in a way that makes it easily searchable in databases. It's characterized by orderliness, which makes it the easiest to analyze.

Unstructured data is the exact opposite, and does not adhere to rules of organization, form, or function. It can be text and numbers, videos, images, audio, social media postings... you name it. Unstructured data can hold a wealth of knowledge when analyzed, but getting to the point of analysis requires more sophisticated methods than our structured data, like text analytics or image recognition.

Semi-structured data sits right between the two. It may not reside in a database, but still contains tags and markers that help you more easily categorize it and enforce hierarchies of records and fields.[7]

Here are some other ways we categorize data:

- Quantitative vs. qualitative:
  - Quantitative data is numerical and can be measured and quantified
  - Qualitative data is descriptive, and can be observed but not measured
- Primary vs. secondary:
  - Primary data is collected directly by your organization for a specific purpose
  - Secondary data was collected for some other purpose but is being utilized for a different kind of study or analysis
- Time series vs. cross-sectional:
  - Time series data is collected over set intervals or periods of time, and used to analyze trends over time
  - Cross-sectional data is collected at a single point in time, and often used to compare different groups or categories at a given moment
- Internal vs. external:
  - Internal data is data generated from within the organization
  - External data is data sourced from outside the organization
- Anonymized vs. identified:
  - Anonymized data is data that has been either collected or processed to remove or alter information that makes it possible to identify individuals
  - Identified data is data that contains identifiable information about individuals
- Nominal, ordinal, interval, and ratio(levels of measurement):
  - Nominal data is data you can classify into categories without needing any kind of order or ranking

- o Ordinal data involves order or ranking, but without a consistent interval between the ranks

- o Interval data has an order and there is a consistent interval between values, but no true zero point

- o Ratio data is similar to interval data but includes a true zero point, allowing for the calculation of ratios[8]

Understanding these various ways we classify and categorize data and the associated attributes is essential. It helps us choose the right analysis methods and tools, ensure data integrity, and comply with appropriate data regulations and protections.

Each type of data has its own strengths and limitations, and the choice of which to use depends on the specific requirements of your analytics. So let's talk about analytics!

Analytics refers to the systematic computational analysis of data or statistics.[9] It's a methodology that allows you to extract meaningful insights from raw data and inform your decision-making processes. Analytics can reveal patterns, trends, and relationships that you might otherwise not be able to see, and help you optimize your operations, improve customer engagement, and create innovative products and services.

Before we get too far ahead of the fundamentals, let's take a quick sideways trip into not just what data is, but what we need to do to protect it, our analytics, and, most importantly, the privacy and safety of our people.

A Quick Introduction to Data Governance

Data governance is "the process of managing the availability, usability, integrity, and security of the data in enterprise systems, based on internal data standards and policies that also control data usage."[10] For all the data we collect, we need to have a plan for protecting it, and that includes understanding the nature of the data—and the policies, regulations, and sensitivities surrounding it that tell us how we should be protecting it, who should be able to access it and at what level of aggregation, and what the key governance roles are.

Your organization should have a data framework that sets standards and processes that help you manage and protect your framework. This basically sets the rules of the road for data use—who can see and access what, who is in charge of organizing and curating data, what kind of data the system can and can't collect, program and workflow management, and who grants permission for different types of data collection efforts or studies. This might also include the tools you plan to use to keep visibility on data sharing and data use, such as smart data catalogs, code repositories, data visualization tools, and so forth.

Your organization's chief data officer, if you have one, is ultimately responsible for all of this. In some cases, they might also have a data manager and team, data stewards who are responsible for individual data sets, and other important roles. The larger the organization, the more people you will need to plan on having involved full time in the curation, protection, and monitoring of your data. Many organizations make the mistake of making this a secondary job or part-time role; if you're going to have a truly data-driven organization, you'll need this to be a primary focus.

This is especially important in the human domain. When you start talking about sensitive data, we on the government side immediately think in terms of classification and security. However, those programs have nothing on the complexity you'll encounter in the realm of personnel data. Human resources and talent management data includes many sensitive items, such as personal and personally identifiable information (PII),[11] contact details, health records, performance evaluations, and financial information. Protecting this information is critical. We have all seen the negative results of high-profile data breaches where this information has been stolen, both in terms of violation of privacy and legal trouble for the individual, and sometimes irrevocable damage to the trust between organization and employee.

A key component of a data governance plan is simple regulatory compliance. Laws like the General Data Protection Regulation (GDPR)[12] in the EU and Health Insurance Portability and Accountability Act (HIPAA)[13] in the US set stringent guidelines for data handling. GDPR emphasizes the right of an individual to their data, requiring explicit consent for data collection and providing rights to access and erase personal information. HIPAA protects sensitive patient health information from being disclosed without consent.

For your organization's people offices, understanding and adhering to these regulations is crucial to avoid legal repercussions and ensure ethical standards are met. So let's cover some best practices in this space:

Regular audits. Conducting regular data audits helps you ensure that personal data is being used and stored in compliance with relevant laws, regulations, and policies.

Access control. Limiting access to sensitive data to authorized personnel only, by role and function, helps ensure that the only people who access sensitive data are those who are both trained in proper handling and who have a need to see it.

Employee training. Regular training sessions for all employees to understand the importance of data, data protection, and the role they play in it can help keep people from inadvertently compromising information.

Secure storage and transmission. Secure data and encrypted communication channels can help you keep your data out of the wrong hands. Keep in mind that like in any good heist, the most likely place something is going to get stolen is in transit.

Ethical considerations also play a significant role, especially in the context of using employee data. These involve respecting privacy, ensuring transparency about how data is being used, and securing informed consent when it comes to collecting personal data. Anonymity and confidentiality of employee data in reports and analytics also builds trust between the employee and the organization and reduces the ability of outsiders to access personal information.

As you build out your data-driven talent management plan and your governance plan along with it, build a balance between how you employ data-driven insights and human judgment. Data can provide a wealth of information, but it might not capture the nuances of human behavior and individual circumstances. Ensuring that you maintain the "human in the loop" for quality control and review purposes helps you keep your models making sense, consider how to most effectively use the insights you uncover through analytics, and see if something is happening with your data that violates policies or ethical principles.

Okay, now that we've talked about how to protect your data, let's talk about how to use it.

Analytics and Their Applications

If you're going to have data-driven decisions, understanding what the different types of analytics do to transform your data into insights is essential. Without understanding the purpose of these different tools, you risk integrating them into the wrong place in your strategy, or expecting them to perform a function they're not designed to perform. Each type of analytics—and there are four—offers unique insights and opportunities. The four types of analytics, in order of complexity, are **descriptive**, **diagnostic**, **predictive**, and **prescriptive**. Here's how they differ in application.

Descriptive Analytics: What Happened?

Descriptive analytics is akin to looking in the rear-view mirror; it helps you understand what has happened in the past. By collecting, processing, and presenting historical data, descriptive analytics reveal patterns and trends. This is what you'll commonly see represented in common daily use, because the methodology is simple and the results are easy to contextualize in data visualizations, like charts and dashboards.

If you do anything in sales, you're likely to see descriptive analytics in financial analysis or sales trends. Financial statements provide information about trends and let you compare different spending amounts over time either in raw numbers or as ratios, as part of a whole. In sales and demand trends, you'll look at customer purchases over time and be able to see if there are rises and falls in your customers' interest in a particular product.

This is also what you'll likely see when you get the results of a survey. Aggregated responses and trends can help you see if there are any potential relationships between variables, like location and the likelihood to see a particular marketing message favorably. By looking at these trends, you can make decisions about whether or not your messages are resonating with the groups you're trying to reach and whether to dig deeper into those relationships.

However, descriptive analytics just report what's happening. Even if you see what looks like a relationship between variables, you need to dig deeper into the data. That's where diagnostics come into play.

Diagnostic Analytics: Why Did It Happen?

Diagnostic analytics delves a level deeper, seeking to understand the 'why' behind past events. It's the perfect next step to investigate your data when you notice a couple of variables that seem to be related, like age and approval of messaging content in a survey, for example.

This involves a number of different techniques, from testing a hypothesis to statistical analysis that helps you determine if your variables are related through correlation. For your hypothesis, you make an assumption and use data and statistics to prove or disprove it. If you're looking for *correlation* (which means there is a statistically significant relationship between your variables), you need to do statistical modeling such as regression analysis to prove that there is an actual relationship. If you're looking for *causality* (meaning there's more than just a relationship, but a change in one variable actually impacts the other variable), you might need to do controlled experiments. Think about how you plan to use the information. It might be enough for you to know that the variables are just related, or at other times, you might need to pinpoint a cause.

This might seem complicated, but here's a very simple example of employing diagnostic analytics immediately after a customer response to a message. Let's think about our customer behavior in the previous example, knowing that a message didn't resonate with a particular group of people. Now think about if we're using responses to a message on, say, Facebook for example. When you select" "I don't want to see this ad," a survey pops up to ask you why you selected not to see the ad. Based on your response and the information Facebook has about you, they can relay information to the advertiser about why people are selecting to not see their ads to better inform message targeting.

Predictive Analytics: What Might Happen?

Predictive analytics uses historical data to forecast future events and outcomes. These can be simple or complex analyses, using anything from simple regression to machine-learning algorithms. It all has to do with figuring out, based on past trends, what's likely to happen.

Keeping with our messaging example, predictive analytics can be leveraged to help you examine customer behavior. Looking at past trends and behaviors, you can better predict whether someone in a particular demographic is going to enter the marketing funnel and convert from awareness to engagement to purchase, or maybe if they're likely to balk midstream, or whether they're going to select "I don't want to see this ad." This will help you make decisions about whether or not you want to change your message with that demographic if they don't want to see your message, or if you need to implement a change somewhere along the funnel where they're most likely to balk.

However you're collecting and using data, predictive analytics can play a pivotal role in your strategy. If you develop the right models, they will help you get a feel for customer behavior along seasonal models, responses to various events (e.g. let's predict what products are most likely to sell to our demographics fastest when there's a storm warning), and whether or not we want to continue with a product where predicted interest is waning.

Of course, all of these methods so far leave what to do about these trends very much up to you, but there is a way to use analytics to help you decide what decisions might work best.

Prescriptive Analytics: What Should I Do?

Prescriptive analytics is the most advanced form of analytics. It doesn't just provide you with an understanding of what is happening and what might happen, it tells you what you should do about it to stay on course and meet your objectives. This type of analytics uses machine learning algorithms to process very large amounts of data and often incorporates simulation and optimization to test scenarios and outcomes.

Let's take our messaging example on Facebook, or any other social media platform. Platforms capture tons of data about your engagement history, and what kinds of things you like, click on, watch, ignore, or close because you don't want to see them anymore. These platforms benefit from showing you more things you'll like and fewer things you don't, and they can make recommendations based on customer behavior of new demographic groups you might want to target with your message, or new types of content you might want to create based on what's popular and being clicked.

Another familiar example of prescriptive analytics is the technology behind navigation apps like Waze and Google Maps. These tools analyze real-time data on traffic patterns, weather conditions, and other factors to recommend the most efficient driving routes. This not only saves time for the users but also exemplifies how prescriptive analytics can lead to practical, real-world solutions.

Integrating the Four Analytics Together

You shouldn't just focus on one type of analytics to reach your goals. You get true power out of data when you plan to use all four types. Descriptive analytics can provide you with the foundational understanding of past trends and outcomes, and can lead you to ask questions about the relationships of certain variables or patterns in your data. Diagnostic analytics will help you answer those questions about relationships, and dig into the *why* of those trends. Predictive analytics builds off this understanding to figure out where future trends are likely to go. And finally, prescriptive analytics helps you figure out what actions you take are most likely to positively affect future trends and lead to success.

Each type of analytics plays a distinct role, and together, they can help you create a comprehensive understanding of the behavior of your business system.

Now let's take that over to talent management. Let's say we're trying to understand the skillset of our organization and how to plan for workforce development in the future. *Descriptive analytics*, provided we've collected the right amount of skills data, will help us understand exactly who we've hired and who is in our inventory. We can layer in performance and productivity data also to see who is succeeding, and if there are any trends to show that certain skills are helping people be more productive than others. If we see these trends, we can use *diagnostic analytics* to dig a little deeper and see whether there's a correlation between, say, data literacy training and data skills and better performance. We can do hypothesis testing or controlled experimentation to see whether giving people training on data skills improves their productivity. We can then use historical data over time to see what types of skills we have in our inventory and how those skills have changed, and if we're seeing more acquisition and training of data skills. We can contrast those with hiring datasets from Monster, Indeed, and LinkedIn and see whether or not the demand for those kinds of skills is increasing, and being incorporated into job descriptions where we don't currently have that requirement. Finally, prescriptive analytics might help us figure out what roles should get more data training in order to close any gaps between our office and industry best practices.

You can see how all of these things fit together to form a data-rich understanding of our capabilities, and also how that understanding can lead to analytics that can help us make decisions about what to do next. With the vast amount of information available, we need to incorporate these kinds of analytics "teammates" into our business strategy. While analytics are not going to replace some kinds of human decision making anytime soon, they can definitely replace some of our bulky and slow data collection, aggregation, and analysis processes. In the competitive global market of today, you certainly don't want to go up against an organization armed with the ability to harness and use vast amounts of information in their decisions with a notepad and a stubby pencil.

Artificial Intelligence in Business

Artificial intelligence is the next logical step in analytics from prescriptive analytics. Descriptive analytics helps show you the current description of your organization in terms of data, diagnostic helps you answer questions about why your organization is the way it is, predictive analytics helps you understand what's likely to happen, and prescriptive analytics shows you the best consequence of decisions based on those trends. AI uses decision algorithms to make that decision and act on those trends for you.

It's no secret that AI has exploded in business applications over the past few years, with the advent of innovative and easy-to-use interfaces that put their power in the hands of the average user instead of the advanced developer. But let's talk about what it is, what it can do for your business, and what it can do for talent management.

Artificial intelligence (AI) is a field of science that enables computers to do the things we expect the human intellect to do.[14] By combining "smart" algorithms and automation, with or without "human-in-the-loop" supervision, computers can interpret speech and text, drive cars, perform customer service functions, and monitor human biofunctions.

But what does that actually mean? Why do we call things "smart?" In the context of the algorithms that power AI, it means that they have "maximally valid/desirable output with minimally valid/desirable input."[15] It means the learning functions within the algorithm are able to approximate correct responses from errors by associating them with things the system has effectively learned about what the user meant to do. Even systems like ChatGPT, even if they don't always do exactly what you meant for them to do, return what is essentially a linguistically valid and correct product when you ask a bare minimum question.

Let's talk about those learning functions and how they work by digging into the main building blocks of artificial intelligence, **machine learning** and **deep learning**.

Machine learning is a subset of AI that uses statistical techniques to enable computers to receive feedback on tasks performed and uses reward and punishment functions to improve their performance. Essentially, this allows a computer to "learn" from its "experience," much like a mathematical form of operant conditioning in psychology. The functions in machine learning have objective functions they are trying to maximize; correct performance of a task improves the performance toward that objective, and incorrect performance moves it farther away from achieving that objective.

Deep learning is a more advanced subset of machine learning that uses neural networks with many layers to analyze data. Neural networks are computational functions that act very similarly to the neurons and networks of axons and dendrites that make up our own nervous system. This allows extremely statistically complex processes to find patterns in the data and mimic the kind of inferences you normally would need a human brain to perform. This kind of learning is especially good at processing unstructured data such as images, sound, and text.

The difference between machine learning and deep learning is in their complexity and their capabilities. Machine learning is good for handling structured data and linear relationships, and deep learning is better when dealing with complex, unstructured data and nonlinear relationships.[16] And depending on what tasks you want your AI to perform, you'll also need to incorporate automation and robotics, natural language processing, and other functions that help it imitate the human brain performing those tasks.

Okay, so now we have a better understanding of what artificial intelligence is. Now do we know what it's *for*? Well, who doesn't want an automated assistant to help you out on the various tasks, especially digital ones, that you're working on? Think of the benefits of that automation. A computer doesn't get tired or bored, it doesn't need to sleep, it doesn't need a bathroom or a coffee break, and an AI system is very literal—it does what you tell it to. That can be a problem sometimes, because you may need that human quality control, the human-in-the-loop supervision we talked about earlier, to come in and adjust performance if there is model drift or model decay, terms we use to indicate that the model's performance has declined over time.

In the U.S. Army human resources space, we've begun using machine learning and AI to conduct preliminary screens of files, flag files with derogatory information for further review, flag high performance files, and otherwise do the laborious task of reading and ranking narratives so that a much smaller set could be reviewed by a panel than previously. This is just the beginning of the work we're planning on doing in this space, but this was a small change that created a large amount of efficiency for us.

Let's talk about how you're already seeing AI at work:

Customer service. You probably interface often with AI-powered chatbots when trying to find useful information from your bank, your airline, or other service providers. They can provide 24–7 customer service and quickly either resolve issues or elevate to a human agent when it's outside their ability to resolve.

Marketing. AI tools can quickly identify purchasing patterns and preferences from consumer data, and generate recommendations, tailored marketing strategies, and personalized customer experiences, like in the marketing and messaging examples we talked about earlier.

Supply chain management. Our logisticians are big consumers of AI. Predicting inventory needs, optimizing supply chain logistics, and improving delivery efficiency through route optimization are just a few applications in this space.

Fraud detection. All across the finance sector, AI algorithms can identify deviations in patterns and behaviors that might indicate fraudulent activities. These have gotten extremely robust over the years, so that you have to worry a lot less about your card getting used where you're not or getting erroneously shut off when you travel.

Human resources. AI is used prevalently in recruiting and hiring by analyzing resumés and matching candidates to job descriptions. We're also increasingly seeing it used in developmental and learning platforms, to provide education to the right level of experience by expanding or curtailing lessons.

So we've talked about what AI can do. Now, just a quick word of warning on what you shouldn't expect it to do. And that's unfortunately what we hear a lot of leaders in government and business saying: "We need AI to make better decisions for us." AI is not going to do that. AI is, if nothing else, going to take the same data we're consuming and, based on what it has learned, make the same decisions, just faster. We don't need AI to be thinking for us in that way.

What we do need it to do is free us up to do the kinds of things humans do best and do the more administrative tasks, like collecting, sorting, and contextualizing our data for us. I like to think of this in terms of the Zone of Genius framework proposed by Gay Hendricks.[17]

This framework categorizes the things we do into four zones: Genius, Excellence, Competence, and Incompetence. The Zone of Genius at the top consists of the things you are uniquely capable of doing and the things you should be doing, and the Zone of Incompetence at the bottom is the things you're not good at doing but have to do simply because, well, someone needs to get them done.

My philosophy toward using algorithms and artificial intelligence in business processes mirrors Hendrics' philosophy on tasks—automate away as much as you can that falls into the lower zones, processes that are boring, time consuming, repetitive, or too hard so that you can spend more time in those upper echelons, doing the things that you, as a human, are uniquely

FIGURE 3.1 Zone of Genius Framework, Based on Gay Hendricks' *The Big Leap*

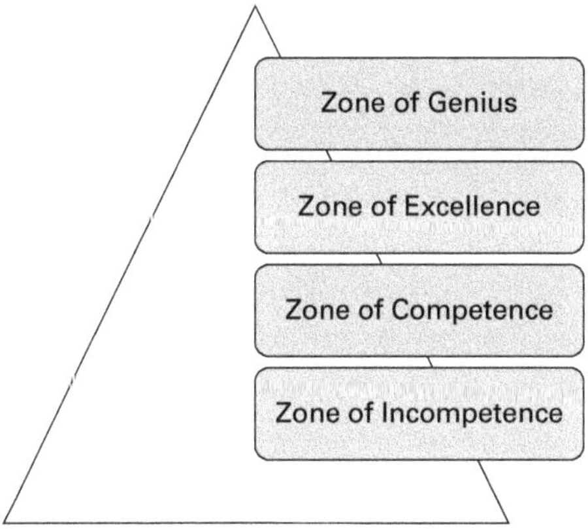

capable of doing. Thinking this way about your business processes can help you free up more time for you and your human employees to do the kinds of things that humans do best—things that require intuition and innovation.

Why the Use Case Matters Most

We keep referring to the "use case," so let's talk about what that is. It's a practical narrative that tells the story of how you are going to collect and leverage data and analytics to gain insights, answer tangible business questions, and inform decisions. It helps everyone from your data professionals to your decision makers have a common understanding of why we're collecting this data and what we intend to do with it.

When we're looking at building either a new analytic model or modernizing our processes with a new system, it's easy to get distracted by the technical challenge. The sophistication of a new tool or a slick interface might draw you toward a solution before you know whether it's right for the problem you're solving, or you may not have fully developed the question you're trying to answer with data. You might answer the question, but that answer might not fit in the context of the decision you're trying to make.

There are many different methods out there for doing this, but I'll share the one my team and I use. These are the four components we consider:

Decision objective. While we talk a lot about data-driven decisions, it really is the decision that drives the process, or the question you want to answer. What is the outcome we want to get from doing this experiment or building this analytic?

Decision maker. Getting an answer to a question or a decision can be difficult if we don't fully understand who the decision maker is in this case. It might be the person who is accountable for making the decision we're informing, or it might be the expert who evaluates whether or not the solution or answer we generate is a good one.

Decision information. Once we know the context of the decision and the decision maker, or how the data we collect and analyze will be used, we can go out and start looking for what information we need to answer the question. This might be data, this might be the results of our analytics, but we really need to know what we need to provide the decision maker with in order to achieve the decision objectives.

Decision method. Okay, here's the fun part for analysts. This is where we get to design the experiment, or what data we're going to analyze in what way to answer the question. This is where we go back through all the different types of data and methods we can use to analyze it or transform it to answer our question.

And once we decide on the decision method, we walk that back up through the information, decision maker, and objective to make sure we didn't lose context along the way. This method, for me, is the outline of a research paper and helps me figure out what we need to fill in and what might just be a distracting shiny object. Those are easy to find when you get excited about your work.

Let's walk our way through an example use case that we're working on right now in my office. We'll break into the different components of the Talent Management Model in the next chapter, but retention of quality service members is always high on our priority list. Let's use that and talk about a data and analytics use case we'd want to explore in this space:

The decision objective: We offer a lot of different retention incentives. How do we know which ones we should select that work for a specific group?

The decision maker: This decision is owned by our director of military personnel policy, so the solution we create must be something she can use and values.

The decision information. We need to identify the people we want to retain who want to leave and identify what they would take as an incentive to stay.

The decision method. We need data or analytics that help us determine who wants to leave, so this probably needs to be a predictive model telling us the likelihood that a person or group is going to attrit. We need data or analytics on the incentives those people who are likely to leave are most willing to take in exchange to stay in service, and we can get that from surveys, focus groups, and hypothesis testing.

From there, you can determine how you will collect and protect your data, whether or not you need a review board or other permission to collect data or conduct experiments, and how you will analyze the data to produce information to support your decision maker's objectives. Structuring the use case like this will keep the model, as an old mentor of mine told me, as detailed as necessary and as simple as possible.

We've developed a library of human resource and talent management use cases with this simple framework, and it helps us not only get after new projects but review old ones that might need to be refined, or provide work when we have analysts or individuals in continuing education or degree programs who need research projects. It's also something we can develop quickly and, even if we don't have the manpower or resources to get after the project immediately, have on hand for future work.

Chapter Summary

We've covered the basic and essential foundations of data, analytics, and artificial intelligence, how to govern and protect our data, and how to develop use cases that let us develop analytics as a project or experiment to support a data-driven decision. Each layer of this process gives us the opportunity for unique and actionable insights, opportunities for process improvement, and the ability to balance the power of learning algorithms with human intuition. While algorithms can process and analyze at unprecedented speeds and volume, they sometimes miss the forest for the trees. Human beings, with our ability to better perceive context and nuance than machines, at least at the moment, still play a critical role in interpreting the outcomes of these models and processes accurately and holistically.

This might have seemed like a complicated journey, but hopefully we were, like our good friend Holmes, able to break it down into digestible chunks. You might ask why we didn't get deeper into the technology, but that ties back into the power of the use case—the decision being driven by our data and analytics is, in fact, the driving factor.

And that's anything but elementary, my dear Watson.

Notes

1   Sir Arthur Conan Doyle (republished 1986) *Sherlock Holmes: The Complete Novels and Stories, vol. 1*, Bantam Classics

2   Online Etymology Dictionary (2024) "Data," www.etymonline.com/word/data (archived at https://perma.cc/5CYJ-XD7T)

3   Merriam-Webster Dictionary Online (2024) "Data," www.merriam-webster.com/dictionary/data (archived at https://perma.cc/2JF3-9KUW)

4   Merriam-Webster Dictionary Online (2023) "Analytics," www.merriam-webster.com/dictionary/analytics (archived at https://perma.cc/2PFP-RX7Y)

5   Merriam-Webster Dictionary Online (2024) "Artificial Intelligence," www.merriam-webster.com/dictionary/artificial%20intelligence (archived at https://perma.cc/SCX7-U5DM)

6   Google Cloud Learn (nd) "What is Big Data?" https://cloud.google.com/learn/what-is-big-data (archived at https://perma.cc/SL3S-RG5E)

7   Jeffrey L. Whitten and Lonnie D. Bentley (2005) *Systems Analysis and Design Methods, 7th ed*, McGraw-Hill Irwin, 37

8   Ibid., 337

9   Gartner Glossary (nd) "Analytics," www.gartner.com/en/information-technology/glossary/analytics (archived at https://perma.cc/R3KW-HDCN)

10 Craig Stedman and Jack Vaughan (2022) "What is Data Governance and Why Does It Matter?" TechTarget, www.techtarget.com/searchdatamanagement/definition/data-governance (archived at https://perma.cc/YT3R-CP23)

11 U.S. Department of Labor (nd) "Guidance on the Protection of Personal Identifiable Information," www.dol.gov/general/ppii (archived at https://perma.cc/T3GR-3W4U)

12 GDPR.EU (nd) "What is GDPR, the EU's New Data Protection Law?" https://gdpr.eu/what-is-gdpr/ (archived at https://perma.cc/C5TK-VS76)

13 Centers for Disease Control and Prevention (nd) "Health Insurance Portability and Accountability Act of 1996 (HIPAA)," www.cdc.gov/phlp/publications/topic/hipaa.html (archived at https://perma.cc/X35Y-6JAR)

14 Merriam-Webster Dictionary Online (2024) "Artificial Intelligence," www.merriam-webster.com/dictionary/artificial%20intelligence (archived at https://perma.cc/MC7M-G37X)

15 R. Harvey (2023) "Smart Algorithms," Bootcamp, https://bootcamp.uxdesign.cc/smart-algorithms-5f76ad1e8945 (archived at https://perma.cc/3F2F-SVTY)

16 Rashi Maheshwari (2023) "What is Artificial Intelligence (AI) and How Does It Work?" Forbes, www.forbes.com/advisor/in/business/software/what-is-ai/ (archived at https://perma.cc/5QCE-QH8G)

17 Gay Hendricks (2010) *The Big Leap*, HarperOne

4

Talent Management

One of the greatest talents of all is the talent to recognize and develop talent in others.

GENERAL COLIN POWELL, AMERICAN SECRETARY OF STATE[1]

Working with Unique Abilities and Talents

There's a common and inspiring theme in the adventures of the Avengers, the Justice League, the X-Men, and other extraordinary pop-culture teams. All of these journeys start with individuals, distributed throughout society, each uncovering their separate unique abilities, and coming together— admittedly through some storming and norming—to form incredible teams that work collaboratively toward fighting the battles no one else can fight. I want that also to inspire our vision for talent management here.

Let's think of ourselves as Nick Fury for the Avengers or Professor Xavier for the X-Men, or even potentially as one of the various emerging leaders in the self-organized Justice League. How would we develop a system to identify, develop, and harness the unique abilities of each of our people? Okay, that's a superhero-worthy challenge. But what about taking all of those abilities and synchronizing them together into a team? Even more difficult. And those abilities are going to develop and change over time, and we'll need to bring on and integrate new people, and...

You get it. Going from the concept of "how many" to "who," and changing from transactional human resources to data-driven talent management is important but it's also incredibly complicated. The key to all of this lies in effective **talent management**—the art and science of acquiring, developing, employing, and retaining the right talent for the right job at the right time over time.[2]

Talent management is an art and a science. Thinking about it in the context of the X-Men, your data-driven talent management plan is the Cerebro (the powerful machine that allowed Professor Xavier to amplify his telepathic powers and connect with mutants around the world), helping you identify talents you need across the globe and tap into their potential.

And think of it also as the next step in the use case, as we talked about in the last chapter, of how you work back from your *decision objective*—creating that talented team capable of great creativity and innovation, with you as the decision maker—into talent management, the *decision information* you need to have about people in order to make the decisions you need about your team—your diverse, talented, and motivated workforce.

Here, we'll delve into the foundational components of that decision information, the definitions and components of talent. We'll explore how that talent can be measured and nurtured, and talk about how to use the Talent Management Model. We'll also discuss some challenges you'll run into in talent management, and address the challenges in collecting and utilizing talent management data effectively.

This chapter will help guide you through the complexities of identifying the capabilities of a workforce as diverse and dynamic as any you've seen in your favorite superhero comic book or movie, and hopefully get you thinking about how to manage those capabilities with agility, creativity, and innovation.

What Is Talent?

My office and I have gotten into a number of debates about the exact definition of talent, especially when we were first starting out. You would think that would be one of the first things we defined, but unfortunately, while we knew we needed to harness it, we hadn't defined it in a way that we could successfully measure and collect data against. This led to the creation of the Army Talent Attribute Framework, which we're still refining as we continue to learn more about our requirements and what we need to know about our people.

Our definitions here will not follow those definitions exactly, since we tend to be somewhat oblique with our doctrinal language. But we'll definitely take from the same spirit of those definitions—and some of those spirited debates!

Talent is a term that refers to a person's collections of abilities, aptitudes, knowledge, or skills. It's the capacity to perform a particular task or activity exceptionally well, often with relative ease and proficiency. Talents are typically considered innate or acquired abilities that set individuals apart from others in a specific area.[3]

Talent manifests in various forms, each significant in its own right, and contributes uniquely to individual and organizational growth. Let's explore these diverse forms of talent with real-world examples:

1 **Artistic talent.** Artistic talent includes abilities in creative arts, like music, painting, drawing, dance, acting, and more.

2 **Athletic talent.** Athletic talent refers to prowess in sports, demonstrating exceptional physical abilities and coordination. This isn't confined to professional sports alone, but anywhere people can exhibit fitness and wellness.

3 **Intellectual talent.** Intellectual talent involves cognitive abilities like problem solving, mathematical aptitude, and linguistic skills.

4 **Leadership talent.** Leadership talent is the art of inspiring and guiding others effectively. There are dozens of different leadership models out there, but almost all of them share those qualities of inspiration and direction.

5 **Technical talent.** Technical talent includes skills in technology, engineering, programming, and scientific areas.

6 **Interpersonal talent.** Interpersonal talent involves exceptional communication skills crucial for building relationships and working effectively with others. In the corporate sector, roles in human resources and customer relations heavily rely on interpersonal talent.

Talent can be both inherent (innate gifts a person is born with) or developed (things that are taught and honed over time through education, practice, and experience). But whether it's a natural skill or one developed through practice or training, identifying these talents is pivotal for building talented teams and managing a creative and innovative workforce. We'll talk about how we can identify that talent through the different types of talent data and how to set up your own data framework for how you want to classify and stratify talent, but first, let's talk about what you're going to do with it.

What Is Talent Management?

There are a multitude of different talent management definitions out there. McKinsey defines it as "the way your organization attracts, retains, and develops its employees."[4] Indeed says talent management is "attracting, motivating, and retaining top-performing employees or the workforce."[5] The U.S. Army People Strategy lists key components in its mission, to "acquire develop, employ, and retain" soldier and civilian talent.[6] For the purpose of this book, I've pulled pieces from those definitions and others to get a working definition that I use whenever I work projects and speak about data-driven talent management.

Talent management is a multifaceted strategic approach that enables organizations to identify, acquire, develop, employ, and retain the talents and skills of their workforce to achieve business objectives. It encompasses a range of activities and practices, but the goal is ensuring that the right people are in the right jobs and equipped with the right skills, knowledge, and resources to drive an organization's success.

Wait... isn't that human resources?

Not quite. These are two very closely related fields—and it's likely that your human resources professionals will handle a lot of your talent management—but they focus on different aspects of managing people. Most people consider talent management a subset of HR that specifically focuses on acquiring, developing, employing, and retaining the most talented and high-potential employees in the organization, and that's largely what this book focuses on. Human resources includes the broad variety of functions that go into managing people in addition to that, including payroll functions, benefits, compliance with labor laws, and other operational, transactional, and administrative tasks. Even though human resources is playing an increasingly strategic role in our organizations, most of the development and future growth-oriented activities in that space are ones we claim under the subset of talent management.

At its core, talent management hinges on the recognition that an organization's greatest asset and its most necessary component to achieving its objectives now and in the future, even in this world of data and automation, is its people. And it's about attracting and building the capabilities, competencies and potential of the individuals and teams that can make or break our ability to achieve or organizational goals.

While talent management is about people, it's not limited to a specific department or set of activities. People comprise all your departments, and

FIGURE 4.1 The Talent Management Model

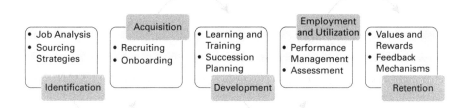

they're being counseled, mentored, and led in those departments, developed by your learning and development plan, their needs seen to by a number of different offices, and impacted by your decisions and visions as a leader. Talent management encompasses every stage of the employee lifecycle, from recruitment to retirement and afterward in many cases, particularly in the case of veterans of military service. And it involves stakeholders from throughout your organization.

Let's talk about the different component activities of the Talent Management Model. As in the definition, we're going to define those activities as Identification, Acquisition, Development, Employment and Utilization, and Retention. As I've done with the definition, I've culled through dozens of documents and books on talent management, and redefined these activities with the best practical language I can.

Talent identification. Talent management begins with the identification and recruitment of individuals who possess the skills and competencies needed to fill specific roles within your organization. There are two key pieces to this step, and that's identifying what talent you need through job analysis (which can also include a gap analysis between your requirements and what talents you have in your inventory) and sourcing strategies, figuring out where the talent you require lives and works and how to get them.

Talent acquisition. Once you've identified your talent, the next step is to acquire it—to recruit and onboard it into the organization. Recruiting is tied closely to marketing, and involves a similar funnel from awareness to purchase, except in this case, the "purchase" you want your target to make is signing on with your company! From there, you need an effective onboarding plan to make sure your people understand your culture, values, and expectations, and where to find and use the tools necessary for success.

Talent development. Your requirements aren't static, and you should not expect your employees to be static also, if you want to reach your objectives. Your employees will join your organization with a set of knowledge, skills, and other attributes, but you will need to have a plan for learning and training, in order to both help them develop to meet promotion and advancement goals, and to help keep everyone armed with the right skills to do their job. A critical part of this that not every model considers is succession planning. You can't count on your ability to retain a critical person in an important role forever, or for that role to not outgrow their skillset, so you need to be looking at your talent inventory, internal and external to your organization, and figuring out who you might be able to acquire or develop into that role next.

Talent employment and utilization. How are you planning on utilizing your talent to their fullest, so they are valuable contributors to your business vision and objectives? This is a combination of performance management and continual assessment. Performance management involves setting expectations and providing feedback on performance, and assessment helps your employees benchmark their activities and development against goals and standards for current and future jobs. Assessments are important to other parts of the Talent Management Model, but we'll discuss that in Chapter 5.

Talent retention. Your organization should have a healthy amount of turnover so that you can bring in new blood and new ideas and sustain diversity of skills and experiences. However, to maintain institutional knowledge or leverage top performers for emerging requirements, you need a plan to compensate and incentivize the employees you would like to stick around. This is everything from creating a work environment that meets their needs and drives performance to developing compensation packages and recognition programs.

There's a bit of overlap in these activities. I think of both talent identification and talent acquisition as continuous activities in your organization. You should always be looking to update your definitions of talents and job descriptions to keep up with the state of your field, and keep updated data on employee knowledge, skills, abilities, and preferences. And for talent acquisition, that's not an activity that happens just when you get someone hired into one of your roles; it also happens when you look at hiring and promoting from within. You've just acquired talent within your organization instead of outside.

We'll get into acquisition, development, employment and utilization, and retention later in the book, but for now we're going to start with the building blocks of talent, and that's the data we need in order to operate our Talent Management Model effectively.

The Types of Talent Data

Our Talent Management Model hinges on our ability to collect, analyze, and make decisions based on relevant talent data. A leader or a human resources professional without access to the right talent data and the analytics needed to put that data into proper context cannot effectively manage talent. Let's take a look at what types of talent data we should be looking to collect at each step of the Talent Management Model:

Talent identification. To identify talent, we need data on two functions: The competencies required by the job, and the sources of that talent, whether internal or external to your organization. Job descriptions, knowledge and skills possessed by previous successful occupants of the role, and an understanding of the state of the field, particularly emerging skill requirements, can help you ensure your job descriptions are updated and tailor both your acquisition and development plans. You can use this also to find pools of talent in the competencies you're looking for, and keep those updated.

Talent acquisition. This data includes information you need in order to make a decision about who to recruit and who to hire for various positions. That may include candidate information, qualifications, interview performance, and reasons for job offer acceptance or rejection. You should also look at the positions you've considered candidates for and keep an eye on how goodness of fit to those position requirements may or may not have correlated with performance. That can inform how much leeway you give your hiring managers.

Talent development. There are many pieces of data that support talent development, from analytics identifying competency gaps between employees and current and future requirements, utilization of and engagement with learning systems, data on development over time, and assessments of skills and performance. These can be used in a one-to-many relationship analysis between a given employee and available future positions, either helping them to choose positions to play to their strengths, or in many-to-one relationships between employees and a key leader position where you want a succession plan and need to see the pool of the most eligible candidates.

Talent employment and utilization. Performance data, which might include your employee performance evaluations, productivity metrics, and goal achievement, can help you understand if you have someone in the right job or how you can improve them through development, mentorship, or tailored performance plans. Continued assessments and tracking of your learning and development plans can also help you understand how your employees are developing, not just from your development plans but from on-the-job training and skill knowledge gained through experience in their role.

Talent retention. Many different factors play into why top-performing people choose to stay at or leave a company, but most of these boil down to factors assessing perceived quality of life and quality of work. Quality-of-life data can be anything from compensation and benefits to satisfaction with work schedules, but in some cases, it might also be ensuring satisfaction with location-based challenges like the ability to balance two jobs in a dual-income home, access to childcare, quality of schools, and purchasing power. Quality-of-work data might include job satisfaction, feelings about growth and development potential within the organization, productivity, sentiment analysis regarding work announcements on social networks, and more. All of these things are important both for retaining talent and attracting new talent.

Other important data. Your organizational climate, social responsibility scale, inclusiveness, environmental scale, perceptions of your company in the news and on social media, perception of leaders, and similar information might be more about your organization than about your talent, but these factors absolutely have an effect on whether or not people will choose to work at your company or work with you. These are all things you should monitor and include in your assessments of your company's ability to acquire, develop, employ, and retain top talent.

Challenges in Collecting and Using Talent Data

As we talked about in the previous chapter, the adoption of data-driven talent management isn't without its challenges, particularly when you start looking at the challenges posed just by the inherent nature of the data itself. When you're working with personal data, especially when it's identifiable or potentially sensitive, you not only have legal and statutory restrictions around the use of the data, but the moral and ethical responsibility to use it well.

Much of your personnel data will be Personal Identifiable Information (PII). The U.S. Department of Labor defines PII as:

> Any representation of information that permits the identity of an individual
> to whom the information applies to be reasonably inferred by either direct or
> indirect means. Further, PII is defined as information: (i) that directly identifies
> an individual (e.g. name, address, social security number or other identifying
> number or code, telephone number, email address, etc.) or (ii) by which agency
> intends to identify specific individuals in conjunction with other data elements,
> i.e. indirect identification. (These data elements may include a combination
> of gender, race, birth data, geographic indicator, and other descriptors).
> Additionally, information permitting the physical or online contacting of
> a specific individual is the same as personal identifiable information. This
> information can be maintained in either paper, electronic, or other media.[7]

This kind of data is tightly regulated by law and statute, to include in the U.S. the Privacy Act of 1974,[8] the General Data Protection Regulation (GDPR),[9] and the Health Insurance Portability and Accountability Act (HIPAA)[10] to name a few, and limits the amount and type of information that an organization can collect, share, aggregate, and make decisions using. National and international restrictions are very different for public vs. private entities as well, so ensure you are looking broadly when you look to collect data, especially if your organization crosses international boundaries or has globally distributed employees.

We talked earlier in the data chapter about the need to have a solid data governance plan, given the restrictions surrounding PII and other types of sensitive personnel data. As you develop your Talent Management Model and start identifying and collecting talent data, ensure you know who does and doesn't need access to it, and how it should be aggregated and/or de-identified. We'll talk about assessment data specifically in Chapter 5 because that data in particular is tricky in that it poses a number of sensitivities, but is not regulated by policy, law, or statute in a way that is truly actionable.

Secondly, *data quality* is an imperative for this type of data. Inaccurate, outdated, or incomplete data can lead to uninformed or badly informed decision making and hinder your efforts. When you're updating your framework for job competencies, skills, assessments, or even employee records, you must determine standards for data quality. How frequently does your data need to be updated? How complete does the record need to be to be useful? What degree of consistency do you need to have between records? What error rate in files are you willing to accept? Remember that the more complex your analytics, the more complete your data needs to be. Putting analytics on top of bad data doesn't improve the data, it just helps you make bad decisions faster.

Third, look out for data silos and promote data sharing. Many organizations struggle with getting access to or even finding fragmented data stored in various systems and departments. This can often contribute to survey fatigue. If you ask repeatedly on surveys or forms for the same pieces of data that people in your organizations have already submitted, they can be less willing to supply that data for your use, and you can impact trust. You might also be paying to collect and store data that you already have elsewhere in your organization. Multiple data storage points like this can reduce your data quality, giving you multiple different fields that either need to be reconciled or leaving you with the unfortunate task of declaring an authoritative data source to rule them all—or at least that one data object.

If you can create governance to allow and protect the use of data, set standards to ensure data quality, and break down data silos and encourage data sharing, you've broken through the major challenges to having a data-driven organization. However, there are two more challenges you need to address in the rest of your organization. Those challenges are resistance to change and skill gaps.

Resistance to data-driven practices can be a considerable hurdle. Employees and leaders alike can be hesitant to adopt new methods or share their data. They may fear a loss of privacy or autonomy or misuse of data, a lack of understanding on the part of those receiving and using their data, or be struggling with their own lack of understanding on the proper collection, storage, sharing, and use of data objects.

Finally, skill gaps can be a large obstacle to leveraging data and compound the resistance to change. Just from experience in this space, I'd recommend introducing a data literacy program into your human resources and talent management department or office as soon as possible if you don't already have a program. A great place to get started on this is Jordan Morrow's book, *Be Data Literate.*[11]

Talent management professionals must possess the necessary data chops to be able to successfully run a data program and use that data to inform talent decisions. Identifying and addressing skill gaps not just in the population but in your talent management professionals, and creating a workforce development plan prior to becoming a data-driven organization, are critical steps.

Creating a Common Language for Talent

The success of data-driven talent management depends on establishing a common language that bridges the gap between HR professionals and data analysts. A shared vocabulary and understanding are crucial for effective communication and collaboration.

We're talking about the language we use to describe talent itself, and not just common terms for talent management. Thinking back to the questions we posed earlier in this chapter, when we asked, "What is talent?," we know we need a common language—and a common framework for how we're going to collect and evaluate talent data.

The most important part of whether or not something constitutes a talent in this equation is whether or not we, as an organization, choose to value that talent. That choice can greatly impact how we see ourselves and how we work to execute the Talent Management Model. For example, we frequently hear anecdotes about talent leaving military service, and how we are "losing" talent. One story I heard early on in my talent management journey was that of an infantry officer with a degree in advanced chemistry who was not promoted and not retained by the service. The narrator of this tale used it as an example of how we were continuing to experience "brain drain,"[12] but it is far more a story about how talent that might be valued in other places was not valued where that officer was being managed and employed.

We value many things about our officers in the maneuver forces. Decisiveness, mental endurance, and physical fitness are high on the list. Up until recently, we did not see technical capability or education as something we valued in the infantry, or at least that we valued as much as we valued these other characteristics. So we had to ask, was not advancing or retaining this officer actually losing a talent that we valued?

In the case of the infantry, that officer's talent was not one he would have used, but it was one we considered "brain drain" just the same. That was a talent we could have used in other branches of service and in other parts of the Army, which, as we delve more into emerging technologies, we are continually finding business cases for employing.

So how do we categorize and quantify these talents so that we can see them across our employees and better understand our inventory and align those talents where they're needed in other parts of the organization? Maybe we can even forecast where they might grow and whether our infantry branch actually did need more folks with an understanding of advanced chemistry.

This underwrites the critical need for understanding and quantifying talent, which can't be done without a common language. This includes the definition and measurement standards for important attributes. In the U.S. Army, the baseline categories for measuring talent are knowledge, skills, and behaviors (KSBs),[13] which is a riff on the industry standard of knowledge, skills, and abilities (KSAs).[14]

The Army doesn't have knowledge, skills, or behaviors specifically defined, but my team has had to create working definitions for our data purposes. This is how we've defined them:

Knowledge. Knowledge represents the theoretical or factual understanding that an individual possesses. It includes information, concepts, principles, and facts relevant to their field, role, or industry. In talent management, assessing an individual's knowledge is crucial for understanding their level of expertise, subject matter proficiency, and depth of understanding in specific areas. Knowledge forms the foundation upon which skills and behaviors are built.

Skills. Skills are practical and demonstrable competencies that individuals acquire through training, practice, and experience. These abilities allow individuals to perform specific tasks or functions effectively. Skills are a critical aspect of talent management as they directly impact an individual's ability to contribute to the organization. Assessing and developing skills can lead to improved job performance and the ability to meet job requirements.

Behaviors. Behaviors refer to the actions and conduct of an individual in the workplace. It includes how they interact with colleagues, clients, and their overall work ethic. The U.S. Army made the deliberate decision to assess behaviors rather than abilities. These are essential for effective talent management, especially in terms of teamwork, leadership, adaptability, and overall cultural fit within the organization. Desired behaviors should align with the company's values, mission, vision, and objectives.

Assessing and managing talent when quantified in essential components—in our case, knowledge, skills, and behaviors— collectively allows organizations to identify talents in their inventory, help identify areas for recruiting, retention, and development improvement, provide targeted training and development, and make informed decisions regarding hiring, promotion, and talent retention.

Just like the components of the Talent Management Model, the components of how we define talent also overlap. Addressing one area can easily influence and change others. For example, improving knowledge through training can also enhance an individual's skills, and fostering positive behaviors can contribute to a more collaborative and productive work environment.

So now that we've talked about the components of talent management, talent, and the kind of data we want to collect, how can this help us address challenges in talent management? Let's explore that a little.

Challenges in Talent Management and How Data Helps

Talent management is complex and multifaceted, and not without significant challenges. While data-driven talent management conceptually gives us more visibility of our talent, more flexibility to fill our requirements, and more tailored and personalized ways to meet our workforce's needs and inspire them to their best performance, it also illuminates a number of challenges we might not see otherwise. But now that data has made these challenges visible, we can start working on strategies to get after them.

Talent scarcity: Navigating skill shortages and competitive markets. We might know what talent we need, but can we get it? In certain industries, finding the right kind of expertise to grow our organizational business plans can be nearly impossible. Data can tell us where that talent is and whether or not we can offer a competitive compensation plan and intriguing work to attract that talent, and, if we can't, ways we can invest in training programs to develop some of those skills in-house.

Talent development: Catering to diverse learning needs. We now know that one-size-fits-all doesn't work for learning and development plans, not when you add in the variety of knowledge, skills, learning styles, preferences, and engagement you'll have to plan for. Each of your employees is going to have a relatively unique learning style, starting spot, and professional aspirations. However, there are programs that use data, analytics, and AI to create adaptive learning programs that assess employee proficiency as they go, making it a more tailored and more rewarding experience for the employee. You can also adopt team teaching programs, like the "Googler-to-Googler" program,[15] where employees teach each other anything from coding to public speaking.

Retention: Keeping top talent in a competitive landscape. Remember the talent scarcity problem? That means that top talent might not be leaving your company just because they're dissatisfied, but because they're being attracted and recruited by another opportunity that might offer some of the things they want. So you need to think about what your employees want, and it's not just competitive salaries and compensation packages, but career development opportunities, work culture, recognition of contributions, and other less tangible factors. Pulse surveys, focus groups, and other means of engaging your people help you keep informed of what they really want, not just in terms of money, but how to grow and achieve.

Belonging: Building a truly inclusive workforce. Getting the range of experiences, backgrounds, knowledge, skills, learning styles, thinking styles, and other key attributes you want as part of a creative and innovative workforce can be a continuous challenge. It means you have to think about how you really want to bring people into your culture, and how you make them feel they are valued and belong. We'll talk about how to address bringing these diverse skillsets—and often these diverse and strong opinions—together in a future chapter, but this is a place where organizational culture inventories, feedback surveys, and other qualitative data collection on your workplace can help.

Rising to the Talent Management Challenge

In conclusion, the challenges of talent management in today's dynamic business environment are multifaceted and demand a strategic, nuanced approach. Whether it's addressing talent scarcity through innovative recruitment and development strategies, enhancing retention by fostering a positive work culture, committing to genuine diversity and inclusion, or navigating the complex landscape of regulatory compliance, each challenge presents an opportunity for organizations to rethink and reinvigorate their approach to talent management.

The key to overcoming these challenges lies in a deep understanding of both the workforce and the broader market dynamics, coupled with a willingness to innovate and adapt. By embracing these challenges as opportunities, organizations can not only enhance their talent management practices but also build a workforce that is skilled, engaged, diverse, and well-equipped to drive business success in an ever-changing world.

So how do we get after this?

Let's look at some of the most significant advances in decision processes and how they might be used to improve your talent management processes:

Big data and analytics. We've discussed this at length, but if you weren't convinced that we needed to explore big data in the human resources and talent management space, maybe this section has illuminated that big data and analytics just might be what you need to change your approach to your talent management decision processes! The ability to collect and analyze massive datasets will let you get deeper and more personalized insights into workforce trends, employee behavior, and the impact of your strategies, policies, and incentives.

Artificial intelligence and machine learning. These tools will help you extract meaningful insights from your data faster, but they can also help you automate and decrease the time various human resources processes might take to complete. Remember the example we used about pre-screening files and flagging them for further review in the selection process? You can do that in talent management by using AI to flag high-value candidates, identify patterns in employee performance, and provide personalized learning recommendations.

Predictive talent analytics. If you build the right foundation of quality talent data, you can begin to predict and forecast a number of things and assess when you need to take action. You can predict future talent trends, like the growth of skills in a particular field, or assess when and which employees might be at most risk of leaving. You can predict potential of current talent based on assessment and learning patterns, and make informed decisions about your succession planning.

Skill mapping and development. Skill mapping, driven by data, helps you focus less on job titles and inventory and track the competencies you both have on hand and your work demands. This, in turn, can inform targeted development and training programs, and let you know whether you need to invest in new programs or potentially target new types of talent for hiring.

Employee experience. Engagement surveys, pulse checks, and other feedback mechanisms that help you collect data on the employee experience get you a much richer view of all the factors that can potentially influence recruiting, retention, productivity, and overall job satisfaction. Getting real-time insights into employee sentiment gives you the ability to not only hear your employees, but to grow their trust as you act on things that concern them.

Remote work adaptation. Four years and change since the Covid-19 pandemic forced offices to figure out how to adopt remote work and telework strategies, some organizations have made the push to return to the office while others have fully embraced staying distributed. Data and analytics can allow organizations to make better decisions about what work models are right for them and their employees, and whether they choose to work remotely, in person, or in a hybrid model, analytics can help track productivity, engagement, and well-being, things that you should monitor no matter where and how you work.

Holistic employee well-being. On the topic of well-being, we want to keep tabs on the physical, mental, and emotional health of our workforce. By collecting and analyzing data relating to well-being, we can offer support and resources to promote greater health, less stress, more fitness, and mental health support.

Chapter Summary

Now we're feeling empowered, continuing our journey through our use case here! We understand that to meet our objective of getting that creative and innovative culture and those high-performing teams, we need to make better decisions along the Talent Management Model. Now we know what talent is and what the components of the Talent Management Model are—talent identification, talent acquisition, talent development, talent employment and utilization, and talent retention—and how the types of talent data can apply to these.

Okay, so how do we get started?

We're going to step into the Talent Management Model and spend some time on the first and most important part—identifying the competencies we need to accomplish our organization's goals. And we're going to start at the individual level. If you're ready to learn more about leveraging talent data, turn the page!

Notes

1 Biz Penho (2018) "101 Colin Powell Quotes on Leadership & Success," https://succeedfeed.com/colin-powell-quotes/ (archived at https://perma.cc/HV97-QWK8)

2 Army Talent Management (nd) "Talent Management 101," https://talent.army.mil/ (archived at https://perma.cc/5HVN-42AB)

3 Merriam-Webster Online Dictionary (2024) "Talent," www.merriam-webster.com/dictionary/talent (archived at https://perma.cc/6F8G-UYYM)

4 McKinsey & Co. (2023) "What is Talent Management?" www.mckinsey.com/featured-insights/mckinsey-explainers/what-is-talent-management (archived at https://perma.cc/4KJ3-MEZU)

5 Indeed Editorial Team (2023) "What is Talent Management? Importance, Strategy, and Process," https://in.indeed.com/career-advice/career-development/what-is-talent-management (archived at https://perma.cc/9FV5-GFN9)

6 US Army (2019) "The Army People Strategy," https://people.army.mil/wordpress/wp-content/uploads/2019/10/The-2020-Army-People-Strategy-Final.pdf (archived at https://perma.cc/9J8N-MZ7J)

7 U.S. Department of Labor (nd) "Guidance on the Protection of Personal Identifiable Information," www.dol.gov/general/ppii (archived at https://perma.cc/MC5F-MVVK)

8 Office of Privacy and Civil Liberties (2022) "Privacy Act of 1974," www.justice.gov/opcl/privacy-act-1974 (archived at https://perma.cc/5PG8-6GV9)

9 18 GDPR.EU (nd) "What is GDPR, the EU's New Data Protection Law?" https://gdpr.eu/what-is-gdpr/ (archived at https://perma.cc/LC5S-2LP2)

10 Centers for Disease Control and Prevention (nd) "Health Insurance Portability and Accountability Act of 1996 (HIPAA)," www.cdc.gov/phlp/publications/topic/hipaa.html (archived at https://perma.cc/WQ9A-HCZV)

11 Jordan Morrow (2021) *Be Data Literate: The data literacy skills everyone needs to succeed*, Kogan Page

12 David Barno and Nora Bensahel (2015) "Can the U.S. Military Halt its Brain Drain?" *The Atlantic*, www.theatlantic.com/politics/archive/2015/11/us-military-tries-halt-brain-drain/413965/ (archived at https://perma.cc/G46R-QXF4)

13 US Army (2019) "The Army People Strategy," https://people.army.mil/wordpress/wp-content/uploads/2019/10/The-2020-Army-People-Strategy-Final.pdf (archived at https://perma.cc/9J8N-MZ7J)

14 Jennifer Herrity (2023) "Knowledge, Skills, and Abilities (KSAs): Definitions and Examples," Indeed.com, www.indeed.com/career-advice/career-development/knowledge-skills-and-abilities (archived at https://perma.cc/6M8N-23NF)

15 Albert Hwang (2013) "Finding the Inner Programmer in Every Googler," The Keyword, https://blog.google/outreach-initiatives/education/finding-inner-programmer-in-every/ (archived at https://perma.cc/YK9K-FHE3)

5

Leveraging Data to Understand Competencies

Take care of your people… by people, I do not mean "personnel." I do not mean "end strength." I do not mean "percent of full" or any of those other labels which refer to people as a commodity. I mean living, breathing, serving human beings. They have needs and interests and desires. They have spirit, and will, and strengths, and abilities. They have weaknesses and faults, and they have names.

GENERAL CREIGHTON ABRAMS[1]

How Do You Know What People Are Good At?

We've discussed how to create a vision for creativity, flexibility, innovation, and inclusion. We've also talked about some common definitions for talent management and roughly what kind of functions we should integrate data and analytics into for a data-driven talent management program. Central to all of this is understanding the unique strengths and competencies of each individual on your team. Leveraging data to achieve this understanding is no longer a choice but a necessity for effective talent management.

Let's talk about the different considerations we need to explore that will allow your organization to harness the power of data, uncover individual strengths, nurture creativity, and foster innovation. Let's start with the most basic question you must ask.

How do we define… good?

Understanding what people are good at is at the core of talent management, but the first part of that is defining what "good" is. For that, we have to look back to the organizational vision we discussed. What is your mission, what are your values, and what are the actions we expect people to take to contribute?

That can be the most difficult item, especially as we need to quantify good along the lines we talked about at the beginning of this book. "Good" doesn't have just one archetype people should be assessed against. An American football team needs people who are good quarterbacks, people who are good defenders, people who are good coaches, people who are good medics, people who are good general managers... you get the picture.

So, if that's the case, how do you know what people *need* to be good at so that you can determine whether they're actually good?

We'll look at that in this chapter, along with a few other key tools for our kit bag:

- What do we have to understand about jobs and people to define "good"?
- How do we collect the right data and measure the right things to see "good"?
- What does a good key performance indicator look like?
- How do we find and hire the right talent?
- How do we develop that talent?
- And finally, how do we keep that talent?

Let's talk about understanding the necessary competencies and attributes you need in order to assess and align individual strengths within your organization.

Understanding Job Competencies to Provide Context

To provide context for any kind of a supply program, which talent management is at its heart, you need to provide context for both the supply and the demand. Job competencies do this for talent management. **Job competencies** refer to the specific skills, knowledge, and behaviors required for success in a particular role.[2] These competencies serve as a roadmap for identifying and developing the right talent.

There are two primary approaches we've looked at to figure out what sets of knowledge, skills, and behaviors you need in a work role. There are many others out there, but we've considered primarily job analysis and competency mapping.

Job analysis. A job analysis decomposes the tasks, working conditions, and other attributes of the job in a way that tells you what specific things are to be performed in that job.[3] It's an evaluation of the position requirements itself, not the employee in the job. To conduct a job analysis, you want to gather information about a position. This can be through interviews, industry benchmarking, a review of job descriptions, productivity or task data, or research. Once you have your requirement list, prioritize the importance of each task. Sometimes it's helpful to categorize these tasks as "must have" and "nice to have." Now you have the starting point that you'll use for comparison.

Competency mapping. Competency mapping is similar to job analysis, but while job analysis considers the functions required by the job, competency mapping analyzes the abilities of the existing employees within your organization.[4] Rather than inferring the knowledge, skills, and behaviors from the task list, this inventories the top-performing people in your organization. To conduct competency mapping, you inventory your employees. What are the core competencies people across your organization need to possess to be successful? What are the job-specific competencies your top performers have? What behavioral traits do people have that contribute to their performance?

The key differences between these two are the focus—job analysis focuses on the work role and competency mapping focuses on the person—but I bring both up for a reason, and that reason is that you should consider doing both as complementary collection efforts. If you have a thorough analysis of the requirements of the job and an analysis of the capabilities of the person, you can compare and contrast the two. That comparison should tell you if there are things that should be updated in the job description. For example, let's say that you hired a human resource analyst to do data entry and basic analysis but that person actually is a capable Python or SAS coder and is successful because he/she has automated processes. You should probably update the technical responsibilities in the job description. Conversely, let's say your job description requires an employee to have a particular type of degree and your star employees in those roles don't have those degrees but have advanced industry certifications instead. It might be worth it to consider eliminating the degree requirement in favor of certifications or skills-based assessments.

Okay, now that we know what our people should be good at and how we define good, how should we go about figuring out whether or not they have the necessary skills and competencies we just mapped out?

Collect employee data. The best way to figure out how your employees stack up against your requirements is a combination of self-assessment, validated assessments, peer feedback, and analytics. *Self-assessment* tools and exercises and skill inventories let employees provide their own ratings and rankings on their performance, and are a great opportunity for them to stop and evaluate where they are, and maybe compare their ratings with their supervisor's assessment or a trusted peer or mentor. *Validated assessments* are formal assessments that have been developed to evaluate specific measures of a person's capabilities, and we'll talk about how to administer those in the next chapter. *Peer feedback* gains people valuable perspectives on their strengths and competencies. Often gained through surveys and evaluations, this can also help supervisors see how others view the employee's performance when they're not observing. And finally, *analytics* can help derive insights on employees from performance data, learning and development history, and other relevant data that might highlight areas of proficiency.

Conduct a gap analysis. This is fairly straightforward, but you'll compare the data you've collected on your employees against the data you've collected on your job competencies and figure out where there's a gap. You'll want to identify areas where your employees excel and where they need additional development, and you can even incorporate analytics and automation to highlight opportunities for self-initiated learning and training to employees.

Create development plans. We'll talk in depth about workforce development in Chapter 8, but in short, using your gap analysis, you can create personalized development plans based on those gaps for each of your employees. If you do this, ensure you have the resources or incentives needed for your employees to get the necessary training and support.

In this chapter and the next, we'll talk about different techniques of measuring competencies, outcomes, and key performance indicators, and then how to do the gap analysis and create your workforce development plan.

But first, data!

Evaluating Assessments... or the Other Way Around?

Effective data collection and analysis is essential in uncovering individual talent data. First, though, I want to talk about the two types of categories where we need to understand what employees can do: Competencies and performance. To measure these, we should start by defining what they are. As we discussed previously, **competencies** refer to the specific skills, knowledge, and behaviors required for success in a particular role.[5] **Performance** is a measurement of the productivity, quality of work, and effectiveness of an individual team member. Both of these involve qualitative and quantitative data to be fully captured. I've studied how a number of different organizations try to currently capture this data, but much of it is collected through the use of proxy measures with varying effectiveness.

To help us develop a useful framework for collecting employee talent data, I'll submit to you that we need to *assess* competencies and *evaluate* performance.

Assessment is a process that collects and integrates domain-specific information from one or more measurement sources and is scored using a standardized process.[6]

Evaluation is a process of determining and assessing the value and significance of a subject using criteria governed by a set of standards.[7]

The difference is that assessment is a broader process that involves gathering information and evidence to understand a person's knowledge, skills, and abilities, and an evaluation involves a subjective interpretation and judgment of that data.

We'll tackle how to leverage some flexible frameworks to collect data for performance evaluation in the next chapter, but in this chapter, let's dig into how we can use assessments to better understand our employee competencies.

There's a natural distrust of assessments, tests, and evaluations. Think about the wizarding world of Harry Potter, where they take plenty of tests, are evaluated by the teachers for their performance, and start off their time in school with an assessment from the Sorting Hat.[8] While most of our organizations don't have a snarky talking hat to figure out people's strengths, weaknesses, and other attributes, the process isn't totally dissimilar to what we can use data to do when we are assessing our people for roles. Just as the Sorting Hat helps guide new students to where they're most likely to succeed, effectively collected and analyzed assessment data can steer the growth and development of your employees.

The kind of data collection and analysis you can get through an assessment process is incredibly important to your talent management program. These can illuminate strengths you can capitalize on and areas needing improvement, letting you capitalize on opportunities for hiring, retention, growth, and development. So let's dig into the mechanics of collecting and leveraging assessment data in your organization's talent management plan and talk about how to create a culture that both values and effectively uses assessment data. Creating a culture of assessments has been a critical step on the U.S. Army's talent management journey and it will be a necessary one on yours as well.

So let's roll up our sleeves and talk about how to unlock the magic of assessment data. No wands needed (unless you insist, of course).

Putting Assessment Data in a Business Context

We can conduct talent assessments at various stages in the Talent Management Model, but let's talk about where it makes the most sense to collect and to use this information. I have it included under Employment and Utilization in the diagram, but you should be regularly and longitudinally assessing your employees in order to create the most robust data model you can on their knowledge, skills, behaviors, abilities, and preferences.

For our intents and purposes, there are three types of talent assessments we need to consider: *Developmental*, *diagnostic*, and *predictive*. These types of assessments and their definitions are loosely based on those outlined in *Standards for Educational and Psychological Testing*, but I will admit, we've taken some practical liberties with them both in the U.S. Army and for the purposes of this book. They are still predominantly administered by professional research psychologists in from the Army Research Institute, however.

> **Developmental assessments** are used to provide individuals with information about themselves in order to support their professional growth and performance. These assessments are designed to provide individuals with insights on how to enhance their performance, or how to work on their own personal development in preparation for competing for future positions. Results from these assessments are considered confidential, and individuals should be able to control whether or not they share the results with anyone.

Diagnostic assessments are used to determine or verify an individual's status or level on their knowledge, skills, and attributes. These assessments are a primary source for data across the Talent Management Model, and should be used by both individuals and the organization. They can be used to both understand the capabilities of the individual and to support organizations in meeting their goals and objectives. Individuals can use them to track their capability development, and communicate their capabilities to interested parties. They can also be used for other talent management purposes.

Predictive assessments are used solely by the organization to make personnel decisions, like promotion and selection. These are "high stakes" assessments and the organization needs to prioritize protecting this content and security in order to preserve their predictive value. However, to the greatest extent possible, results from these assessments can be made available for use with access restrictions and appropriate steps (i.e. aggregation) to protect the assessment content.[9]

So where in the context of the Talent Management Model do we want to employ assessments?

Talent acquisition. You can use a number of different assessments during the talent acquisition process, from skills and personality assessments to assessments generated from past recruitment processes and new hire performance. For example, if data shows that candidates possessing certain skills at the onset performed better, you might prioritize candidates with those skills for future hiring and develop skills assessment to evaluate a candidate's capability.

Onboarding. Assessment data can help you personalize your onboarding processes. For example, if the performance you're seeing for your existing employees suggests that new employees with certain backgrounds or characteristics struggle with adopting one of your software programs, you should think about incorporating additional training into your onboarding program.

Learning and training. Ongoing skill and behavior assessments can inform how you select or develop your training programs. This is a great place to link multiple types of systems and data. For example, if performance data reveals a gap in your organization's digital fluency, you can implement targeted sessions. Rolling out self-initiated or gamified assessments can help you with this, as your employees can play a game or perform a task to get feedback on their abilities in a certain area and can help you see what sessions they might benefit most from. You can use these findings to recommend development modules on your organization's learning management system as well.

Succession planning. Performance evaluations and skill assessments, both individually and when analyzed longitudinally, can tell you who has the capabilities and who has the learning trajectory to take on more challenging roles. You can also incorporate quantitative assessments into this as well, collecting feedback from supervisors and other employees about an individual's motivation, collaboration, and other similar variables.

So what kind of data do we need to inform these assessments? How do we collect it?

Let's think back to what we talked about in the previous chapter, in terms of developing metrics and KPIs. We talked about defining competency objectives, establishing measurement methods, setting benchmark criteria, then creating the specific metrics and KPIs for each competency, and ensuring all of these align with your broader organizational objectives.

As we look at the competency objectives needed in each of these areas, we can decompose these into different things we can measure and collect data against. Here are some examples.

Talent acquisition

- Base skill competencies—are we attracting and selecting quality hires with the right skill competencies needed to start out successfully in the role we're examining?

- Behavioral assessments—are we attracting people with the personality, work style, problem-solving and decision-making skills needed for the role?

- Teamwork and collaboration skills—what skills do we want people to come into the organization with and which ones do we want to train?

- Leadership potential—for roles that require leadership skills, assessments can help identify the ability to motivate others, build coalitions, manage conflicts, communicate vision and intent, and lead by example.

Onboarding

- New hire skills—what kind of company processes, tools, and procedures do we expect our employees to learn while onboarding? Are they learning them effectively?

- Time to productivity—looking at performance, how long does it take our new hires in various roles to reach expected productivity?

- Employee integration and collaboration—how effectively are we incorporating new employees into the processes and projects? Is this happening in a timely manner?

Learning and training

- Skill development—did the employee participate in the training, and how effectively did that employee learn the desired skills from the training event?

- Employee engagement—how do our employees engage with the training offered? Does that engagement lead to skill development? Can we determine why/why not?

Succession planning

- Leadership skills—similarly to talent acquisition, we can look at leadership skills and the ability to inspire, motivate, and guide others along with strategic thinking and decision-making

- Business acumen—how well does the employee understand the organization's business model, market, and industry trends, particularly in the area of the role you are looking at them to potentially fill?

- Emotional intelligence—leaders need a combination of self-awareness, empathy, and relationship management skills you can assess through emotional intelligence assessments.

- Change management—how well does your employee adapt to changing circumstances, lead through transitions, and drive organizational change?

- Specialized skills and expertise—similar to business acumen, does the employee have the breadth and depth of technical skills that are needed for positions of greater responsibility?

So, what kind of data would we look for to inform these areas and questions? Let's think about what kinds of tests we could administer, evaluation we could conduct, assessments we could develop, and how to bring it all together:

- Test scores from skill assessments
- Interview evaluations
- Behavioral assessments

- Situational judgment test scores
- Responses to teamwork scenarios
- Past team experiences
- Feedback from group interview activities
- Leadership assessment scores
- Past leadership experiences
- Responses to leadership scenarios
- Training completion rates
- Test scores on processes and tools, before and after
- Trainer and teacher feedback
- Time-tracking data
- Supervisor feedback
- Integration milestones
- Application of skills in job tasks
- Project efficiency
- Engagement scores
- Post-training survey responses
- Personality test scores

These are just a few ideas for the things you can collect in order to answer the questions you've laid out in each of the key areas of talent management. Now let's think about how to collect those.

Collecting Assessment Data

Having an effective plan to capture and govern your assessment data is critical. Think about the sensitivity of personal data that we spoke about in earlier chapters. We spoke about identifying relevant data, data storage, and data management, but those become incredibly important when you start looking at the kind of data that comes from assessments.

To protect the privacy of individuals and maintain the confidence and trust of your people, talent data should largely be aggregated and de-identified in some way after collection. The baseline form for assessment collection should be standard scores, but these can be masked through aggregation into categories (e.g. deciles, quintiles, tiers). Aggregating across populations for the purpose of strategic planning also helps protect individuals.

Access to this kind of data should be governed on a role basis at least. The individual requesting access and the type of assessment that produces the data should be used to govern who has access to what kind of information, what data can be viewed, the level of aggregation and identification that will be applied, and what sources of the assessment data are viewable. Personnel systems of record should also incorporate the ability to distinguish between these user roles and provide appropriate access and protection on that basis.

Table 5.1 shows the rough schema that we use.[10]

When developing assessments, attention should be paid to several factors—assessment fairness, assessment validity, construct validity, content validity, and criterion validity. Let's talk quickly about what each of those things are.

Assessment fairness is the extent to which assessment scores are unrelated to individual characteristics irrelevant to the assessed domain. These can include gender, race, ethnicity, religious affiliation, national origin, or disability status. Assessment fairness is critical for assessments used to make personnel decisions and should be examined through differential prediction statistical techniques.[11]

Assessment validity is the rationale and evidence supporting each of the intended interpretations of assessment scores for the intended uses of the assessments. Scores of validity evidence include construct, content, and criterion validity information, which we'll discuss briefly below.[12]

Construct validity is the extent to which an assessment measures content of the domain of interest and does not measure non-domain content. Evidence of construct validity normally includes the pattern of statistical relationships between the focal assessment and other tests or assessments of domain and non-domain content.[13]

Content validity is the extent to which the content of an assessment accurately and fully represents the domain of interest to be assessed. Evidence of content validity normally includes an evaluation of the overlap and representativeness of assessment content with the content of the domain of interest, including the proportion of domain-relevant content compared to the domain-irrelevant content within the assessment.[14]

Criterion validity is the extent to which assessment is related to job-related performance or behavior which should be related to the assessed domain. Evidence of criterion validity normally includes the pattern of statistical relationships between the focal assessment and observed job-related performance or behavior.[15]

TABLE 5.1 Defining Assessment Types Through Validity Requirements, Maintenance, and Use

CLASS OF ASSESSMENT	DEFINITION— Intended Use	VALIDITY EVIDENCE REQUIREMENTS	MAINTENANCE COSTS	INTENDED USE
Developmental Assessments	Assessments used to provide individuals with information about their strengths & weaknesses for personal development	Minimum: Content Validity Preferred: Content Validity & Construct Validity	>Lowest ($) Evaluate/refresh test content 3–5 years Maintain population norms	>Individual development Strategic and institutional analysis
Diagnostic Assessment	Assessment used to determine or verify an individual's status or level on their talents and KSBs; Primary source for KSB data across the TM enterprise	Minimum: Construct Validity Preferred: Construct Validity & Criterion Validity across multiple Army occupations	Moderate ($$–$$$) Regular refresh of test content (2–4 years); Set and maintain population norms	All purposes except institutionally imposed personnel decisions
Predictive Assessment	Assessment used to make personnel assignment, selection, promotion decisions	Minimum: Construct Validity & Criterion Validity for specific position/ assignment	High ($$$$$) Constant update or CAT/Item banking Set and maintain population norms	Specific personnel decisions (Select, Promote, Screen); Strategic Analysis

Finally, above, we reference the concept of a high-stakes assessment. A *high stakes assessment* is an assessment that is used to make high-value decisions about individuals, typically associated with granting access to valued resources, programs, or outcomes to some individuals and denying outcomes to others.[16] These conditions may motivate the assessed individuals to intentionally attempt to affect their assessment scores in order to obtain access to resources or outcomes. An assessment used to inform or make promotion and selection decisions is an example of a high-stakes assessment.

There are many methods for collecting this kind of information, and some major considerations. We're talking about using validated psychological instruments with potentially high-stakes repercussions on an individual's career, so no matter whether the assessment is developmental and will be shared just with the individual wanting to learn, or predictive where it might determine how someone advances or is selected, you should think about the following.

Informed consent. Make sure people fully understand the nature of the assessment they're going to participate in and what you're going to do with the data. Is it for them for self-development, or is it going to be research to improve development programs, or is it going to be used as part of a selection process?

Confidentiality. Ensure the confidentiality of the respondents' data and make sure they know who is going to see it and just how much of it they will see. To protect confidentiality, assessment data should be anonymized as much as possible.

Voluntary participation. Participation in assessments should be voluntary, and participants should be free to withdraw at any time without consequences. That goes to say that they might not be invited to compete for the opportunity where you're requiring an assessment, but there should be no negative repercussions on their current position.

Competence. Make sure you have qualified and competent individuals administering the tools, who have taken part in appropriate certifications to handle this kind of information. To handle assessment and research data in the U.S. Army, we use the Collaborative Institutional Training Initiative (CITI) program to ensure people are appropriately trained.[17]

Appropriate use. Assessments should be used for their intended purpose, and you should consider their use and purpose before anyone applies to use the data for another purpose. Misuse of assessment data or misrepresentation of the findings can disrupt your entire talent management program.

Feedback. Participants should receive appropriate feedback about the purpose and results of the assessment, including information about the study's objectives, any blind experiment conducted, how the data will be stored, and what information they will be able to access.[18]

If you are selecting an assessment, make sure you have professional advice on what the assessment is designed to test for, and how to make sure the results are interpreted correctly for your people. Personally, I recommend taking the assessment yourself to get a sense for the experience and to make sure the outbrief is something you and your employees will be comfortable with. You'll also want to consider how to make the testing environment comfortable to minimize test anxiety, and make sure you are providing proper considerations to those who might need accommodations in their testing environment.

Analyzing Assessment Data

All of this planning and collecting of assessment data is just the beginning of building out your talent assessment plan. Now let's think about how we're going to process it through analysis to gain the actionable insights you need. The true value of this data lies in what you do in terms of your analytics and interpretation. This crucial phase turns raw data into the fuel you need to drive the important decisions you need for your talent management strategy.

Fortunately, you have a few tools in your kit bag that you can use to make sense of all this data you're going to collect.

Your top two tools are statistical analysis and thematic analysis. **Statistical analysis** is "the process of collecting and analyzing large volumes of data in order to identify trends and develop valuable insights."[19] **Thematic analysis** is "a method for identifying, analyzing, and interpreting patterns of meaning ('themes') within qualitative data."[20]

For quantitative data, like your performance metrics, survey scores, and test results, you're going to want to use statistical analysis. The techniques you'll want to apply range from basic descriptive statistics, which summarize data (like mean, median, mode, and standard deviation), to more complex inferential statistics, which allow you to build predictive models and identify correlations and trends in your data. For instance, regression will help you determine the relationship between an employee's engagement level (the independent variable in this case) and their performance ratings (the dependent variable). Similarly, factor analysis can be used to identify the underlying factors that explain patterns in response to a survey.

So, that's your quantitative data. For your qualitative data, such as responses from interviews or open-ended survey questions, you'll need a different approach. Thematic analysis involves identifying, analyzing, and reporting themes within data. It's about making sense of text strings and understanding the patterns and narratives those text strings present. An example would be the analysis of interview transcripts to identify common themes in employees' perception of your workplace's culture, classifying or clustering the terms through any number of techniques depending on the size of the dataset you're analyzing.

The interpretation of talent assessment data is as crucial as the collection and analysis. Here, you'll transform your analytical findings into practical insights. You'll start by *connecting data to objectives*. Begin by revisiting the goals of your assessment. Whether it's understanding workforce competencies, identifying potential leaders, or improving employee engagement, ensure that the data interpretation aligns with these goals.

Next, let's *look beyond the numbers*. Quantitative analysis might tell you that 70 percent of your employees rate their job satisfaction as high, but let's delve deeper. What does this mean for employee retention or performance? Similarly, if thematic analysis of interview data reveals concerns about leadership, consider the implications for training and development.

When we can *identify actionable insights*, we're close to our ultimate goal—to turn those insights into action. If data reveals skill gaps in certain parts of your organization, you can target training programs. If certain leadership qualities correlate with high-performing teams, this can inform succession planning and optimal team building.

None of this matters if we can't successfully complete the last step, though, which is *communicating our findings*. Data that isn't successfully communicated is the proverbial tree that fell in the woods. Effectively communicate your findings to your stakeholders in a clear, concise manner. Use visual aids like graphs and charts where appropriate, and ensure that the implications and recommended actions are clear.

Analyzing talent assessment data is a multifaceted process involving a variety of techniques and tools, each suited to different types of data. The critical part of this process is interpreting the data in a way that yields meaningful and actionable insights. This analysis forms the backbone of informed decision-making in talent management, enabling organizations to strategically address their workforce needs and challenges.

Leveraging Assessment Data for Talent Management

Let's talk about how we can strategically leverage our talent assessment data, analysis and insights to optimize our employee development, tailor career paths to individual strengths and aspirations, and ensure a robust pipeline for succession planning and leadership development.

Employee development and training are vital for maintaining a competitive workforce. Assessment data provides a wealth of information that can be used to identify both organizational and individual training needs.

Identifying skills gaps. Assessment data, such as performance evaluations and skills assessments, can highlight areas where employees may need additional training. For example, if data reveals that a significant portion of the sales team lacks advanced negotiation skills, targeted training programs can be developed to address this gap.

Customized training programs. The insights gained from assessment data allow for the creation of customized training programs that cater to the specific needs of employees. For instance, an employee showing potential in leadership but lacking in certain leadership competencies can be enrolled in a leadership development program.

Measuring training effectiveness. Post-training assessments can measure the effectiveness of training programs, helping organizations refine their approach to employee development. This continuous feedback loop ensures that training initiatives deliver the desired outcomes.

Assessment data is powerful when it comes to providing customized training needs, but it can also help you tailor personalized career paths, and guide your employees through where they might best fit in your organization, or help them close the gaps between where they are and where they might want to go.

Personalized career development paths. By understanding an employee's strengths, weaknesses, aspirations, and performance, you can work with them to develop personalized career development plans. For instance, an employee with a strong aptitude for analytical thinking and a desire to move into a managerial role might be guided toward opportunities in data-driven decision making, decision science, or a technical manager role.

Employee engagement and retention. Personalized career paths based on assessment data not only cater to the professional growth of employees but also enhance engagement and retention. Employees are more likely to feel valued and motivated when their organization takes an active interest in their career development.

Talent utilization. Effective use of assessment data ensures that employees are in roles that fully utilize their talents and skills, thereby maximizing organizational efficiency and employee satisfaction.

Any discussion on personalizing career paths often leads into succession planning. Succession planning is crucial for the long-term success and stability of any organization. Assessment data plays a key role in identifying and developing the next generation of leaders.

Identifying potential leaders. Assessment data, 360-degree feedback, leadership assessments, and other information can help you identify your employees who have the potential to take on larger leadership roles. This proactive approach to identifying potential leaders ensures a steady pipeline for succession.

Developing future leaders. Once you've identified potential future leaders, you can start to develop and implement targeted development plans. This might include specialized training, mentorship programs, and stretch assignments that help you prepare these employees for future roles, so that when one of those roles comes open, you have a nice portfolio of potential candidates who not only have the necessary skills but already have a knowledge of your organization's business model, portfolios, and culture.

Monitoring progress. Continuous assessment is necessary to monitor the progress of individuals in leadership development programs. This includes regular performance evaluations, feedback sessions, and potentially reassessments to ensure your employees are on track to meet the demands of leadership roles. You can tailor and adjust the pathways you've developed as well, because the role demands will change dynamically over time. This keeps your skill development programs and leader development programs from stagnating as well.

Again, as you're leveraging this information and these insights, it's imperative to maintain your ethical standards and ensure fairness. This means using your data in a way that's transparent, respects employee privacy, and avoids biases that could lead to unfair treatment.

Leveraging assessment data enhances your overall organizational strategy, from fine-tuning employee development and training to customizing career paths and ensuring effective succession planning. The informed use of assessment data can significantly improve all of these functions, and the alignment between individual employee goals and organizational objectives.

This alignment not only boosts employee morale and productivity but also contributes to the organization's agility and resilience in the face of changing business landscapes. As organizations continue to navigate an increasingly data-driven world, the ability to effectively harness and apply assessment data will remain a key differentiator in successful talent management.

Driving Organizational Strategy with Assessment Data

The strategic alignment of your workforce's capabilities with organizational goals is pivotal for success. We've talked about that before, but let's talk about how to actually do this through the leveraging of your assessment data, which provides a factual basis for data-driven decision-making in your talent management space. A data-driven approach not only strengthens the organization's talent management but also drives overall strategic objectives.

Let's explore how assessment data can be utilized to align workforce capabilities with organizational goals, the role of data-driven decision-making in talent management, and examine a couple of case studies that highlight successful implementations.

So what do we need to do in order to align our workforce capability with organizational goals?

We've talked before about what we need to do for the *identification of talent needs*. Assessment data informs everything we've talked about in identifying the strengths of our current workforce and juxtaposing those strengths and capabilities against current and future workforce needs. For instance, a technology company eying expansion into new markets might launch a skills assessment into its employees to determine if the current team already has the new skills they need to adapt to that market, or if additional training or hiring is needed.

We probably should touch on the subject of *strategic workforce planning*. Strategic workforce planning is a process of human resource planning that aligns with business strategy and identifies the workforce needs of the organization in the present and in the future, and charts out projected growth areas needed to move from the former to the latter. The goal of strategic workforce planning is to ensure the organization has the right mix of talent, technology, and talent management models to achieve its objectives, and to avoid over- or understaffing. Insights from assessment data can help us chart out these development plans between current and future workforce needs. This can involve not just identifying potential skill gaps, but assessing learning and development potential, forecasting future requirements and emerging talent requirements, and planning for workforce expansion or restructuring.

Another key alignment we need to consider is *enhancing employee performance*. By aligning individual employee goals and development plans where we can with broader organizational perspectives, and levering everything we talked about previously with preference and motivation, we can ensure a more engaged and productive workforce. Performance evaluations and feedback can be used to set individual targets that contribute to the overall strategy.

Assessment data aids in *refining the recruitment process* to ensure that you're pulling from a pool of new hires that possess the skills and attitudes aligned with company culture and strategic goals. Behavioral and skills assessments can predict candidate success in specific roles throughout the organization.

Data analysis helps you with *customized training and development* that address both individual needs and organizational skill requirements. This ensures that training investments are directly contributing to strategic objectives.

Finally, data-driven *succession planning* ensures that potential leaders are identified and nurtured early, guaranteeing a steady pipeline of leadership aligned with the future strategic direction of the organization.

The use of assessment data in driving organizational strategy represents a paradigm shift in human resource and talent management practices. This approach allows organizations to align their workforce capabilities with their strategic objectives more effectively, ensuring that every HR decision, from hiring to training to succession planning, is contributing to the overarching goals of the organization.

As businesses continue to navigate an increasingly complex and competitive landscape, the ability to effectively leverage assessment data will be a key differentiator in achieving strategic alignment and sustained growth.

Looking into the Future of Assessments

All the considerations and challenges with collecting and handling assessment data aside, the future of assessment data in organizations is set to be truly transformative. Emerging capabilities in artificial intelligence, built into assessments and into other people analytics functions, coupled with the increasing size, complexity, and depth of big data, are reshaping the land-scape of talent management and organizational learning and development. These advancements promise more nuanced, efficient, and forward-looking approaches to managing and nurturing talent. Let's talk about a few of the exciting emerging trends in this space, and where we think those could go in the near future.

AI in assessments. The integration of AI into talent assessments is not the future; it's happening now, and it's revolutionizing the way organizations evaluate and understand their workforce. AI algorithms can analyze vast amounts of data more quickly and accurately than traditional methods, offering insights into employee performance, potential, and developmental needs. For instance, AI can analyze responses from personality tests and predict job performance or cultural fit, thereby refining the recruitment process. In learning and development, AI-driven assessments can proactively identify gaps in skills and knowledge, tailoring training programs to individual needs, learning styles, work styles, and other preferences based on understanding of engagement.

Predictive analytics. Predictive analytics, as we've discussed earlier, uses historical data to forecast future outcomes, and the capabilities we have to do this are only becoming stronger. In talent management, this means we can better predict employee behaviors, career progression, and potential turnover. Such insights allow organizations to proactively address issues before they become problematic. A practical application for this is identifying potential leadership candidates. By analyzing past data, feedback, learning cycles, soft skill demonstrations, and other data, predictive models can flag employees who are likely to develop and succeed in leadership roles for further development and evaluation, so that employers can have a full portfolio of potential candidates for succession into key leadership positions.

Gamification in assessments. Gamification, or the application of game design elements in a non-game context, is increasingly being used to collect data in many different ways. In assessments, it's being used to enhance engagement and accuracy. Gamified assessments, especially in recruitment, can provide a more dynamic evaluation of a candidate's skills and personality. It allows different nuances into the timeliness and tactical or strategic nature of decisions as well, as candidates are presented with a scenario and must demonstrate how they actively make a certain type of structured decision in real time. All these things are enhanced by the increasing availability of quality big data sets. The explosion of big data has come with its advantages and disadvantages, but now that it's been around for a while and techniques for ensuring the quality or engineering of the data sets have greatly improved, these sets offer unprecedented opportunities.

Evidence vs. intuition. The largest benefit of having big data sets is that fewer and fewer traditional human resource decisions need to be left up to assumption and intuition. While we still like to have the human in the loop to provide quality control and "common sense" checks, we can make more decisions based on concrete evidence rather than guesswork. This includes everything from whom to hire, promote, or develop, to understanding the drivers of employee engagement and retention. For example, we can identify patterns and reasons why employees leave and predict their likelihood of attrition, leading to more effective incentives and targeted retention strategies.

Personalized employee experiences. Leveraging big data allows for a more personalized approach to employee management. By understanding individual preferences, strengths, and development areas, organizations can offer personalized career paths, training programs, and even benefits, enhancing employee satisfaction and productivity.

Workforce planning and talent pipeline development. Big data facilitates strategic workforce planning, helping organizations anticipate future talent needs and develop a robust talent pipeline. This is particularly important in rapidly changing industries where the skill requirements are constantly evolving—which in this day and age is nearly all industries!

As the role of artificial intelligence and big data in talent management grows, organizations must continue to develop tools to assist in navigating challenges such as data privacy concerns, the risk of algorithmic biases, and ensuring the ethical use of these tools. Maintaining a balance between data-driven decisions and the human element is more important than ever, and the organizations that coordinate these two sides of the decision space well are the ones that are poised for success, not just in terms of leveraging this information but in maintaining employee trust, confidence, and willingness to share data.

The future of assessment data in organizations is undeniably tied to the advancements in technology and analytics, particularly predictive analytics, and our ability to collect, store, and utilize big data. These technologies are not only enhancing the accuracy and efficiency of talent assessments but also enabling a more personalized and proactive approach to talent management. As organizations continue to harness the power of these technologies, the potential for transformative changes in the way talent is managed and developed is immense. With this comes a responsibility to navigate the ethical implications and ensure that the human aspect of human resources remains at the forefront of our operations.

Chapter Summary

It matters not what someone is born, but what they grow to be.

J.K. ROWLING, *THE GOBLET OF FIRE*[21]

It matters a lot less how someone came into your organization than what they have the potential to become, and that you're able to unlock that potential through the use of assessments coupled with learning and development plans. Talent assessments provide critical insights for strategic workforce planning and strategic talent management, driving organizational success. They remind us to understand and effectively value the unique talents and abilities of each individual.

We've dug into the intricacies here, highlighting the strategic importance of talent assessments and the data they collect, and the necessity for continuous learning and adaptation in data practices. We defined and explored different types of assessment data and data collection methods. We talked through some considerations in effectively analyzing assessment data, and the ethical considerations and governance that come along with that. We discussed leveraging assessment data and the insights it provides for practical data-driven talent management, and how these things should align with the overall organizational strategy. And we took a look into current trending technologies and how we think those are going to shape the near future of talent management.

Just as the Sorting Hat's assessments were crucial for the development of young witches and wizards at Hogwarts, in the corporate world, assessment data is vital for organizational success. It informs the decisions that shape a workforce, aligning talents and skills with business strategies and identifying top challengers for future roles. We hope that all of us can continue to evolve our assessment practices, embrace new technologies and methodologies, and keep ethical considerations and the reduction of biases in mind, ensuring that your talent management strategies remain relevant and effective.

Even if we don't have a snarky talking hat to tell us how to manage our people, we can create some pretty amazing tools and insights with our data. Let's take our inspiration, though, from the stories and approach talent assessment with the same wisdom, care, and foresight, ensuring a magical blend of success and innovation.

Notes

1 Robert A. Fitton (1997) *Leadership: Quotes from the world's greatest motivators*, Routledge

2 Andy Przystanski (2020) "What are Job Competencies and Why Do They Matter?" Lattice, https://lattice.com/library/what-are-job-competencies-and-why-do-they-matter (archived at https://perma.cc/438A-VBWZ)

3 Indeed Editorial Team (2022) "How to Conduct a Job Analysis," Indeed.com, www.indeed.com/career-advice/career-development/how-to-conduct-a-job-analysis (archived at https://perma.cc/AS4C-9JEC)

4 Indeed Editorial Team (2023) "What Is Competency Mapping? (Plus Benefits and Steps)," Indeed.com, www.indeed.com/career-advice/career-development/what-is-competency-mapping (archived at https://perma.cc/23KM-BSTT)

5 Andy Przystanski (2020) "What Are Job Competencies and Why Do They Matter?" Lattice, https://lattice.com/library/what-are-job-competencies-and-why-do-they-matter (archived at https://perma.cc/HP68-CQF4)

6 Rubina Khan (2018) *Assessment and Evaluation: Basic concepts in testing and assessment*, Wiley

7 Dana Linnell Wanzer (2020) "What Is Evaluation? Perspectives of How Evaluation Differs (or not) From Research," *American Evaluation Association*, 42 (1), https://journals.sagepub.com/doi/full/10.1177/1098214020920710 (archived at https://perma.cc/UX8A-YLYE)

8 J.K. Rowling (1998) *Harry Potter and the Sorcerer's Stone*, Scholastic

9 American Educational Research Association, American Psychological Association, National Council on Measurement in Education (2014) "Standards for Educational and Psychological Testing," www.testingstandards.net/uploads/7/6/6/4/76643089/9780935302356.pdf (archived at https://perma.cc/Z5H4-KWQ3)

10 Schema developed by the Army Research Institute for a cooperatively authored directive, used with permission

11 Robin Tierney (2016) "Fairness in Educational Assessment," *Encyclopedia of Educational Philosophy and Theory*, Singer

12 Pamela A. Moss, Brian J. Girard, and Laura C. Haniford (2006) "Validity in Educational Assessment," *Review of Research in Education*, 30, pp. 109–62

13 Charlotte Nickerson (2023) "Construct Validity: Definition and Examples," Simply Psychology, www.simplypsychology.org/construct-validity-definition-examples.html (archived at https://perma.cc/94GU-K8QQ)

14 Charlotte Nickerson (2023) "Content Validity in Research: Definition and Examples," Simply Psychology, www.simplypsychology.org/content-validity-in-research-definition-examples.html (archived at https://perma.cc/3LCV-KW9A)

15 Charlotte Nickerson (2023) "Criterion Validity: Definition and Examples," Simply Psychology, www.simplypsychology.org/criterion-validity-definition-examples.html (archived at https://perma.cc/J6CF-DDUR)

16 Sarah French, Ashton Dickerson, and Raoul A. Mulder (2023) "A Review of the Benefits and Drawbacks of High-Stakes Final Examinations in Higher Education," *Higher Education*, Springer

17 CITI Program, https://about.citiprogram.org (archived at https://perma.cc/K6RP-3PZR)

18 APA Task Force on Psychological Assessment and Evaluation Guidelines (2020) "APA Guidelines for Psychological Assessment and Evaluation," American Psychological Association, www.apa.org/about/policy/guidelines-psychological-assessment-evaluation.pdf (archived at https://perma.cc/A5S7-QPXK)

19 Coursera Editors (nd) "What Is Statistical Analysis? Definition, Types, and Jobs," www.coursera.org/articles/statistical-analytics (archived at https://perma.cc/ZP4N-NV54)

20 Victoria Clarke and Virginia Braun (2016) "Thematic Analysis," *The Journal of Positive Psychology*, 12 (3), pp. 1–2

21 J.K Rowling (2002) *Harry Potter and the Goblet of Fire*, Scholastic

6

Leveraging Data for Performance Management

There is a fine line between performance improvement and employee surveillance and companies that have overstepped this mark have faced huge backlashes.

BERNARD MARR[1]

Mixing Competency and Motivation to Understand Performance

In the arena of employee performance, evaluation can rapidly become a high-stakes competition. I've been in too many meetings about evaluation reports and rating profiles that have felt a bit like choosing tributes for the Hunger Games,[2] having to decide not who has performed in what way, but who makes it to the next level and who might potentially be released from service. But one of my biggest hopes for data-driven talent management and talent-based systems is that we are able to rely less on these evaluations and more on the combined power of data-driven competency assessment and performance evaluation to show when people are most qualified for advancement into new positions and when they need further development. One can dream.

In the meantime, I want to come back to one of the concepts we raised in the previous chapter, about how we understand the total data profile of our employees. We talked about needing to understand two different sides of employee talent—competencies and performance. We stated that to develop a useful framework for collecting employee talent data, we need to *assess* competencies and *evaluate* performance. In this chapter, we're going to talk about how to evaluate performance, but before we get to that, I'd like to think about how we should combine our assessments and evaluations.

I proposed to one of my mentor researchers at the Office of Economic and Manpower Analysis[3] that we needed a version of the von Moltke Square[4] that, instead of considering people in terms of intelligence and work ethic, considered them in terms of our competency assessments and performance evaluations. That led us to a discussion of the different things that comprised performance. There's a lot of existing literature that combines these things into the COM-B Model, or a system that shows that B = Behavior is a result of the combined factors of C = Capability, O = Opportunity, and M = Motivation.[5]

We decided to adopt that model for talent management, but to not directly include the "opportunity" part of the function. Opportunity to succeed has to be there for a person to realize their full potential through performance but that's something we couldn't include in our data collection effort, although we are trying to develop assessments that better capture a range of possible performance and not just performance on a given day.

What happened instead was a model with a version of the von Moltke Square that looked at the results when you had low or high competency, or low or high motivation. That wasn't enough, however; because I'm a big comic book nerd, we had to add in demonstration examples, and I insisted that those be individuals from the comic book universe.

FIGURE 6.1 A Way to Think About the Interaction Between Competencies and Motivation Using a Variation on the Von Moltke Square

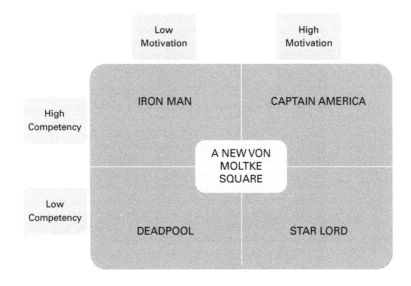

Let me explain why I chose the examples I did and what those might mean for our understanding of our workforce, the superheroes we have to manage on our teams:

High Competency/High Motivation: Captain America. Steve Rogers is highly competent and highly motivated, demonstrating a combination of skills and commitment to the greater good. He is the leader we want to follow, because he is demonstrating the best of what he is.

High Competency/Low Motivation: Iron Man. Tony Stark is a certifiable genius and creates amazing inventions, but he very much does his own thing. He can be motivated to participate with the team in some circumstances, but he's highly unreliable and follows fickle whims.

Low Competency/High Motivation: Star Lord. Peter Quill might not have the highest abilities in terms of superpowers or intelligence, but he demonstrates a high level of motivation and commitment to his friends, to the Guardians, and to doing the right thing.

Low Competency/Low Motivation: Deadpool. Wade Wilson has moments of great competency as a superhero and moments where he demonstrates the full range of his ability to survive anything. And his motivation is usually driven by his own interests rather than goals or any kind of higher calling.

We talked in the previous chapter about how to assess competencies. Once we've gone through how to collect, analyze, and derive insights from performance data, think about how you could use a model like this to make some determinations about your team. We can find ways through learning and development to create higher levels of competency in the team. We'll talk in the next chapter about how to leverage data to understand and impact motivation. But understanding where everyone fits on this square helps you understand what kind of developmental paths you might be dealing with, and how to appropriately apply them!

So now let's talk about what evaluation is and how we can apply that to our understanding of performance. **Evaluation** is a process of determining and assessing the value and significance of a subject using criteria governed by a set of standards.[6] The problem with evaluation, despite this definition, is that it's often very subjective whereas assessments are governed by a rigorous set of scientific standards. Take the motivation example above. Who decides what high motivation or low motivation is? There are mechanisms we can use for this, and we'll talk about those in the next chapter. But because that part of the function is subjective, the overall evaluation of performance is also subjective.[7]

However, there are ways we can grade the results of the combination of competency and motivation in a somewhat objective fashion. For us to do this, though, we need to dig deeper into how to effectively measure outcome-based performance.

This is an essential part of your data-driven talent management system no matter how your office works, whether in-person and synchronous or fully distributed. I bring this up, however, because performance metrics have been illuminated significantly as organizations wrestle with the decision of whether to return to the office or stay distributed. One of the primary objections to distributed work people have brought up is measuring performance by hours worked or observed working. This is not a good measure of performance; it tells you whether someone sat at their desk, but not whether they got anything done.

So let's not beat that poor metric up any further. Let's talk instead about how to measure individual performance.

Metrics and Measures for Individual Performance

If performance is the outcome of the combination of motivation and competency, it only makes sense to contextualize them in a framework of outcome-based measurement. The most natural framework for this, for us, has been one of Objectives and Key Results (OKRs) and Key Performance Indicators (KPIs). These can be used to effectively measure performance at the team and individual level respectively.

Objectives and key results (OKRs) are a simple and flexible goal-setting methodology that encourages you to pair your objective with the results you'll use to measure progress. In short, "I will (objective) as measured by (key result)."[8] These can be used by both teams and individuals, but I've personally found that it's most effective to determine the objective by what the team will contribute, and then assign the key results to different members of the team who are responsible for actions that will create that result.

Objectives are "significant, concrete, action oriented, and (ideally) inspirational."[9] This basically means that when you set an objective, it should be specific and clear, lend itself to measurement, be feasible and bound in terms of time, be challenging but achievable, be owned and understandable by your team, and be something you can support with your **key results**, which are in turn specific, measurable, and directly contribute to the achievement of the objective. This ends up being a very tidy measurement strategy if you do it right, and it can definitely help you pinpoint the actions your team needs to perform in a given timeframe in order to be considered successful.

So how do we then measure the success of your team's individual and total performance?

To measure individual performance effectively, you should develop a process for collecting and evaluating metrics and key performance indicators (KPIs). These provide a quantifiable way to evaluate and track individual strengths. Developing and measuring the right metrics and KPIs is essential for ensuring that an individual's competencies align with your organizational goals and expectations and the job competencies you're looking to fill.

So what exactly is a **key performance indicator (KPI)**? A KPI is a "critical quantifiable indicator of progress toward an intended result. KPIs provide a focus for strategic and operational improvement, create an analytical basis for decision making, and help focus attention on what matters most."[10] When that intended result is one of your key results from your team's overall OKR plan, setting good, measurable KPIs helps you evaluate whether or not individuals on your team are performing productively. So let's talk about how to create good KPIs!

Developing Your KPIs

Step 1: Define performance objectives. Start by defining the things that need to be accomplished to achieve your objectives and align the ones that are essential for each role in your organization. Clearly articulate the skills, knowledge, and behaviors that are required for success. These serve as the foundational elements for developing metrics and KPIs.

Example. In a project management role, competencies may include effective time management, problem-solving, and communication skills.

Step 2: Establish measurement methods. Identify the most effective measurement methods for each competency. Consider both quantitative and qualitative approaches, depending on the nature of the competency.

Example. To measure communication skills, you may use a combination of quantitative metrics like response times to emails and qualitative metrics such as feedback from peers and superiors.

Step 3: Set benchmark criteria. Define benchmark criteria that indicate success for each competency. These criteria provide a clear target for individuals to strive towards.

Example. If one of the competencies is time management, you might set a benchmark for meeting project deadlines consistently.

Step 4: Create KPIs. With your objectives, measurement methods, and benchmark criteria in mind, create specific KPIs that will tell you (indicate!) whether you have achieved the key results you're looking to achieve. These should be quantifiable and give you a way to better quantify the information you're looking for in performance evaluation.

Here are a few examples of good KPIs linked to OKRs you're likely to find in a business setting.

- Example 1: You are wrestling with minimizing defective products for shipment.

  o Objective: Improve product quality

  o Key result: Reduce the defect rate of your product to 1 percent

  o KPI: Defect rate

  o Measurement method: Quality control inspections

- Example 2: Your employees aren't engaging with a training module you want them to take.

  o Objective: Improve employee engagement

  o Key result: Achieve an employee engagement score with this module of 75 percent

  o KPI: Employee engagement survey scores

  o Measurement method: Employee surveys and feedback

- Example 3: You want to encourage employees to share more ideas

  o Objective: Foster innovation in your workforce

  o Key result: Launch three new products based on ideas within the calendar year

  o KPI: Number of new products based on suggested ideas launched

  o Measurement method: Idea pipeline data and launch records

- Example 4: You want your employees to better articulate your brand

  o Objective: Improve employee brand adoption and articulation

  o Key result: Increase employee brand awareness

- o KPI: Employee brand awareness index
- o Measurement method: Brand perception surveys and employee feedback

Hopefully this gives you a good feeling for how to align your thoughts for improvement for your organization into concrete objectives and then create the results you need to measure to see if you achieved them, link those with key performance indicators that will tell you about your measurement success, and the measurement methods you need to capture the data. All of this also helps align your employee performance with your organization's goals, which should be one of your primary goals for your talent management program to begin with.

Now that we've seen a few examples, let's talk about how to evaluate what makes a good KPI.

What Makes a Good KPI?

KPIs serve as a compass that guides both individuals and organizations towards success. An effective KPI is much more than a mere target; it is a well-crafted measure that aligns with broader goals, provides clear direction, and is adaptable to changing circumstances. Even though we've seen a few good examples, let's talk about what actually goes into making a good, understandable, relevant, and measurable KPI.

Clarity: The foundation of understandable goals. KPIs must be clear and specific, leaving no room for ambiguity. This clarity ensures that your people understand exactly what is expected of them. For instance, a sales team KPI might be to "Increase customer base by 15 percent by the end of Q4." This is a specific measure the team can understand and work towards.

Relevance: Ensuring KPIs connect with roles. KPIs need to be directly linked to the essential productivity expected of a specific role. For a customer service representative, a relevant KPI could be "Achieve an average customer satisfaction rating of 90 percent or above." This KPI directly reflects how we want the representative to perform.

Measurability: The key to objective assessment. KPIs should be quantifiable, to allow for objective measurement of performance. If your KPI for your marketing department is "Generate 500 qualified leads per month," it gives you an objective to compare performance against, making it difficult to argue subjectivity.

Benchmarking: Setting standards for success. Benchmark criteria are crucial for indicating successful performance. Do research and take a look at industry standards, and use those as benchmarks. It sets a clear standard for successful performance that is clear, understandable, and linked to proven processes in other organizations throughout your field.

Alignment: Harmonizing individual and organizational goals. KPIs should not only reflect individual performance but also contribute to broader organizational goals. If a company's goal is to enhance its digital presence, a KPI for the IT department could be "Complete the development and launch of the new customer interface app by the end of the fiscal year." This one is binary, but still measurable, clear, and relevant.

Regular evaluation: Monitoring progress and adapting. Continuous monitoring and assessment of KPIs are critical to track progress and make necessary adjustments. A financial analyst might have a KPI to "Reduce reporting errors by 25 percent within six months." You might not want to review their error percentages only at the end of the six months, but give them monthly progress reports so they can get a sense of how they're doing and what might or might not be working to meet their goals.

Feedback loop: Fostering growth and development. An effective KPI framework includes mechanisms for feedback and coaching. KPIs aren't just about measuring performance, but also about helping your employees achieve. Regular feedback sessions can help identify challenges faced in meeting KPIs and provide guidance on how to overcome them.

All in all, this isn't just about setting targets. It's about working together with your teams to set clear goals and tell them how you'll measure everyone's progress and efficiency taking care of the tasks needed to accomplish those goals. This gives you a simple and easy-to-communicate framework to collect data on performance, iteratively adjust performance, and tell people whether or not they're performing the way you want them to. The measurements are powerful, but more powerful are the discussions you'll have with your employees as you develop the robust feedback loop needed to make this process work effectively.

Let's put this into practice and talk about how to not only use data to execute parts of the Talent Management Model, but how we can utilize OKRs and KPIs to see if we're doing that effectively.

OKRs and KPIs for Talent Acquisition

We're going to use data in all parts of our Talent Management Model, as we've discussed before, but now I want to take a look at how we can harness our data-driven approach of measuring performance through OKRs and KPIs to measure how we actually do our talent acquisition process. Here's a look at how we can use this same performance management plan to measure the performance of our talent management processes!

Before you can use data to recruit the right talent, you must clearly define your talent needs, as we referenced in the beginning of this chapter, and understand the specific skills, qualifications, and cultural attributes required for each role. To bring people in with these skills, you need to create detailed job descriptions that outline the key responsibilities and competencies, but also keep a repository of the associated attributes you need, how you will assess them, and how they are prioritized. From that, you can create talent profiles—the skills, experiences, and preferences that make an ideal candidate for a particular role. Let's evaluate that.

- Example: You need to understand what talent you are trying to acquire.

    o   Objective: Clearly define talent needs for each role

    o   Key result: Develop detailed job descriptions outlining competencies

    o   Key result: Establish a framework for measuring attributes, skills, and fit

    o   KPI: Percentage of roles with well-defined talent fit

    o   Measurement method: Conduct regular audits to assess the presence and quality of your talent profiles, and track completion status of profiles for each role

Once you have a clear talent profile, use it to craft targeted job advertisements. Focus on the specific skills, qualifications, and attributes you've identified. A data-driven approach enables you to optimize your job postings for relevant keywords and search terms, increasing the visibility of your listings to potential candidates. You can also collect data or contract services that collect data on the locations of particular talent pools you need to advertise to—and not just physical locations, but the digital locations (websites and platforms, social media, etc.) they are most likely to frequent. Here's how we'd evaluate that.

- Example: You need your target audience to see when you have vacancies.
  - o Objective: Craft job ads targeting specific skills and attributes
  - o Key result: Use talent profiles to optimize job postings for relevant keywords
  - o Key result: Use data to identify physical and digital locations of your target talent pools
  - o KPI: Ad performance metrics, like click-through and conversion rates
  - o Measurement method: Utilize analytic tools to monitor ad performance metrics, and regularly review data to optimize ad content and placement

Let's assume that you've had success with your talent profiles and targeted ads and you have a large number of resumés flowing in for your various positions. Your hiring officials and hiring panels don't have the ability to go through each and every resumé, but you're worried about losing good candidates because of some of the questionable screening software out there. Let's figure out a way to evaluate a method for getting top-tier candidates to your hiring panel and allowing them to focus.

- Example: You need to focus your hiring panels on the top candidate packets.
  - o Objective: Screen and evaluate applicants using data analytics
  - o Key result: Implement resumé-parsing software for quick candidate assessment
  - o Key result: Use skills assessments and initial interviews to elevate top candidates
  - o KPI: Effectiveness in shortlisting top candidates
  - o Measurement method: Track the time taken at each stage of the screening process and the quality of the candidates that make it to the top of the funnel fastest

You see how this works? This is a methodology you can use to set goals throughout your company business plan, and when you set the results and tasks you need to accomplish to achieve those goals, the performance indicators you're going to use to measure success, and measurement methodologies, all of a sudden you have a system where you're not only able to measure employee performance, but able to measure your organization's performance toward pretty much any objective you want to set that fits in this framework!

Chapter Summary

We've talked about a number of important things in this chapter. We started with a concept for combining assessment of competency and evaluation of motivation to figure out how to best manage and develop our people, and then established a system we can use to better quantify subjective evaluations of motivation and performance. Through the use of OKRs and KPIs, we explored how to set clear objectives, align those with critical tasks to be performed and results to be achieved, figured out the necessary performance indicators that would let us evaluate the achievement of a key result, and discussed measurement methods to collect data toward these KPIs. This systematic performance gives us a way to not only evaluate and enhance employee performance, but inform strategic decision making.

We've shown that OKRs and KPIs play pivotal roles in the performance management process. OKRs can provide a framework for setting and aligning strategic objectives across the organization with the things we want our team to achieve, bringing the somewhat lofty goals of the organization down into something tangible we can get after. OKRs create a shared understanding of priorities and guide employees toward achieving common goals. KPIs link well into this process by giving us quantifiable metrics that measure the success of the activities we've identified and lead to the accomplishment of our objectives. Together, OKRs and KPIs establish a structured approach to performance measurement and improvement.

The feedback loop we create here by measuring individual performance also lets us measure other performance throughout the organization. It creates the systems we need to collect information and feedback on a variety of objectives, and creates an open dialogue where discussing performance reviews and regular check-ins leads into discussing the organization's performance and things that can be used to evaluate key functions beyond just those in the talent management space. The continual discussion of evaluation measures in what should hopefully be a transparent and collaborative work environment can help you take the distrust of assessment and the dislike of evaluation your employees might have struggled with before and create an open, sharing culture of trust. If your people know that evaluation and assessment, measurement, and benchmarking are all done openly and objectively with an eye toward achieving organizational goals and creating process and personal improvement, they may be more willing to trust you with their data and their feedback.

Notes

1   Bernard Marr (2018) *Data Driven HR*, Kogan Page

2   Suzanne Collins (2008) *The Hunger Games*, Scholastic Press

3   U.S. Army Office of Economic and Manpower Analysis (nd) https://oema. army.mil (archived at https://perma.cc/PC6Q-UNSH)

4   Quote Research (nd) "The Person Who Is Clever and Lazy Qualifies for the Highest Leadership Posts," https://quoteinvestigator.com/2014/02/28/clever-lazy/ (archived at https://perma.cc/EE72-5ATV)

5   Susan Michie, Maartje M. van Stralen, and Robert West (2011) "The Behaviour Change Wheel: A New Method For Characterizing and Designing Behaviour Change Interventions," *Implementation Science*, 6 (42)

6   Dana Linnell Wanzer (2020) "What Is Evaluation? Perspectives of How Evaluation Differs (or Not) From Research," *American Evaluation Association*, 42 (1), https://journals.sagepub.com/doi/full/10.1177/1098214020920710 (archived at https://perma.cc/W2V9-P73A)

7   Utin Hermina and Sri Yosepha (2019) "The Model of Employee Performance," *International Review of Management and Marketing*, 9-69—73, www.researchgate.net/publication/332793540_The_Model_of_Employee_Performance (archived at https://perma.cc/X7NK-3PK8)

8   John Doerr (2018) *Measure What Matters: OKRs: The simple idea that drives 10x growth*, Portfolio Penguin

9   Ryan Panchadsaram (2020) "What is an OKR? Definition and Examples," What Matters, www.whatmatters.com/faqs/okr-meaning-definition-example (archived at https://perma.cc/NYQ9-3GTM)

10 KPI Basics (nd) "What is a Key Performance Indicator (KPI)?" www.kpi.org/KPI-Basics/ (archived at https://perma.cc/9C9Q-F4SK)

7

Leveraging Data to Understand Engagement and Motivation

Ability is what you're capable of doing. Motivation determines what you do. Attitude determines how well you do it.
LOU HOLTZ, AMERICAN FOOTBALL COACH AND TELEVISION ANALYST[1]

We Can… But Do We Want To?

Just as we need to understand both the supply and demand sides of talent management (using the assessments, metrics, and KPIs we discussed in the last couple of chapters), we also need to understand not just the outcomes of capability and motivation—performance—but how to impact the motivation side of the superhero square we came up with earlier. To put it simply, people can do the things that you need them to do… but do they actually want to do these things? How do you know?

One of the biggest challenges we face as leaders is creating the environment we need to get the optimal performance out of our people, to provide them with both the opportunities and challenges they need to grow, develop, and succeed, and to balance external and internal motivation so that they are willing to do their best. So if, as the previous chapter suggests, we can get a good handle on what our people are capable of, how do we see how motivated and engaged they are with our vision and mission?

Let's talk about how we can figure that out.

ABILITY VS. CAPABILITY

These words are seemingly used interchangeably, but they have some different nuances. Ability typically refers to the skill and expertise to do something, while capability refers to the potential to do something, perhaps something not yet achieved. Most assessments are designed to test abilities, but research is moving toward broader assessments that can identify not just a single instance of performance but a potential performance range.

Motivation Models in Talent Management

There are many theories in human resource management that explain a large amount of human behavior as a function of both their ability or capability to perform certain things and their willingness to do so. One of the most prevalent models is the AMO model,[2] which states performance is a combination of an individual's abilities (A), motivation (M), and their opportunities (O), which we discussed in the beginning of the previous chapter.

Industrial and social psychologists added an opportunity factor for performance after the original models published initially by Victor Vroom in the 1960s only accounted for performance as a function of ability and motivation. In sports, we might think of this as a wind-aided sprint. A star athlete might be capable of great speed and incredibly motivated, but might be able to squeeze out just a little more speed with a strong wind behind them.

Still, that's one of the things we can't impact. Opportunities will happen or they won't. Competencies likewise might be there or they won't. We have the ability to affect some competencies through learning, training, and development, but that is a process that takes time and deliberate planning (and we'll talk about how to do that at length in the next chapter). But one of the things that we can impact a little more rapidly is that third very important factor in the equation: Motivation.

Let's talk a little about models that help us understand motivation.

Maslow's Hierarchy of Needs

The hierarchy of needs is Abraham Maslow's psychological theory proposed in his 1943 paper, "A Theory of Human Motivation."[3] He assessed five levels of human needs, from the most basic to the most advanced, and asserted that an individual would need the most basic needs met before he

FIGURE 7.1 Maslow's Hierarchy of Needs

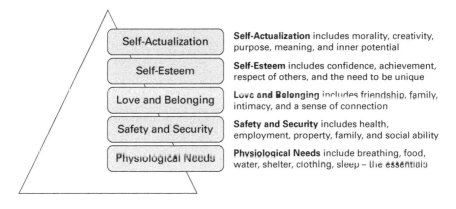

or she would focus their effort on meeting secondary or higher-level needs. The five levels of needs are pictured in Figure 7.1.[4]

This hierarchy is still foundational to most talent management efforts as it directly relates to how people perceive their quality of life and quality of work. How an organization meets these needs is reflected in people's perceptions of their physical and psychological safety at work, their compensation and benefits, rewards, recognition, training, and development.

Herzberg's Two-Factor Theory

Frederick Herzberg developed his two-factor theory, also called the motivation hygiene theory, in the 1950s.[5] It divides factors that influence employee motivation into two categories: hygiene factors and motivators:

Hygiene factors are those that, if lacking, can lead to employee dissatisfaction—things like compensation, safe working conditions, and relationships with managers, peers, and leaders.

Motivators are things that increase levels of motivation—like recognition, achievement, opportunities for development and growth, and valuable work.

According to Herzberg, leaders need to influence both sides—the reduction of factors that create employee dissatisfaction and the increase of factors that create employee motivation—to create a motivated and productive workforce.

Self-Determination Theory (SDT)

SDT was developed by Edward Deci and Richard M. Ryan in the 1980s, and focuses on differentiating internal and external motivation in an individual, or intrinsic and extrinsic motivation:[6]

Intrinsic motivation is internal motivation, or a person's propensity to act on things due to internal impetus. Activities are performed for personal satisfaction, like choosing books or studying a subject just for your own interest and enjoyment.

Extrinsic motivation is external motivation, or a person acting on things due to external factors, like receiving a reward or avoiding a reprimand. Unlike the former example, you wouldn't be choosing books or a subject to study for your own enjoyment, but to increase your salary or to get good grades.[7]

Deci and Ryan believed that intrinsic motivation was the better of the two, and led to better quality of life and psychological health. Individuals likely to demonstrate more intrinsic motivation were those who possessed three psychological needs the two researchers deemed essential: Autonomy, competence, and relatedness, or belonging. They proposed that in environments where these three needs were valued and encouraged, individuals would achieve higher levels of intrinsic motivation, quality of life, and psychological health, and that in environments where those three needs were not present or not valued, motivation would suffer.

We're not going to talk much more about the three psychological needs, but we will talk a lot more about intrinsic and extrinsic motivation!

Expectancy Theory

Expectancy theory was also part of Victor Vroom's work as he looked at ability and motivation.[8] His theory states roughly that motivation is a function of an individual's expectation of achieving a certain outcome and the expected value of the outcome. There are three key components to this:

Expectancy: The individual's expectation that he or she will achieve a certain outcome.

Instrumentality: The belief that if an individual meets certain expectations, they will receive a greater reward

Valence: This is the value that the individual places on expected rewards[9]

This theory states that you can expect much higher levels of effort from an employee when there's a strong belief in effort and performance being rewarded in a particular way, and when the value of that reward is one the employee desires highly.

While all four of these different motivation theories discuss concepts and functions to predict employee motivation, they give you very little actionable information on how to actually measure things like autonomy, competence, relatedness, ability, expectancy, instrumentality… you get the idea.

These concepts are loosely applied in talent management, particularly under the categories of performance management and learning and development, and there is not a lot of information out there about how to make them data-driven. Let's think about how we can measure what makes people work.

What Makes People Work?

Let's tie some of this theory work back into what we've been trying to create: Teams of talented individuals that demonstrate creativity and innovation and a culture that fosters them. Let's add in the factors from the last few chapters that tell us we want people that we can recruit with or coach to high levels of competencies as well, and we also want them to display high levels of motivation. And let's assume that Deci and Ryan are right, and we want to encourage intrinsic motivation. We want a team that is internally motivated and possesses a high desire for autonomy, competence, and relatedness.

Why do you want intrinsic motivation? It's really for your sanity. In a fast-paced environment, you cannot manage everyone's actions 100 percent of the time and expect a good result. The more time you have to spend giving directions and approving decisions, the less time your team—and you—actually have to get things done.

You want *autonomy*, or for your people to be self-disciplined and regulated, capable of seeking out answers from a variety of resources when they need them and help from their teammates without waiting for direction. You want them to pounce on problems when they emerge and not simply observe them going by. You want them to explore new ideas, take risks, and invest their energy in problem-solving and innovation, and that takes autonomy.

You want *competence*. This one might seem like a given, because doesn't everyone want a competent team? Creating a team that values competence doesn't mean you don't do developmental work on your team or corrective training when needed, but coupled with autonomy, you want your team to seek out ways to better themselves and their knowledge of the space because they value competence.

You want *relatedness*, because fostering a sense of belonging and cohesion in your team enables people to feel like they can seek out assistance from others when needed, talk through problems, self-develop, get ideas, and collectively solve problems. This value enables the other two in a very great sense.

This might sound like you have a "fire and forget" team, that you want one that will just work on its own without any intervention from you. That's definitely not the case. It takes a lot of hard work, vision, communication, and trust from a leader to develop this kind of environment. You must ensure that you have an open stream of communication to your team and that they fully understand your vision and mission and their operating lanes. The more they understand what you are trying to do and what they are empowered to do, the more flexible they can be. Think of it as setting constraints around a feasible region—some are hard and fast, like law and statute, and some, like policy, are much more flexible and can be given slack. You must know when to trust them to try and to push back, and when to give clear direction when you need something done, and set conditions so that they can tell the difference. You must correct and develop without sacrificing someone's ability to self-develop and self-motivate. All of these are difficult tasks, and ones you must develop your own philosophy for, based on how your team operates and how you lead.

It's often hard for leaders to create this kind of environment. We have to resist the urge to start with exact instructions and not intent and vision. The urge to strictly manage (or "backseat coding," as some of my team call it) can be a strong one. Encouraging intrinsic motivation involves understanding the unique desires and passions of each employee, and what each needs to feel autonomous, competent, and connected to their work and team.

With small teams, leaders can tackle these differences in desires and passions by putting in the hard work getting to know their people. However, even on small teams, collecting data can help.

How Data Can Reveal Indicators of Intrinsic Motivation

Intrinsic motivation is complex and multi-dimensional. You definitely should not put all your money on one metric or one measurement technique alone to tell whether or not your employees are intrinsically motivated. But what are you looking for?

Data-driven assessments of your work environment and your employee experience, including measures of autonomy, job satisfaction, meaningful work, and opportunities for skill development, can all help you understand whether or not your employees are intrinsically motivated. Let's talk about how you can develop these:

Employee experience models [10] These provide a structured framework to analyze all the different factors likely to influence your people's journeys and their experiences within your organization. If you understand drivers of engagement in every aspect of an employee's interaction, from their initial recruitment to their onboarding, their learning and development, their performance, growth, and eventual exit, you can understand how to influence their motivation. This also allows you to look for opportunities to personalize the employee experience, a necessary factor when you recognize that your employees have different skills, preferences, passions, and needs that must be addressed.

Job enrichment and task involvement metrics. [11] How are your employees responding to opportunities for job enrichment and development? Do they seek out and apply for new challenges, learning opportunities, or increased responsibility? Do they participate in voluntary projects, committees, or other offered activities? What kind of activities do they most like to participate in? These can all be indicators not only of intrinsic motivation, but of the kind of experiences that motivate your employees.

Learning and development engagement. Are your employees driven to self-develop? What kind of opportunities motivate them to pursue additional skills? By monitoring people's likelihood to volunteer for these opportunities and their persistence and performance in completing them, you can gain a lot of insight into their potential for career growth. Having a learning management system that both offers opportunities and collects data on their utilization and individual performance is a key factor here.

Self-reported measure. Engage with your employees and ask them to rate their own levels of passion and interest in their work. You can't expect everyone to love their job all of the time, of course, but getting a pulse on how often people enjoy their work, find value in it, and are passionate about it can tell you how their work needs are being met.

Performance reviews and feedback. These are tools that should not just look at performance but should include assessments on how employees approach their work, their enthusiasm, their creativity, and their commitment. Feedback from managers and peers alike can also indicate whether someone brings their A-game all the time or only turns it on in certain situations.

Employee surveys. A well-developed survey can capture employee sentiment about their work, job satisfaction, engagement, personal fulfillment, and things that would help them better pursue their passions. There are a number of characteristics that make a good survey, but even the best survey unactioned is the proverbial tree that falls in the woods, and the reason most employees hate surveys—not that they take time to fill out, but unless you have a plan to draw actionable items to execute from them immediately, they are useless. Ensure that you have a plan to draw actionable insights and communicate findings to your employees.

Sentiment analysis. With proper consent to monitor, you can employ text analytics on your feedback, communication, emails, and surveys. These analytics can assess the emotions expressed by your employees and determine whether and how employees derive personal satisfaction from their work. Results from these should be largely anonymized, but can lead to productive discussions during focus groups and feedback sessions about how you can offer more of what provides satisfaction and remove obstacles.

Out of all of these, your employee experience model is likely to be the most powerful tool you have in understanding drivers of engagement. These other techniques can be applied at various parts of the journey, depending on how your people engage with your organization at each step, to collect data for your job enrichment and involvement metrics, performance metrics, and even retention rates, and get a holistic understanding of how the employee experiences your organization, your mission, and their work.

Longitudinal data along this employee experience model can reveal a lot about how employees develop and are motivated over their lifecycle, about how your organizational culture encourages intrinsic motivation, and where to sustain and improve employee well-being and work-life balance.

Extrinsic Motivation in Employee Engagement

Understanding employee experience is a critical piece of understanding intrinsic motivation, but it can also help you understand the other side of the equation—extrinsic motivation. Don't think of looking at methods of affecting extrinsic motivation as a negative or as a lack of intrinsic motivation, but as tools at your disposal to shore up employee motivation where intrinsic motivation isn't sufficient to do the trick. Also, don't underestimate the influence of rewards and recognition, even on the most internally motivated individuals, when it comes to taking on tasks or achieving goals they might not normally seek out.

Extrinsic motivation just refers to external motivation, whether receiving a reward like a bonus, promotion, or recognition, or avoiding a punishment, like developmental counseling or a reprimand. All of these, when used properly, are tools in the leader's toolbox to shape employee behavior and motivation.

As mentioned previously, your employee experience model is important here. You understand drivers of engagement and indicators of intrinsic motivation, but that will also help you apply drivers of extrinsic motivation where employees avoid certain tasks or opportunities or are likely to balk out of the system.

Organizations can introduce data into the mix here as well by analyzing performance metrics, key achievements, and individual contributions. This data helps to identify the biggest contributors and ensure that rewards are distributed in a system that's equitable, transparent, and understood, supporting what we talked about in Expectancy Theory previously. If employees understand how performance is rewarded in a way that meets their expectancy, instrumentality, and valence, they're more likely to achieve.

Any data you collect to help you understand factors of extrinsic motivation should focus on the impact they make on employee behaviors and performance. All too often, organizations grapple with a problem we jokingly call *habeus program*—we have a program, therefore we assume that people can use it or want to use it. This is not always the case! Just because we offer bonuses, we can't assume they actually work for the desired purpose.

So to reveal impacts of our reward, performance management, promotion plans, developmental plans, or other extrinsic motivation programs, we have to look at whether or not those programs 1) are used at the points in the employee experience we think they should be used to have the desired effect, and 2) have the desired effect, improving performance and productivity.

Let's talk about how you can measure the potential impact of external motivation on your team:

Performance metrics. I'll come back again and again to Chapter 6 and setting KPIs for individual strengths and performance, not just because you need to have them, but because they'll inform many different decisions on your employee journey and need to be designed accordingly. In this particular instance, we need to make sure they're designed for longitudinal collection, so you can see trends in employee behavior over time, especially before and after the application of an external motivation factor!

Engagement and satisfaction surveys. You need a system to collect feedback on employee engagement with and satisfaction with your reward system. How do employees perceive your programs? Are they using them? Why or why not? Are they applying to use them and getting denied? All of these things can inform your understanding of whether or not your programs are desirable and whether or not you're meeting the various psychological needs we discussed in the motivational model section.

Participation in incentive programs. Separately from the engagement surveys, track participation rates in programs like employee referral bonuses, stock options, developmental programs, and others. Don't just track binary participation, either. If you model and collect data on the whole path from application to engagement with the incentive, you may identify improvement points for your program in areas that are causing employees to balk.

Goal achievement rates. How are you monitoring how your employees are meeting or exceeding their targets and objectives, particularly when you have these objectives tied to a specific reward or incentive? Again, remember that you might have the program but that doesn't mean people are using it or that it's effective. You might be offering what you think is a great incentive for a particular objective, but if no one is meeting the objective, that incentive might not be what your people are looking for.

Performance reviews and feedback. Especially in the case of developmental programs, what are your employees saying about the program? Where has it helped them and where has it just made them frustrated or disgruntled? Feedback mechanisms should be in place and used to adjust the effectiveness of your strategies.

In all cases, compare the data you've collected before and after the introduction of initiatives designed to provide extrinsic motivation. Assess whether there has been a noticeable impact on your team's engagement, creativity, and innovation.

You should also look at the team dynamics as well when you introduce these variables. Are you noticing performance metric variance in other team members when one of their teammates receives a reward or a developmental intervention? If you are, this doesn't necessarily mean you should stop applying them, but one of the things we hear often when developing targeted reward and retention incentive programs is that leaders are wary of creating a perception of unfairness. The better your communication plan and the better your team understands how they are being graded and whether or not they are eligible for certain rewards or incentives, the better chance you have at mitigating this.

You'll also run into situations where the metrics you're collecting are very different for different people and different populations. Some people are just not as motivated by some incentives as others. In the U.S. Army, for example, some of our officers are extremely motivated by opportunities to attend the Army War College. For many, this is seen as a gateway into the opportunity for officers to compete for senior leadership positions. It is also a 10-month temporary move to Carlisle, Pennsylvania, which is not desirable for officers who are also trying to balance the careers of their spouses and partners, children in school, or other considerations that might make a temporary move like this difficult or incur a financial loss.

Ultimately, these metrics will help you understand individual motivation, but motivation is not one-size-fits-all. We have to recognize variations in individual motivation and how to balance these out across teams and organizations in a way that is equitable, transparent, and well understood. So how do we do that? We'll discuss that in the next section.

Recognizing Individual Variations in Motivation

Different people value different things. Not everyone is going to respond the same way to the offer of a bonus, paid time off, developmental opportunities, or even free coffee and pastries in the break room. Due to the diverse nature of our people (remember, not "how many" but "who"), people respond to incentives differently! Understanding the factors that can influence individual responses to different incentives is hugely important for designing effective strategies to increase motivation and therefore performance. Let's talk about what kinds of things might change the way different incentives influence people:

Personality traits. People have very different personalities, different likes, different preferences. They set very different goals and aspirations, and value different things. These can all influence how they perceive and respond to different incentives.

Cultural differences. Cultural norms, values, and expectations can significantly impact how people interpret and respond to different incentives. Even your most independent folks have likely been influenced by social norms in the communities where they grew up, and these will have an impact on how they see and value incentives.

Cognitive factors. As individual perceptions vary, so can the perceived value of different rewards. What one person finds rewarding or pleasing might not appeal to another.

Temporal factors. Different personalities handle delayed gratification differently. Some respond better to immediate rewards, while others will hold out for long-term benefits. Different life stages can impact how different temporal factors impact how we value incentives as well.

Social influences. Social dynamics and peers can shape how we perceive different incentives. It's hard to fight the urge to keep up with the Joneses; things that align with social approval or recognition, things our friends might want to celebrate, might be more effective incentives.

Any plan you have to measure and monitor motivation and engagement has to be highly individualized, and your approach to increasing employee engagement has to be more personalized to be effective.

This has proven difficult in the past except on small teams where leaders had the access and the flexibility to get to know their teams extremely well. Data and analytics allow you to do that better with small teams, and more broadly with larger organizations, as we can use technology to collect, analyze, and contextualize data on our people in a way that gives us a much better picture of their goals and preferences.

Through the use of employee experience models, as we mentioned previously, we can create data-driven profiles for each employee, outlining their strengths, preferences, and motivational triggers. These profiles should serve as a foundation for tailoring engagement and incentive strategies for your employees. These can include customized learning and development opportunities, recognition programs, preference surveys, or adjustments to job roles to better align with individual strengths, desired development, or other goals.

Synchronizing Different Motivations Across the Team

Teamwork is integral to creativity and innovation in the workplace, which means a team of diverse skills, abilities, knowledge, preferences, passions, values, and motivations needs to be synchronized in order to collaborate. We'll talk more about this in Chapter 11 (Rethinking Work from Individual to Team), but let's touch on team dynamics in terms of the data we're collecting, centering around motivation here for a moment.

We discussed earlier that when you're applying different incentives to members of a team, it's helpful to monitor the motivation, job satisfaction, and other metrics of the team members to see if and how that incentive impacted the rest of the team. This data can reveal potential areas where more communication and development are needed, either to explain the logic of the incentive, or to resolve issues of jealousy. Even in the most professional high-performing teams, you are often relying on people to be extremely motivated, high-achieving, and competitive, and it isn't always easy for them to turn off that competitive nature, even with each other.

As you're conducting your individual assessments and surveys, it's helpful to also conduct regular assessment of team performance, motivation, dynamics, climate, and culture. Where is the team working well together and where is there friction? Where does a leadership style resonate and where does it create resentment? You want to think about these things as you design your incentive plan and how you communicate it, so that you don't end up doing more harm than good.

How Do We See Our Teams Engaging Over Time?

One of the lessons we can pull from dynamic career mapping, assessing motivation, and the reason we need motivation mixed with ability in the first place is that to be effective organizations, we need continuous learning and growth. In the ever-evolving world of work, new requirements constantly emerge and the talent to address those requirements either has not broadly developed or is scarce. It's not always possible to hire all the talent your organization needs, so instead you need to prioritize developing from within.

By offering learning opportunities and engaging employees through development of intrinsic and extrinsic motivation, not only to you encourage performance in the immediate timeframe, but you ensure the growth of ability and motivation over time for future demands. Learning opportunities boost employee skills and enable them to take charge of their professional growth, and you can combine that with other incentives to urge them to develop in the direction of the skills you need the most.

As you look at what learning and development programs to offer, prioritize the long-term growth of employees. You can integrate mentorship and coaching into your employee experience model that helps employees make sense of the data you're collecting. Your tools and your analysis should contextualize the data for them as well. While you might have a learning and development official in your organization, it again becomes a problem of scale. We cautioned you as the leader against trying to manage too many aspects of your employees' performance, and you should caution your supervisors and LDOs against directly managing too many aspects of employee development. Employ automation, self-initiated learning and development opportunities, and incentives, of course, to distribute that workload.

Use the data you collect to assess your learning and development programs. How are they being used and are they effective? Identify areas for improvement, for communication, for efficiency, and for ensuring you're getting the value you desire. The data you collect should guide a cycle of continuous improvement, and prioritize learning and development programs to nurture the talent you need as new requirements emerge, either from the dynamics of your business model or from the desires of your workforce to grow and evolve. This way, you can keep your workforce engaged, motivated, and well-prepared for the challenges and opportunities of the future.

Chapter Summary

In American football, each player's diverse skills and drive, the coach's leadership, and the collective spirit of the team are essential for success. Similarly, in the realm of talent management, understanding motivational models, acknowledging individual differences in what drives people, and fostering long-term engagement are key components of organizational triumph. Just as a skilled football coach understands each player's strengths, weaknesses, and motivators, effective leaders in the workplace recognize the importance of diverse motivation models. Whether it's Maslow's hierarchy of needs reflecting a player's drive for achievement and recognition, or Herzberg's two-factor theory mirroring the desire for a supportive team environment and meaningful roles, these models provide a playbook for understanding what propels individuals in their careers—and what makes people want to work.

In football, a player might be driven by the thrill of competition, loyalty to their team, or the personal goal of excellence. In the workplace, similar forces are at play. Employees may be motivated by challenges, a sense of belonging, recognition, or personal growth. Understanding these driving forces is like decoding an opponent's strategy in football—it's crucial for developing tactics that maximize individual and team performance, and for creating the motivated and engaged workforce you want, ready to tackle challenges and race toward success.

Notes

1 Jim Afremow (2011) "Your Attitude Is a Decision," Psychology Today, www.psychologytoday.com/us/blog/trust-the-talent/201110/your-attitude-is-decision (archived at https://perma.cc/Q3DP-ZNYL)

2 J. Purcell, S. Hutchinson, N. Kinnie, B. Rayton, and J. Swart (2003) *Understanding the People and Performance Link: Unlocking the Black Box*, CIPD Publishing

3 Abraham Maslow (1943) "A Theory of Human Motivation," *Psychological Review*, 50 (4), pp. 370–96, https://psycnet.apa.org/record/1943-03751-001 (archived at https://perma.cc/WL98-WM28)

4 Saul McLeod (2024) "Maslow's Hierarchy of Needs," Simply Psychology, www.simplypsychology.org/maslow.html (archived at https://perma.cc/UEM5-TJ6N)

5 Charlotte Nickerson (2023) "Herzberg's Two-Factor Theory of Motivation-Hygiene," Simply Psychology, www.simplypsychology.org/herzbergs-two-factor-theory.html (archived at https://perma.cc/3Z3V-TL2Q)

6 Richard Ryan and Edward Deci (2017) *Self-Determination Theory: Basic psychological needs in motivation, development, and wellness*, The Guilford Press

7 Ibid.

8 Victor Vroom and Edward Deci (1970) *Management and Motivation*, Penguin

9 Ibid.

10 Erik van Vulpen (2023) "Employee Experience: A Complete Guide for HR," Academy to Innovate HR, www.aihr.com/blog/employee-experience-guide/ (archived at https://perma.cc/R2TV-A5PH)

11 Christopher Orpen (1979) "The Effects of Job Enrichment on Employee Satisfaction, Motivation, Involvement, and Performance: A Field Experiment," *Human Relations*, 32 (3), pp. 198–217

8

Unleashing the Potential
of Different Talents

To have an idea is the easiest thing in the world. Everybody has ideas. But you have to take that idea and make it into something people will respond to—that's hard.

STAN LEE, LEGENDARY COMIC BOOK CREATOR[1]

Sunshine, Spiders, and Other Means of Developing Superpowers

You all might have guessed by this point that I'm a bit of a comic book nerd. Believe it or not, it fits in well with what I love to do in talent management—identify people with superpowers and put them together in powerful teams. That takes a lot more than understanding what kind of powers they have in the here and now. Everyone has an origin story that takes them from people who didn't have superpowers to the start of their journey, or who had them and didn't understand them, or who had some kind of a critical obstacle keeping them from achieving their full potential. Kal-el needed the power of Earth's sun to unleash his powers as Superman, Peter Parker needed an encounter with a radioactive spider, and the X-Men all had different abilities as a result of a genetic mutation in the X-gene (very clever, Stan Lee) that Professor X helped them harness, develop, and unleash.

As our superheroes progress along their journey, either from origin to superhero or as a superhero engaging new kinds of villains and challenges, they constantly discover new means of unleashing their power as their stories progress. Because this is the land of fiction, our creative authors have no problem dropping in things like infinity stones and magical lassos, but we have to find other means of empowering our super-teams out here in our world.

That brings us to the domain of workforce development. **Workforce development**[2] is a strategic practice that lets us do just that, develop and enhance the skills and competencies of our employees.

We're not just talking about employee training, although training is a large component of this. When we're looking at creating a talented, autonomous, and innovative workforce, we're looking at a broad spectrum of activities, geared toward providing pathways and tools for more flexible adaptation and responding to new challenges. These other activities include the skills assessments and gap analyses we've talked about previously: career mapping and planning, cross-functional work and training, performance management, and wellness. We'll outline how to build all of these into your strategy later in this chapter, and how to make them data-driven.

Data-driven workforce development, when done right, is a paradigm shift in how organizations approach the current and future employment of their people. Our ability to collect, analyze, and interpret large quantities of talent data can completely change the game, giving us insights into dynamic skill management over time, from identifying skill gaps and predicting future talent needs to measuring the effectiveness of current learning programs and understanding and influencing employee engagement.

Introducing data into the mix gives us the ability to make informed decisions about where and how to allocate our resources, what kind of learning programs to implement, and how to best support the ongoing development of not just individuals but teams. This lets us make strategic and targeted investments in workforce development.

This also lets us integrate employee preferences and goals into our calculations. We'll be able to see where employees seek work and skills that are meaningful and valuable to them, and we can tailor our development initiatives to match those aspirations and provide additional incentives where they don't match. This customization and incentivization of learning not only can boost employee satisfaction but can encourage additional learning and improvement.

By the end of this chapter, you'll get both a strategic and a practical view of what you'll need, both in terms of your data and your organization, to implement your own data-driven workforce development plan and create the adaptive, innovative, and prepared superheroes you need to meet the challenges of the future head-on. And no radioactive spiders required.

Basic Building Blocks of Workforce Development

Workforce development goes beyond just employee training. It has been defined in many ways over the course of its study. As a term, it first came into use in the 1990s when researchers and employers wanted to connect not only employee skills and training but to include the economy's demand signal and how those skills and training related to industry demand.[3]

For our use here, we'll define it like this: Workforce development is a strategic and comprehensive approach to enhancing the knowledge, skills, and abilities of an organization's employees to meet current and future business needs.

The U.S. Department of Labor states that workforce development covers "policies and programs designed to prepare and improve an individual's employability for the workforce."[4]

Both of these definitions, a practical one and the more authoritative Department of Labor one, highlight the necessity of strategically developing the workforce in the context of industry demand signals, which means we're going to have to consider the following factors as we develop our workforce development plan:

- Look at not just immediate needs but forecast over time—some of the skills we find lacking in our current workforce might be obsolete compared to some of the requirements on the near horizon. Analyzing industry trends, technology changes, and market dynamics can help us figure out what we really need to teach.

- Consider industry demand signals and employability—stay tuned into the shifts in the job market, emerging skills that are cropping up in hiring announcements for roles similar to those of your workforce, and watch the evolving nature of those roles. This helps you make sure you can stay competitive and keep top talent engaged.

- Consider how we can be rapidly adaptive—this is where the culture of creativity and innovation comes in. You want your workforce to be curious and continuous learners. Make sure your employees know how and why you invest in upskilling and reskilling programs, and incentivize them to buy into your logic and motivation.

- Think about both individual career growth and organizational success— this dual focus helps ensure that while you're achieving your company's strategic objectives, your employees are also finding professional fulfillment.

The scope of workforce development is obviously broad, but also very dynamic. Its stakeholders include employers and employees, but also training providers, policy makers, strategists, and industry analysts, and it covers a very wide range of activities—skill development, career planning, leadership training, and work culture. It's a long-term investment, about not just meeting current requirements but proactively preparing to meet future needs.

Let's talk about the key considerations of a **workforce development plan**. By looking at the components, we can make sure that we take care of the needs we discussed above, but we can also start thinking about where we can incorporate data, analytics, and AI in the space:

- **Skills assessment and gap analysis.** Everything we talked about in the early chapters (see Chapters 5 and 6) with regard to benchmarking skills and figuring out what we have vs. what we need still very much applies here! We need a good inventory of our existing skills and a job analysis that tells us what we need for future success, and then we need to identify the gap between those.

- **Training and education.** Once you identify the gaps, figure out how you're going to apply training and education opportunities to close those. Consider what kind of training you're going to offer in-house, what happens on the job through developmental experiences, and what you're going to need to get externally, and think about how you'll get it. Will you offer continuing education credit, credentialing assistance funding, tuition assistance funding, coupons, or other compensation?

- **Career mapping.** Coming back to the career mapping concept, the more you let your people know what is required for them to meet their goals for advancement, the better they will plan how to meet their goals and utilize the resources you provide. You can use this to identify and incentivize high performers, but if you do this part right, autonomy and self-efficacy will create a lot of momentum toward development!

- **Performance management.** If you want your employees to develop, make it part of your performance management plans, your evaluations, and your incentives. Use this system not just for your purposes but to provide feedback to employees on the areas they can grow and develop best.

- **Engagement and retention.** A good development plan is great for retention, especially if you incorporate employee engagement and feedback opportunities, look at workforce development as related to job satisfaction, and recognize and reward performance.

- **Leadership development.** Think of this also as succession planning. One of the great things you can do with a solid workforce development program is create the next generation of your organization's leaders. Think about how to incorporate coaching and mentorship into your development program from this angle.

- **Adaptability and continuous learning.** Remember what we said about creating that culture of curiosity? A curious culture is always looking for new ways to do things and efficiencies. That fosters both innovation and a great interest in learning new techniques and tactics. Think about how to draw on this demand signal and provide answers with your workforce development program.

Much of this is internal to the organization, but workforce development is not just internal. Granted, your major considerations are employee development and organizational success, but that's in the context of the overall industry.

What should we pay attention to in terms of industry benchmarks? And let's think about how we can incorporate data, analytics, and AI into this space as well. Here are some considerations:

- **Technological advancements.** What is the state of the art in the technology for your space and where is it going? The rapid pace of change in this space demands a workforce that is adaptable to new tools and new ways of working. Data literacy, digital literacy, and technical training are incredibly important components of this—but to create those programs, you have to know what the industry standard is.

- **Globalization.** Our industry is not getting any less international, and it won't. Digital collaboration tools let us partner with key folks throughout our industries, and many of those leaders we need to collaborate with will be in other parts of the world. There will be a growing need for cross-cultural communication and understanding of languages, nuances, markets, and culture. Context is everything, and to provide proper context for data-driven decisions, you must understand the environment.

- **Generational shifts.** People are living longer and working longer, and younger generations are entering the workforce with skills that catapult them faster and faster into higher echelons of leadership. Because of this, we are working with teams, especially senior teams, with greater generational gaps than we've seen. There's a significant need to understand and address different expectations, experiences, work styles, and needs of a vastly multigenerational workforce.

- **Economic shifts.** Everyone in the workforce has experienced a significant economic shift. Just looking at the last few years, inflation, global tensions, and not to mention Covid-19 have significantly changed industry demands. Workforce development programs need to be cognizant of these and quickly adapt to these changes, whether those changes are the fairly recent shifts toward a service-based economy, subscription-based living, or the rise of gig work.

- **Soft skills in hard tech.** Even in the most STEM-focused areas, we're seeing significant emphasis on soft skills like critical thinking, communication, teamwork, and problem solving. I have been running extremely technical teams since 2016 and there is more demand than ever to be able to communicate effectively with both a technical and a lay audience. This trend is rising.

Okay, so we've looked at both sides of things, the considerations you need internally to your organization—skills assessment and gap analysis, training and education, career mapping, performance management, engagement and retention, leadership development, adaptability, and continuous learning—and the considerations you need for the business environment external to your organization—technological advancements, globalization, generational shifts, economic shifts, and soft skills.

That's a lot of information to collect inside and outside your organization. However... as you can imagine, there's a lot of data you can collect and use to give insight into those critical factors inside and outside your organization, to link them, identify trends, and create gap-closing measures through workforce development.

Let's talk about the data piece of this puzzle!

Let's Think About Adding Data

You have a lot of information you need to collect and process to build context for decisions from both inside and outside your organization to build a comprehensive workforce development plan. If that doesn't sound like a job for data and analytics, I don't know what does! By harnessing the power of data, your organization can better contextualize all the information we talked about previously in this chapter and better decide how to maneuver in the space.

Let's think about the kind of data we need to understand our workforce's current capabilities better, predict future plans, and implement strategies that address real needs and gaps! Our goal is to create personalized plans that capitalize on our workforce's individual strengths and aptitudes, team functions, goals, preferences, and work styles, and not to default to the previous one-size-fits-all approach.

So what kind of data do we need to get this done?

- **Talent data.** Everything we talked about in Chapter 4, Talent Management, comes into play here. What are we collecting about knowledge, skills, behaviors, and abilities? To do workforce development, we have to be able to benchmark our teammates' current skills, and there's no better way to do that than with good talent data.

- **Performance data.** Let's look at how our folks are meeting their current performance objectives and where improvements are needed for current operations. This will also become important as we start benchmarking future requirements.

- **Training data.** What kind of training, learning, and development programs are our people participating in? We can look at participation rates, learning curves, and other effectiveness measures to include employee satisfaction and applicability of skills learned to workplace requirements.

- **Engagement surveys.** How are folks engaging with training, how do they feel about the skills they're given to successfully meet their goals, how do they feel about the opportunities to progress? All of these are essential for your workforce development program, and can give you insights on training demand signals and gaps your employees identify before your market research can.

- **Workforce demographics.** These are important to note, as age, gender, educational background, certificates, preferences, and interests can give you insights into the composition of your workforce, and let you decide just how specifically you want to tailor your workforce development plan.

- **Career mapping and career progression.** Everything we've collected in career mapping can help us tailor experiences and development for our teammates. What positions and training events develop the abilities needed for the next position? Where are the gaps? Where are employees most interested in progressing? You can use all of these to tailor your workforce development plan for the most interest and engagement.

As we collect this data, you might be thinking, "What is the benefit?" The biggest one is just what we've been focused on throughout this book—moving away from a one-sized-fits-all approach to one that is tailored for and actually works for you, your employees, and your business model! Data allows organizations to pinpoint exact skills gaps and competency shortfalls and can help you develop and invest in the training programs you actually need.

This should lead to enhanced career mapping. By understanding the skills, aspirations, and performance of employees, you can create those personalized development plans but you should also learn from those and feed automated or intelligent recommendations in your career mapping tools, to let people know what kind of paths people have taken, what kind of training they have taken to close gaps, and where they have been the most successful.

This increased return on investment (ROI) on training is key for any organization. By focusing on the areas that lead to the most improvement and the most engagement, you can ensure a much better ROI for your employee development. You can also conduct experiments to determine what programs are the most effective, seeing what is offered and how it is engaged with and varying means of compensation, from an incentive based on completion to different support and assistance packages allowing the employees to get there.

I once brokered a conversation between the U.S. Army and Amazon that discussed these means of developing talent internally to a large extent. Amazon told us that we weren't alone in our struggles for technical talent—that there just wasn't enough available to satisfy the demand, so they had to create it internally. They went through various different studies to figure out how best to create this talent, and ended up establishing a number of different college and university program partnerships, even their own training center, and paying for their employees to go through actual accredited university training.[5] Now, not everyone can do this, but it made sense for Amazon because of all the considerations we talked about above. It was great ROI for them, it got them the talent and the ability to flex the content of the training the way they needed, it provided a great program for employees, resulting in a high degree of employee satisfaction and retention, and it helped them close the skills gap.

All of this should be part of your consideration as you develop your program, and as you identify how you're going to collect and use the relevant data and what kind of obstacles there might be for you in the process.

What Do We Collect and Measure for Our Plan?

Effective data collection and management are pivotal for a successful workforce development program. The right data will give you the right insights and will help you tailor and shape the employee's journey right along the development of the superpowers you both want them to develop. But collecting this data isn't a simple process. There are a lot of nuances that require careful planning and execution.

Let's first talk about what you need to think about for your data collection plan, and how you ensure data quality and integrity.

First off, you need **standardization of data collection methods**. Just like you can't mix apples and oranges, or you can't shoot 7.62 mm ammunition out of a 5.56 mm weapon, you need to figure out how you're going to collect your workforce development data for consistency, comparability, and the ability to develop longitudinal analyses over the lifecycle of a teammate.

You'll need a mechanism to ensure quality, and that means **conducting regular data audits.** Is the data accurate, timely, relevant, valid to the reason you're collecting it, accessible to your systems and your analysts, protected within legal requirements, and tagged with appropriate markings, authorities, and metadata? How are you reviewing your data ingest processes, sources, and storage methods to ensure this is the case?

All of these sensitivities mean **training and sensitization of your data teams**. Make sure your data teams are trained on best practices, policies, and in the case of personnel data, law and statute governing the collection, protection, and use of this data. Emphasize the importance of accuracy and thoroughness in data handling, storage, and protection.

These principles apply across tools, but you also need to consider the **software and tools** you will be using for this program. Many of the functions we're talking about are built into many programs we have for data collection and data management, and that makes your job much easier. Having an intelligent data catalog that tells you when data was curated and accessed, and having people rate its validation can solve a lot of problems. But research before you buy, and make sure you have tools that are reliable, tested, and trusted.

Finally, invest time and resources in **data validation and cross-verification**. Implement validation rules in the data entry system to reduce propagation of erroneous data throughout your system and regularly cross-verify data from different sources to detect and correct inaccuracies.

Tip for validation: In the U.S. Army, we did a comprehensive audit of our legacy systems in preparation for our 2021 migration from those systems to the Integrated Pay and Personnel System-Army (IPPS-A). As we did that, we discovered a number of instances where no one had done proper validation. Across the various systems designated to be replaced by IPPS-A, we found 36 different variations on how people's names were entered. This should have been something we standardized, and yet no one had. Even though we had other identification fields that we used primarily to link records, the vast differences in the way names were entered in systems stymied queries and caused a number of problems. Resolving those led to significant efficiencies when we moved data between systems, as we have to do when, for example, officers commission, moving them from military academy or reserve officer training corps categories into active or reserve duty categories, which all reside in different systems.

So these are all the things you need to do to be effective. What are the obstacles and constraints you face when going after those things?

First off, personnel data is rife with **data privacy and ethical considerations.** You have to comply with data protection laws, local or international. Almost all of these involve different processes for obtaining consent for data collection, informing teammates about how their data will be used, and ensuring the data is used for its intended purpose only.

All of these restrictions come with **security considerations.** You need to store your data in secure, encrypted databases and systems. Restrict access to sensitive data to authorized personnel in appropriate roles and regularly review access rights. You can do this in a lot of dynamic ways if you have policies for how to assign roles through automation and propagating those roles through role-based user authentication.

Just like everything else, **communication** becomes a key factor. Be transparent with your employees about what data is being collected, why it is being collected, and how it will be used. Create feedback mechanisms as well. This will help your employees trust what you are doing enough to share their data with you, and create a means for you to let them know what you're doing with their data, what you've learned from it, and what actions it will inform.

When you can, make the data **anonymous.** Anonymizing data protects employee privacy and helps you avoid biases when conducting analytics.

Unless you're doing operational work that requires you to know who the individual person is, try to anonymize your data.

Finally, maintain your **ethical use of data policies**. When you are designing data collection programs and analytics, make sure you are collecting the data ethically, respecting employee confidentiality, and avoiding the misuse of information for discriminatory or unethical purposes.

So, now that we've talked about how to collect the data, let's talk about the categories of data we suggested before and what kinds of data you might want to collect for these.

- **Talent data.** Capture individual qualifications, experience, knowledge, skills, preferences, certificates, and other pertinent ability data.
- **Performance data.** Performance reviews, if well designed, are a treasure trove of data. Pull in individual performance, feedback, and goal tracking. This is a good opportunity to include performance tools like 360-degree feedback to gain a full view of performance.
- **Training data.** Track the individual's progress and outcome of training programs using your learning management system. These systems can provide data on course completion rates, test scores, feedback on training, and learning curves.
- **Engagement surveys.** The ever-important engagement survey tracks organizational understanding of job satisfaction and workplace morale. Use anonymous surveys to collect honest feedback, and use analytics to look at sentiment and trends over time.
- **Workforce demographics.** This can come easily from HR information systems. Information in this category includes items like age, gender, educational background, location, and other information that helps understand the diversity of the workforce in a way that will help you identify trends you can use to tailor workforce development plans.
- **Career mapping.** Monitor career progression and projected goals and performance using programs that track an employee's growth trajectory, skills acquired, and future aspirations to include future positions, development interests, and other preferences.

The collection and management of employee data in workforce development requires a strategic, methodical approach that prioritizes data quality, integrity, and privacy. As you work through your data collection strategy, keep these things in mind and determine how you'll set and maintain high standards for data quality, adhere to legal and ethical standards for data privacy and consent to use, and provide good research oversight in how you conduct experiments and develop analytics.

Now That We Have Data, Let's Analyze It

Stepping away momentarily from our superheroes, let's take a return to American football to think about how we would collect and analyze individual capability data in a way that would let us identify strengths and weaknesses, as we discussed in Chapters 5 and 6, and generate plans to close those gaps, as we've discussed in this chapter. And, by the way, let's not forget keeping an eye on trends and emerging patterns in what the rest of the league is doing to advance! Because that's the crux of the problem we face when creating a workforce development plan—balancing our individual team needs in the present with what we think they might be in the future, looking at the state of the industry.

So let's think about what kinds of things a football team would need to think about. Stamina, endurance, speed, agility, strength, power, health, fitness? All of these are critically important. Skill proficiency? We need to collect data on specific skills relevant to each player's position, like passing accuracy for midfielders, tackling success for defenders, goal accuracy for kickers. And then we need to expand that view to team play data, tracking individual and team movements during games to understand how teams think about their position and move in relation to others, ball possession and distribution, and choice and execution of team formations.

Then we need to think about each of these things, not for our players but for current standards and for projections of where the industry is going. This is similar to the job analysis we've discussed in previous chapters, but takes a great deal of research and forecasting. Sometimes, we have to use proxy measurements when we don't have an actual industry standard. None of these things are set in stone—sometimes you just have to make an assumption to get started! But this results in a solid collection of metrics you can use to benchmark team performance and make recommendations for improvement.

Gathering all this data together, we can customize a number of different training plans, both for the team and for the individual based on how we analyze it. We should understand the deficiencies between current standards and future goals and the individual and team performance in all of these various areas. Once we do that, we can figure out what we need to do in terms of physical training, skill development, drills, coaching, physiological health and recovery, visualization exercises and simulation, and feedback and review sessions.

All of these things come together to develop a holistic understanding of capabilities, gaps, and how to best develop to meet future requirements.

What Kind of Tools Do I Need to Start Analyzing My Data?

Let's start with the basics—**hardware, software, firmware, cloud**. Whatever kind of information technology solutions your organization uses, you'll need to make sure that you have a safe, secure, and accessible place to store your personnel data, analytics software to make sense of it, and a means to display it.

Many companies will already be familiar with tools like Tableau, Microsoft Power BI, SAS, and other analytic tools, but depending on the size of your company, you may need to look at larger software solutions for scalability. The more mature your analytics program gets, the more you may want to look into larger human resource and people analytics systems, like BambooHR, Talentsoft, Workday, and similar.

Personnel data, as we've discussed, comes with more than its fair share of sensitivities and protections, and you'll need to make sure you take that into account and if you are doing research and not just operational work with your data, you may need to make sure your organization has a Human Research Protection Program.

Next, let's think about how much data you have and how you want to analyze it.

Your goal should be to create a **mature analytics process** so that you have the people, platforms, processes, and culture needed to implement analytic solutions from the descriptive to the prescriptive. However, this is extremely dependent on the quality, quantity, accessibility, and relevance of your data. Much of your work will be descriptive analytics, or describing the current state and what has happened. However, the true power of analytics comes when you can start using predictive analytics.

Predictive analytics let you make robust forecasts about future events. In the case of workforce development, you can predict engagement levels, skill development, and future hiring needs when you don't have sufficient time or engagement to develop employees into emerging positions. Developed properly, your analytics can also help you identify employees who are most likely to succeed in a role or to learn the necessary tasks in an emergent requirement.

For all of this, you don't have to create all of your standards and goals from scratch. **Benchmarking against industry standards** can help you provide valuable context on how your people and your organization compare against peers in like areas. You can also leverage commercial trends like LinkedIn's Talent Insights to see what kinds of skills are emerging in hiring announcements and job descriptions, and use smart automation to recommend that you add those to current and future job descriptions and performance plans.

Finally, you'll need to figure out how you're going to govern and safeguard all of this data. Your chief data officer's data governance plan should cover how you are going to protect your talent data and should identify who (what roles) can access what type of data, the level of aggregation of that data, and whether or not that data is deidentified. The more robust your data and analytics program, however, it might be helpful to consider maturing your program from just data governance to a Human Research Protection Program.

> A Human Research Protection Program (HRPP) is a comprehensive system that helps you ensure that you are treating human subjects involved in research ethically and responsibly. The primary purpose of the program is to protect the rights and well-being of research participants, particularly in studies that involve sensitive personal information. They establish guidelines for the conduct of research and will let you know when you need to run things by an Institutional Review Board (IRB) or another type of ethics committee to review for ethical compliance.
>
> While HRPPs are normally associated with research institutions, the principles and practices they advocate are seeing much broader use across other types of organizations that find themselves doing research-like work. Companies handling sensitive personnel data can and should adopt similar principles to protect employee privacy and ensure data is used ethically!

What Kinds of Patterns and Trends Should I Be Looking For?

Analysis of your talent data can show patterns and trends in **talent acquisition and retention.** Who did you hire for what positions, and were they successful in that position and in future ones? Who stays and who leaves and why? Identifying these things can provide you with a lot of useful information for your recruitment and retention strategies.

Once we have acquired our talent, **performance management** trends are also ones we should be watching for. Identifying high performers, underperformers, and the factors that contribute to their performances allows you to shape behavior through the engagement drivers we've discussed previously, and tailor training and development plans for everything from succession planning and development to remedial training for underperformers.

When we get to the point where we understand current and future skill requirements and the current skills of the workforce, we need to identify and flag **skill gaps**. This is a critical element for us to be able to proactively plan our training and development needs.

Finally, we should be looking at all kinds of **employee engagement** data. Employee motivation, job satisfaction, interests, preferences, and engagement drivers are important for us to offer both programs they engage with and offer them in means they will actually use. Employee experience insights are critical components of shaping future experience offerings.

A QUICK CASE STUDY ON BRIDGING SKILLS GAPS

The U.S. Army released its initial drafts of the Army Cloud Plan and the Army Data Plan in 2019[6] and 2021,[7] directing the force to modernize its digital efforts using cloud-based platforms and data architecture. However, we almost immediately ran into a shortage of capability to execute this plan. Given the urgency to adapt and evolve, we embarked on a strategic talent management initiative to identify the Army's data workforce.

The first step was a comprehensive data scrub of our personnel systems to find not just people who were working in specifically coded data fields or in career field designators for data and IT, but people who had degrees and certificates in this space or who had received performance appraisals or commendations calling out their work in the digital space. This gave us a much broader view of where our digital and data talent lay, and where we had gaps. The largest gap was not our data workforce, which we had developed well, but digital and data literacy in key enablers—the lawyers, contracting officers, operational data stewards, and other people who worked adjacent to our data professionals and needed expertise, though not necessary the experience of having hands on keyboards.

We initiated a pilot program in 2021 based on a Data Literacy 101 course my friend Nick Clark developed while on his operational experience assignment as an Academy Professor at West Point. We taught the course a few times, and tailored it based on experience, skill levels, and the types of data and problems different units would most likely experience. The course caught on, particularly from the standpoint that we could tailor it to specific problems and data sets, not as a one-size-fits-all recorded solution.

The impact of just this initial training was profound. Adoption and effectiveness of data resources in organizations that received data literacy training increased noticeably, and there was a rise in employee engagement and confidence concerning data, digital fluency, and technology throughout those organizations.

From that point, the Army has incorporated different tailored levels of data literacy training, not as a separate course (except for the introductory course) but integrated into our professional military education so that it can cater to various practical applications that are most relevant to the learners.

Conducting a Skills Gap Analysis

Let's talk about the steps to conduct a skills gap analysis so that you can identify where to invest in training and development:

1 **Identify future goals and objectives.** Understanding your business objectives and the direction you want to take is critical. As you identify those objectives, consider market trends, emerging technologies, and industry standards that might impact the growth of skills and the changes you might make to these objectives over time.

2 **Analyze job roles and requirements.** There are two parts to this activity. The first is evaluating what your current workforce is required to do through analyzing job descriptions and industry standards. Use this to determine the knowledge needed for the role. Now let's take a future look at those goals and objectives you just made. What skills do your people need to achieve the goals and objectives of your organization? What is missing from your current requirements, and where will those new skills need to grow?

3 **Assess your team's current skills.** Evaluate the existing skills of your workforce. Performance reviews and skill assessment tools can assist with this, and you can collect data from your Human Resource Information Systems (HRIS) and Learning Management Systems (LMS)

on credentials, resumé items, certificates, and other data points. Make sure you are searching for data on a range of competencies, including those new emerging competencies you identified from that future look.

4 **Identify the gaps.** Compare the current skills of your workforce with both the current and future requirements. This will show you where skills fall short of what is needed, but also where skills will evolve, and where you might need something very different in the future than you need currently (Hint: Don't invest money in building skills that will be obsolete). Prioritize the skill gaps based on your business objectives.

5 **Use data-driven approaches to close the gaps.** Now comes the time to use your data most effectively. You don't want a one-size-fits-all skills approach. You want to create programs and resources that take advantage of how your employees learn and work best. Some of your skills can be closed through on-the-job training, some of them need professional development courses, some need workshops, and some can be self-initiated through online learning programs. Use your data on skills, competencies, preferences, and employee engagement to assess what programs will most likely result in the most engagement and the most success closing that gap.

As a reminder, this is not a one-time activity but something you should be doing regularly. As your business evolves and the economic landscape shifts, you should regularly assess the state of the field against the state of your company's skills and reassess to make sure your workforce stays competent and competitive.

This is also a point where your hard investment into creating that culture of curiosity and innovation will pay off! Creating a culture of learning generally means people will want to learn new things, whereas if you allow people to grow static and get stuck in a rut, you're going to have to do a lot more work to jog them out of it!

Future Trends in Workforce Development

As we look toward the future of work, data-driven workforce development is poised to transform just as the digital landscape continues to transform. Technology offers new and powerful ways to gain insight into talent development, but at the same time, the changes that enable us are things we need to teach our workforce to use as well!

Further integration of AI. No one has to look too far in the news to see the growing rise of AI capabilities and the interest in applying these. The better these tools become (and the better the data we can give them), the more sophisticated and predictive the insights they can generate. Our ability to forecast future trends, skill needs, emerging requirements, and gaps will improve, as will our ability to align these with targeted training and development. Just as with the growth of technology, the growth of AI will see the emergence of new skills and techniques needed to effectively partner with AI. Some roles will be totally replaced with automation, but most will likely see some level of AI integration that your workforce will have to be trained to use properly.

Personalization. The rise of digital collaboration tools and platforms will continue to facilitate more personalized and flexible learning experiences. Extended reality experiences (virtual, augmented, and mixed reality) provide customized and on-demand skill development that is extremely easy to tailor to individual learning styles and can be sped up, slowed down, or repeated as needed.

Monitoring and continuous adaptation. Real-time monitoring of employee performance and new assessments will give businesses not just an idea of how employees perform and learn but how they have the potential to learn. Scoring individuals on a range of performance and effort rather than just a single snapshot at one point in time gives you an understanding of how much additional capability you might be able to train them to achieve, or where they may have reached their peak (and help guide how much effort either of you want to put into growing them in that particular space).

Preparing for these future workforce challenges, it's more important than ever that you lead your organization to remain adaptable and resilient. It's not just about having all the learning technology and data, but emphasizing that culture of continuous learning, curiosity, and innovation. The more your organization believes in having a growth mindset, the more they are willing to improve their abilities and talents as needed.

Chapter Summary

We've covered an important series of topics in this chapter when it comes to the basic building blocks of workforce development, and how we can combine the data we know and collect about our people's performance and competencies with data we gain about how they learn to craft a tailored learning and development plan for each person. Just like all the superhero journeys we've followed, it's important to not treat our people as static, and to know that they have the potential to grow and learn and transform if we provide them with the right incentives and resources. If we can figure out the best ways to identify how to grow everyone's skills, we have a much better chance of unlocking those innovative solutions we need.

Notes

1   Riz Pasha (2018) "43 Super Stan Lee Quotes on Life," SucceedFeed, https://succeedfeed.com/stan-lee-quotes/ (archived at https://perma.cc/23VP-EJCH)

2   Ronald L. Jacobs and Joshua D. Hawley (2009) "The Emergence of 'Workforce Development': Definition, Conceptual Boundaries, and Implications," in *International Handbook of Education for the Changing World of Work*, www.researchgate.net/publication/226306067_The_Emergence_of_%27Workforce_Development%27_Definition_Conceptual_Boundaries_and_Implications (archived at https://perma.cc/ZGJ5-VTE5)

3   Ronald L. Jacobs and Joshua D. Hawley (2009) *International Handbook of Education for the Changing World of Work*, pp. 2537–39

4   Department of Labor (nd) Workforce Innovation and Opportunity Act, www.dol.gov/agencies/eta/wioa (archived at https://perma.cc/BB5T-W4WC)

5   Amazon Staff (2022) "Amazon Pays College Tuition For Front Line Employees," Amazon, www.aboutamazon.com/news/workplace/amazon-to-pay-college-tuition-for-front-line-employees (archived at https://perma.cc/3ZBB-FJZB)

6   Chief Information Officer, U.S. Army (2019) "Army Data Plan 2019," U.S. Army Stand-To! Update, www.army.mil/standto/archive/2019/11/22/ (archived at https://perma.cc/9RCF-ZB6U)

7   Chief Information Officer, U.S. Army (2022) "Army Data Plan 2021," https://api.army.mil/e2/c/downloads/2022/10/13/16061cab/army-data-plan-final.pdf (archived at https://perma.cc/EB79-JPT9)

9

Managing Different Thought and Work Styles

When a measure becomes a target, it ceases to be a good measure.
CHARLES GOODHART, LABOR ECONOMIST[1]

Contagion, Chaos, and Opportunity

We're delving deep into how to build exceptional teams of talent that span across broad capabilities here. As we do that, it's becoming clear that people have different knowledge, skills, abilities, behaviors, preferences, values, and motivations. Because of that, we should also throw out the idea that people think and work the same way and that a *one-size-fits-all* work model will capture everyone you need for your team.

The Covid-19 crisis turned the modern way of work on its head in many ways, but first and foremost, it forced organizations to get people out of close contact with each other. Remote work and individual work existed long before that, but not at scale. It made sense that a lot of our practical and trade work happened at a set location during set times, but for our knowledge workers, especially those who commuted back and forth to a cubicle, we had more flexibility and we used it. Years later, people have dramatically changed the way they look at work and their expectations of work.

Business models have been far less flexible, however. Some businesses adapted to remote work very well, whereas others maintained the office mentality, only copied and pasted into the digital collaboration space. This is a very input-based mentality, focusing on metrics that are easily measurable but don't contribute to productivity. Leaders with this mentality focus on whether or not people are present at meetings, if they chime in for accountability at the right times, and try to determine how to "see" whether or not people are at their desks at home.

This type of focus leads to work methods that not only keep you from capitalizing on all the strengths of distributed work, they just plain don't work. Steve Glaveski[2] calls this Level 2—recreating the office online. He estimates that this is where most offices go and stop innovating, and this probably is what has led many managers to try to push for a return to the office. Even some of their workers, although they might be more productive outside the office, might crave the office under these conditions. At least then they can step away from their desks without feeling like Big Brother[3] is watching them.

A large contributor to keeping businesses from performing well when they moved from in-person conditions to distributed and remote conditions is just what we talked about in Chapter 6—good performance measures and metrics.

It amazes me how many offices default to "hours of work" as a measure of performance. The amount of time someone is sitting at their desk doesn't equate to them being productive. Everyone can probably recount a time when they've walked around and seen someone zoning out, reading a book, or shopping on Amazon while they're at their desk simply because they have to be at work and they haven't found or been tasked with anything more productive to do. One of my favorite moments in the *Avengers* movie is when Tony Stark is causing trouble on the bridge of S.H.I.E.L.D.'s massive airship, points to one of the agents, and accuses, "That man's playing Galaga. Thought we wouldn't notice. But we did."[4] That isn't to say that good outcome-based performance metrics will prevent someone from playing Galaga while at their desk, but—except potentially in the case of the agent who was supposed to be on duty—it might keep that from being something we care about or even monitor.

We've talked about how we can better measure and manage individual performance and the performance of an organization by redefining how we look at productivity metrics. We can apply this to capturing information about the employee experience as well, by looking at the way we expect people to be productive and aligning that with varying methods of work, times for work, and how we batch work into constrained and unconstrained time blocks. And let's think about how we can harmonize across all these different styles of work so that we have a concept that works for the individual and works for the team, and more importantly, works for everyone to collectively achieve their goals and those of the organization.

This may seem at first glance like it's a remote work discussion, but this isn't about remote work. It's about different styles of work, different times for work, different manners of thinking, and the growing need in knowledge work to make room for all these different types of work. Ironically, our distributed work experiments during Covid-19 taught us many things about distributed work, flexible work, and performance that we can use to manage teams of diverse thinkers. We just need to dig into them a little bit deeper than at office space level.

The Importance of Thought and Work Style Diversity

Diverse teams drive innovation. Bringing together individuals with different backgrounds, experiences, perspectives, approaches to problem-solving, and thought processes allows you to attack problems from far more angles than you might otherwise. When people from various backgrounds collaborate, they challenge assumptions and uncover problem areas that a more homogenous team might otherwise be oblivious to.

Let's just cover the subject of language. As a member of the U.S. Army, I spend a lot of time collaborating with our close allies, many of whom speak English as a common language. But when you introduce slang, accents, dialect, idioms, colloquialisms, and other locality-based eccentricities of the language, speaking English in Australia, England, Scotland, Canada, and the United States... we might as well be speaking different languages. Even within the United States, we can get into great debates over the proper word for carbonated beverages. In some parts of the country, it's soda, in others, it's pop, and in still others, it's all Coke, regardless of whether or not it was produced by Coca-Cola.[5] If you want to have some fun, ask your American colleague if they go to drink water from a drinking fountain, a faucet, a cooler, or a bubbler.

These might be humorous examples, but think about what happens sometimes in marketing and advertising, when we need a critical word for a jingle, to name a character, or to spell out an acronym, and it has very different meanings and connotations in our different markets. A team working solely in the American South would not catch some of the potential issues that a team with a more diverse command of language would.

Think about the other kinds of solutions we need to develop, and how some of those solutions might fail if we didn't have all the necessary perspectives at the table. I spent a lot of time working with NATO and USAID on humanitarian assistance and disaster relief (HADR) projects prior to beginning my journey in personnel. This was prior to the Women, Peace, and Security Act of 2017 being signed into law[6] but we were already working with our allies and partners on the meaningful inclusion of women into response plans. One of the major considerations we had for humanitarian aid was creating living spaces with accommodation for women and children. That often failed when you didn't have the right people working on the solution, particularly mothers, because for some reason, male-only planning teams always seemed to equate "child" with "baby." They were good at planning for diapers, but not planning for the accommodations, clothing, and resources needed for six- to twelve-year-olds.

Having these different perspectives doesn't just keep you from making ill-informed decisions. When you turn them loose on a project, they challenge assumptions, ask to amend policies, and figure out new ways of doing business. I spent three years managing the planning team taking on the U.S. Army's data workforce modernization, and we completely pulled apart the concept of career paths and specialties, just because there was so much skill and competency overlap between the different data personas we were trying to manage. The resulting model looked nothing like the typical skill paths or pyramids you might normally see, but was a topography map with dozens of different crisscrossing footpaths to get a person from their starting skill set to where we eventually wanted them to be. This talent topography map became what our Assistant Secretary of the Army for Manpower and Reserve Affairs has referred to as a vision for a "jungle gym model" of career development.[7]

Creativity thrives when you bring in unconventional thinking. When you bring together groups of people who think differently from one another, and you create a permissive and inclusive environment for them to think in, they're far more likely to explore alternative solutions, push boundaries, and break away from conventional norms. If you're looking to create a culture of creative experimentation leading to breakthroughs, you need to both harness and nurture these different perspectives and ways of thinking.

Some take this to mean you need all creative thinkers and people who live outside the box. This isn't true. I've relied heavily on people who understand what life is like inside the box and why the box was there to begin with, as much as I've relied on those who, like me, want to explore broadly outside. The contrasting perspectives these apparent polar opposites bring to your projects are essential.

Consider the people you would want to bring to your house for a home renovation. You wouldn't want to bring all designers—someone might forget that the walls they want to remove are load-bearing and you'd end up with a mess. Likewise, if you want to discover new solutions and ways of doing business, you wouldn't want to bring all engineers to the renovation.

It might be fundamentally impractical to move the plumbing and electrics for a kitchen from one room to the next, but the difference in space usage might make all the difference in the world to the way the home's occupants live.

Organizations that bring a good mixture of the practical and the pioneering to the table broaden their range of problem-solving capabilities. When each individual is encouraged and enabled to bring unique abilities and approaches to the table, you have more opportunities to develop a broad portfolio of solutions for a problem, and to better understand and adapt to changing market conditions and varying customer needs.

So, given that you are looking for such a broad range of perspectives and personalities, and you need them to cooperate with each other on teams, how do you actually manage them?

Recognizing and Valuing Different Work Styles

We recognize a multitude of different elements of diversity in the workplace, but what we're looking at here is largely cognitive diversity. *Cognitive diversity* refers to the variety of ways individuals perceive, think, and approach problem solving.[8] This can be due to differences in background, training, demographics, preferences, education, or a multitude of other factors, but at its heart, the concept of cognitive diversity recognizes that people bring unique cognitive attributes and perspectives to the table. Here are some of the attributes:

Problem-solving styles. People exhibit distinct preferences for different approaches in solving problems, whether through analytical, intuitive, or structured methods.

Decision-making approaches. The ways people make decisions can vary substantially. Some prefer to rely on data and analytics, and others lean toward intuition and experience. Some want to deliberate, either alone or with others in debate, and others make decisions and tend toward action very rapidly.

Communication preferences. People prefer to communicate and share information differently. Some are more verbal, while others favor written or visual communication. Some desire real-time face-to-face interaction and some prefer to be more removed.

Learning styles. Individuals have different preferences for intaking and processing information. Learning and development professionals debate how to best differentiate these styles, but it's sufficient to say that learning is also not a one-size-fits-all proposition.

Cognitive biases. Each person brings their own set of biases to the decision-making process, and those aren't always obvious without different perspectives to highlight or mitigate them.

As we've highlighted, cognitive diversity is an essential piece of fostering creativity and innovation. It leads to more comprehensive problem solving, a better understanding of potential pitfalls and opportunities due to a wider range of perspectives, better risk management, and improved adaptability. But how do we bring together all those different perspectives? How do all of these different people work?

We recognize a number of different work styles in the modern workforce, some structured and some very unstructured. There are a number of different work and personality assessments out there to help categorize how people work, such as DISC[9] and the Predictive Index.[10] Coming back to the home renovation example, I use my own (admittedly unscientific) version, pictured below, as a reminder to listen to the different types of voices at the table when I hold planning meetings. At each one, I want to make sure I have voices from each category, and that I listen for the ideas from my Designers who are looking to tear out walls, and my Engineers who know that we could break a lot of things if we do end up moving that kitchen.

FIGURE 9.1   A method of categorizing different work perspectives

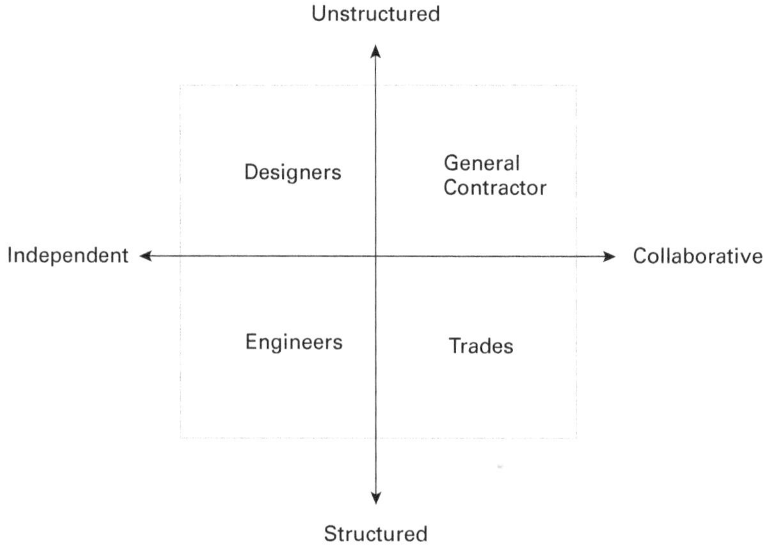

Designers. These are your unstructured, independent, creative thinkers. They are constantly looking for new solutions and they love exploring uncharted territory, challenging the status quo, and finding new ways of doing business. Their strength is in their creativity and ability to look beyond rules and norms, but their weakness is that they sometimes have to be reminded that rules exist for a reason, i.e. that wall might actually be load-bearing and need to be supported.

Engineers. Your structured, independent, analytical thinkers. They thrive on organization, schedules, and planning in detail. They're your best drivers of task completion and will also ask the necessary probing questions about your ideas that help you make sure you didn't miss a critical detail, like a constraint that happens to be written in law and statute. Their strength is in their eye for detail, but that's also their weakness. They sometimes need help seeing a bigger picture.

Trades. Your structured, collaborative thinkers. These are your collaborative team players who excel in group settings and are skilled at building strong interpersonal relationships. While they thrive in a team setting, they also have set expectations and need guidance and direction.

General contractor. These are your unstructured, collaborative thinkers. They tend to be adaptive, creative, and collaborative enough to work with the designer and translate their vision into something practical for the trades to execute. They'll take a grand vision and figure out how to execute it, but they'll also push back on it when it's something the team can't do because it's outside of code.

The key point for understanding all of these work styles in the home renovation example is that all of them bring different strengths and skills to the table, but you don't want a crew made up of all one type. What really makes the project work is having the right application and synergy of each of their strengths, and figuring out how each of them works and communicates enough that you can develop a common language amongst them, a common design plan.

Let's talk about how we can use data to identify different work styles:

1 *Assessments.* There are a number of different assessments you can use to categorize your different methods of work. Choose the one that best fits your organization's business model and combine that with performance evaluations and 360-degree feedback to give people a good understanding of how they work.

2 *Performance metrics.* Yes, those KPIs rear their heads again! When you understand how your team and your organization work, look at whether different work styles align with different work roles. This helps you see where someone might be working in a role aligned with their strengths and where they are misaligned and need development.

3 *Job analysis.* We've talked previously about collecting data about job requirements in terms of knowledge, skills, and behaviors. Let's talk about collecting that data in terms of work styles, structured vs. unstructured work, and independent vs. collaborative work. This will help look at how people best align to roles, and what kind of flexibility we have in designing their work.

4 *Productivity metrics.* As we're looking at how people work best, there are other pieces of information we can collect about how they perform. Are there certain times of day when they're most productive? Do they do better with certain types of management? When and how do they work best?

Armed with this information on how people work, how they're performing, how their roles require them to perform, and when they perform best, we can begin building the work environment we need to capitalize on that performance data. This takes a balance between building a work environment that includes and promotes different styles of working and thinking and collaboration, communication, and trust systems necessary to bring all these different types of workers together when necessary.

Let's talk about how to do that.

Creating an Inclusive, Flexible Work Environment

An inclusive work environment is more than a buzzword. To create an inclusive work environment, it means one that allows and empowers people to work how they work best, not the standard office environment where it fits some with the expectation that everyone else will figure out how to squeeze themselves in. This is a necessary step in actually making use of these talented teams we've been talking about building.

This is a challenging balance for organizations to strike, and it's very much tied to identity. The foundational tenet of data-driven talent management is movement away from an industrial manufacturing model of personnel management to one where we collect, analyze, and contextualize data on the individual; that we move from "how many of what type" to "who" in the questions we ask; that we learn to prioritize the individual when the individual has previously been subsumed by the needs of the organization. The balancing act we must perform is in giving that identity to the individual without losing sight of the needs of the organization.

How do we create a work environment that strikes this balance?

Your organization will need strategies for fostering Individuality and personalized recognition for individuals, and a clear, inclusive organizational culture.

Balance *fostering a culture of inclusivity and respect* with *recognizing and celebrating differences*. Acknowledge and celebrate the uniqueness of each individual as strength that contributes to the overall organization's success. Encourage open dialogue and create safe spaces for sharing ideas, experiences, and debate.

Balance *authenticity* with *opportunities for social connection*. Create an environment where your employees feel comfortable and empowered to be themselves. Authenticity encourages open communication and the sharing of creative ideas. And when you give opportunities for social interaction coupled with open sharing, people are more likely to discover ways they fit into the community and find a sense of belonging.

Balance *autonomy and empowerment* with *collaboration opportunities*. Give your employees a degree of independence in their work and allow them to approach tasks in ways that suit their skills and interests. Encourage them to exercise this autonomy in seeking out partnerships, peer-review, and discovering ways of partnering with others that work best for them.

Clearly communicate organizational goals and values. Aligning individual goals and objectives with the organization's goals and objectives is ideal for creating synergy between the identity of the individual and the collective identity of the organization. Create every opportunity to find compatibility between these identities.

And finally, *support quality of life and quality of work*. Some would say work-life balance, but I avoid that term. It creates a separation and polarity that isn't there in practice. Instead, you should look for a healthy fusion of the two, recognizing that the employee is a whole person instead of just a function at work.

This gives you an inclusive work environment that values the individual. Let's talk about why and how to create work arrangements that accommodate those individuals and their potentially diverse work styles. The key is flexible work.

Flexible work models give organizations flexibility in giving their employees the ability to work where and how they work best. This eschews the typical office 9-to-5 schedule in favor of a more adaptable, employee-centric approach. There are a number of different ways organizations can provide flexibility to their employees, both in and out of an office, but let's start with the geographically different methods:

Remote work is work done outside of a traditional office environment, whether it's done at home, a coffee shop, a shared workspace, or otherwise away from the office.

Distributed work is a blended work model with employees in various locations. This can be a combination of offices, or a combination of in-person and remote workers.

Hybrid work is any combination of in-person work and digital collaboration. This can be done between elements of the same organization or between partner or matrixed organizations.

Telework also means an employee works outside a traditional office environment, but it is typically used to indicate a stronger digital connection than remote work, which might be done completely independently.

Variability in work location is also known as *flexspace*. Employers that offer this give employees a wide range of suitable locations from which they can work. With the expansion of digital technology and digital collaboration tools, the range of suitable locations is expanding as well, although those of us who travel frequently aren't strangers to seeing people taking calls and fielding issues from hotel lobbies, airport lounges, or anywhere there's cell phone reception.

Variation in time is conveniently referred to as *flextime*. Employers giving flextime give employees some amount of choice in their work hours, perhaps starting the day earlier or later based on other requirements or preferences. This can also include compressed workweeks, or time off in lieu (TOIL), where employees get time off to compensate for extra hours worked instead of overtime pay.

Work hours still remain a critical item to track, even in the modern workplace, as a result of work agreements. They also can be important to ensure offices can provide expected service hour availability. However, we've discussed performance and productivity metrics multiple times in this book, and I recommended that work hours not be used as a proxy for productivity or performance. The person spending the most hours at a work location is not always the person who is most productive, or even the person working the hardest.

Working Together and Apart

Think back to the different work styles we discussed, structured vs. unstructured, independent vs. collaborative. This can be very important when we're looking at how often people are expected to work together and how. As we design flexible work arrangements to best accommodate individual productivity, we have to look at how different work roles require people to work, both together and apart.

The way these work roles need to come together is a critical piece that so many offices overlooked when designing their Covid-19 plans and their return-to-office plans. Offices that didn't consider how people needed to collaborate and connect ended up creating calendars full of meetings while working remotely and bringing people in for an arbitrary number of days just to sit on digital meetings with their colleagues when returning to the office. Determining whole-of-office plans is essential.

There are four basic models for how people need to work in a distributed environment:

1 Working together, together

2 Working together, apart

3 Working apart, together

4 Working apart, apart

Working together, together refers to collaborative work done in-person. Even with collaborative tools, many will agree that there are some things that just seem to work best together. Design labs, workshops, panel discussions, and happy hours are all just better when they happen face-to-face.

Working together, apart is when people are working in the office but on separate projects. This idea of togetherness while working on separate projects is largely behind the idea that cubicle farms could bring cohesion to teams, but many people find it annoying because they can't control when people come to interrupt their concentration. Working together,

FIGURE 9.2   A Look at How We Expect People to Work, Together and Apart, Onsite or Remote

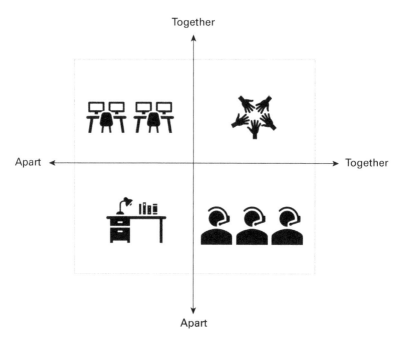

apart is fine when folks are using or working specialized equipment, but otherwise, it is the least effective.

Working apart, together is when people are at distributed locations but working together, over the phone or over digital collaboration tools. This can be highly effective for small groups working on anything where sharing a screen, a coding window, a digital whiteboard, a collaborative document, or anything else that can be worked on simultaneously regardless of where your workers are.

Working apart, apart is when someone is working on a separate project at a separate location from anyone else. That would be me, writing this book in my home office, my noise-canceling headphones on, full of gratitude that I'm not trying to do this in a cubicle and that my husband has been gracious enough during my writing bouts to keep our son and the dog busy. This is also how a number of my data scientists spend their time, blocked out in "productivity bubbles" on their calendars where they are working hard to complete a piece of code independently before they come together, either in-person or virtually, for us to review.

As a note, when it comes to working with data scientists collaboratively, we find that it's actually easier to work *apart, apart* and then work *apart, together*—collaborating digitally and not in person. That way, someone can share their screen and we can go through the code and reference documents from our own machines and see exactly what's going on.

We found this also worked very well for academic conferences during the Covid-19 quarantine, when people were all watching a presentation from their own computers and could see the actual code being reviewed, rather than squinting from the back of a presentation room.

Flexible work requires much more detailed planning than mandating that your employees come to the office at a given time, but it can be highly worthwhile when it comes to quality of life and quality of work. Reducing commute time and potential distractions when there's work that needs to be done apart or can be done together in small collaborative groups just makes sense.

Thinking about the work styles we outlined before, the more collaborative the nature of work, the more likely your team is going to need to meet in person. The more independent the work, the more it can take place wherever it can be done. What you'll need to do is look at how it makes sense for individuals to be able to work, and how it makes sense for your team to synchronize that work. There will be times when almost everyone needs to work *together, together*, and probably times when almost everyone can work *apart, apart*. Creating systems that enable planning and scheduling in a way that maximizes efficiencies and collaboration helps people work where they work best.

Aligning Different Work Styles With Work Together and Apart

The most important factor in matching various styles of work with various ways of working, both together and apart, is coming up with a strategic approach. Your goal as an organization is to optimize productivity, efficiency, and collaboration while respecting individual work preferences, and you can't do this by simply mandating that individuals be in the office a certain number of days per week.

I look at this starting with work requirements. What kind of work requires people to work *together, together*? What kind of work requires people to work *apart, apart*? If I can schedule those times and create hybrid times in between to balance out collaboration between folks who choose to work in the office and those who choose to work elsewhere, it tends to give me the best productivity and the team the most satisfaction. In short, I want to minimize the amount of time spent working together, apart, as that to me is the most inefficient and annoying type of work, and then optimize the other three areas for my team's work preferences.

Still, there's no one-size-fits-all here. A lot of this is based on your understanding of job performance and the nature of work. What kind of work and work styles lend themselves best to independent and structured or unstructured work? Those are the types of jobs and tasks that can most likely be done apart or in a hybrid environment. What kind of work is collaborative in nature? Those are the types of jobs and tasks that should be done in person. How often do your teams have to participate in these types of tasks? Collecting data on each of these might tell you how often you need to allocate space in each instance, and whether or not it's worth your while to have full-time space, part-time space, or just rented space available.

Let's talk about how to develop this kind of strategy.

Determine individual work requirements. This comes back to the work we did in job analysis initially and now requires mapping the tasks and abilities we identified for job requirements to the environment and equipment necessary for getting those duties done. This helps you make the determination whether an individual's work is tied to a location or working with a team or not.

Determine teamwork requirements. Let's broaden the look now from the requirements of the individual to the requirements of the team. What kind of interaction or cooperation do we expect or require? We may not think about these looking at the individual job or the expertise required, but when we factor in workshops, training, counseling, supervision, and other tasks, this may illuminate interactions that may require people to work differently at times.

Determine individual work preferences. Preferences matter, and it's important for you as a leader to attempt to align people's preferences to work where possible. Individual work may not require in-office attendance, but you will still have people who prefer to work in an office environment. Some may not have dedicated workspace at home and some like the separation and decompression time a commute offers. Others will prefer to work independently whenever possible. As long as the individual demonstrates the reliability and autonomy needed to meet their performance objectives, let the individual work where they work best.

FIGURE 9.3 A Methodology to Determine How and When People Should Work Together or Apart

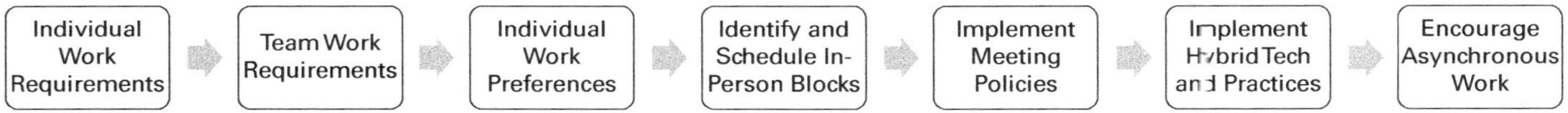

```
┌──────────────┐      ┌──────────────┐      ┌──────────────┐      ┌──────────────┐      ┌──────────────┐      ┌──────────────┐      ┌──────────────┐
│  Individual  │ ──▶  │  Team Work   │ ──▶  │  Individual  │ ──▶  │ Identify and │ ──▶  │  Implement   │ ──▶  │  Implement   │ ──▶  │  Encourage   │
│     Work     │      │ Requirements │      │     Work     │      │ Schedule In- │      │   Meeting    │      │  Hybrid Tech │      │ Asynchronous │
│ Requirements │      │              │      │ Preferences  │      │ Person Blocks│      │   Policies   │      │ and Practices│      │     Work     │
└──────────────┘      └──────────────┘      └──────────────┘      └──────────────┘      └──────────────┘      └──────────────┘      └──────────────┘
```

Identify and schedule in-person blocks. You may want collaboration to happen on your team, but you can't automatically assume that will happen by having people come into the office a certain number of days per week. Deliberately schedule the times you want people to work in-person and what work or collaborative events you want to accomplish during that time. If it's just a routine collaborative check-in or if it's an actual design event, both are fine, but make sure your people know the purpose of the gathering.

Implement meeting policies. In a hybrid environment, supervisors default to meetings more than they should. Ensure you set clear agendas, define when meeting and which meetings are necessary, encourage shorter meetings, and even designate no-meeting days. For the past three years, I have had Fridays designated as no-meeting days so that I don't have to check my calendar for availability when someone wants to schedule a call, a site visit, or a doctor's appointment.

Implement hybrid technology and practices. Sometimes you'll need your team to work together but not for a long enough time to justify the expense and travel time needed to bring them physically together. For that, you'll need to make sure you have digital collaboration technology available (such as Microsoft Teams, Zoom, Google Suite, or similar) and good meeting practices for a hybrid audience. Can your people participate from a distance as if they were in the room? Or are they out of sight, out of mind? The more they can effectively participate, the better your meetings will be.

Encourage asynchronous work. Foster an environment where you demonstrate the value of asynchronous work as much as synchronous activities. Not all work needs to be done in person or simultaneously online, and by fostering a culture—and setting appropriate performance metrics—where people are able to do their work with dedicated focus, without checking in on collaboration tools, knowing that they can do the work when they work best, you'll get the most productivity out of your team.

This kind of work strategy might seem like it takes a lot of planning, but it isn't rigid. It's up to you how often and how far in advance you want to identify and schedule each block, and how often you want to recall your team for in-person meetings. Whatever you decide, make sure you clearly communicate policies and expectations so that people understand what is required of them. Whether you want to have a 24-hour rapidly deployable force or a predictable six-week training calendar, both of which we have in the U.S. Army, your folks need to understand how quickly they need to respond and how far out they can make their own plans.

Promoting Collaboration and Idea Sharing

Collaboration is your greatest ally in turning a collection of empowered individual performers into a high-performing team. Bringing people together to think together is not just beneficial, but essential. No matter which examples we go back to, the high-performing American football team, the Avengers, or your own team, you're bringing together people who all individually perform key functions, and while those are useful, you need all of them together to play the game, to defeat the *bad guys*, or to win at achieving your business objectives respectively! Figuring out how to engineer your environment so that you can manage folks who need to work differently but also need to work together is key.

Proper collaboration allows these diverse strengths and skills you've assembled to be used effectively. You need those different strengths, skills, and perspectives to see the whole picture and assemble the pieces of a total solution, one much more robust than any one individual can achieve alone. It gives you the necessary ingredients for innovation as well, an environment where pieces of a solution and, in fact, pieces of the problem itself can be discussed and challenged. When you have a team full of different perspectives crashing on a problem, they'll challenge assumptions and what you might otherwise have accepted as hard constraints, and let you know that what you thought was a tight feasible region is actually a lot broader.

Over time, this kind of environment and encouraged collaboration allows for learning and growth. Individuals who work together will cross-pollinate understanding and skills faster as you continue to promote a culture of curiosity. If you creatively mix your novices and experts, having people see the practical application of the skills you want them to learn can provide greater context for how the system works and what their place is in it, and where at times you need them to learn and grow to fill a gap.

Collaboration and cooperation also build trust and cohesion. I won't say some team-building events can't be fun (we've all been at corny events, but my team has put together some fantastic ones), but the most powerful team-building event is working cooperatively to successfully solve a problem and achieving that victory together. Break that back down for your team and show how everyone's different skills, working styles, and strengths, which folks will now be more familiar with, contributed to the team victory. This kind of understanding allows your team to be more autonomous, not just with their own work but in seeking out expertise on the team. This creates trust when those needs are met—your team should feel comfortable in knowing they have your support if they make a decision or take a risk aligned with team goals and your vision and intent. That may mean sometimes you have to smooth some ruffled feathers or clean up when a risk doesn't pan out, but that's part of leading a team empowered to take on great challenges and full of expertise that you may not have. You need them exercising and seeking out expertise, thoughts, and ideas from where the expertise lies, and you don't want them waiting for you to tell them to do it.

This also builds a sense of flexibility and adaptability. Collaborative teams, ones where multiple folks are helping guide discussion and ideas, can better flex and adjust to new challenges. Think of the rapidly changing and ambiguous environment of the future as a fog, and the more people you have looking out for obstacles and opportunities, the better your chances of finding and understanding those soon enough to respond. And now you have more people with more perspectives who are properly motivated to help you get after those things in creative ways. You see how all of this builds on itself?

So, while that's all well and good, let's talk about how we get there. How do we create the collaborative processes and practices that support innovation?

Create Cross-Functional Teams

Your team may be a small cross-functional team already, but if you're in a larger organization, figure out ways to seed activities that bring people together across different departments. Bring together people with varied perspectives, skills, experiences, and expertise to address complex problems.

For example, our team working on Customer Experience at U.S. Army Human Resources Command is made up of military and civilian members, some with a lot of experience in the command and some new to the command, or even new to the Army, and brings in collaborative elements from directorates throughout the command to provide advice and ideas. Give them the opportunity to figure out how to work together and give them the tools to help them design their best work solutions when they have plenty of time to experiment, not when you have a crisis.

Design Labs and Idea Workshops[11]

Challenge your folks to think differently, and endorse and empower this from the top. Design labs can help you create an environment where people can come in and deliberately put authority and position aside and share their thoughts and ideas openly. Different thoughts and work styles reveal themselves during these labs, and it definitely helps you break down any existing barriers to see how different people attack different problems—and teaches the organization to value that.

We conducted a design lab when we established the Army People Analytics office to help us figure out how to collaborate and leverage the entirety of research offices, data teams, and other analytic organizations within the space. We had leaders and contributors of all ranks, dressed down so that that rank was far less apparent, and created an open environment to share ideas and concerns openly.

Communicate and Communicate

I can't emphasize enough the power of communication when it comes to building trust, sharing ideas, understanding vision, and empowering a team. And when I say this, I don't simply mean quantity of communication. Focus on the quality of the communication. What is the top-line message people need to understand to execute the vision and mission of the organization? What underlying instructions do you need to give them to help them better understand priorities? Layer those in first, and make sure they are received as broadly as possible.

When we started working to modernize functions in our transformation plan for U.S. Army Human Resources Command, the top-line message from the commander was a focus on being "transparent, agile, and customer-centered."[12] As a team, we walked those three values down through messages and statements that showed how we would demonstrate those values. For example, under being customer-centered, we further defined actions and messages such as, "I am proactive, clear, and concise in the information I provide to avoid confusion and questions," and "I confirm clarity in my responses and offer further assistance with each interaction."

Idea Incubation

Collaborative work in innovation often involves incubation. In the innovation model I use, we always start from taking an idea just from a simple suggestion to full problem understanding and definition. Give people the time and space to refine their ideas so that you can understand how they and their potential solutions fit into the overall ecosystem.

We take idea proposals all the time and maintain a running list. Depending on work capacity and priorities, some of them sit there for a while, but that has worked to our advantage. While they're sitting there on the list (and we keep the list visible on our collaboration chat), people have time to think about not just the idea, but how to write the problem statement and start designing the potential solutions we need to prototype and evaluate.

Innovation Hubs

Whether you're working together or apart, it's helpful to identify dedicated spaces and practitioners to help you and your teams focus on creative thinking and problem solving. This can be a physical space like a design lab with facilitators, which you can create internally if you have the resources or rent as needed, or a digital space, like a meeting room.

A few friends and I keep a standing "Office Hour" calendar invite that can be accessed any time of the day. It provides an alert for anyone subscribing to know that someone is in the calendar event and is interested in brainstorming or talking through a particularly thorny problem. We've had this running for two years now, and it has been extremely helpful.

Recognition and Reward

Simple psychology and mathematical optimization functions both agree that people (and equations) seek out reward and avoid punishment. If you want people to collaborate and innovate together, establish recognition and reward systems that acknowledge and celebrate this. Actions that bring people together to share ideas, solve problems, and contribute to the organization's creative efforts should be recognized and incentivized.

Let's talk about how we can use data to do this.

Data-Driven Ideas to Enhance Collaboration

What kind of things can you do to bolster collaboration among your teammates, and how can you use data to enhance it? Let's talk about a few ideas.

First off, let's **use data-driven team composition** to ensure we have diverse teams.

Consider what data we've collected about individual thought and work styles, preferences, strengths, and abilities. We can employ analytics to show what kinds of skills and strengths best come together to go after certain project types, especially when we start collecting success metrics within the organization, and we can assemble a team to make sure we have the right composition of strengths there. There are personality assessments that can also help understand and predict team dynamics as well.

Setting the right **performance metrics for collaboration** is as important as setting any other performance metrics—and as we've discussed before, those are essential. We need to look at things like project outcomes, team dynamics, communication quality, and so much more to determine the successful composition and collaboration of a team. Over time, your data will tell you what teams, processes, or practices are the most effective in driving innovation.

We need to make sure we have all the right **tools for collaboration**. Again, remember "habeas program?" Just because you have a tool doesn't mean people will use it or use it effectively. Leverage data to see how effective your collaboration tools and technologies are. You can measure things like user engagement, adoption rates, and do focus groups and surveys to gather employee feedback on how well the tools are working for them. This information can help guide your acquisition strategies and shore up gaps.

You'll want to **gather and act on employee feedback** to gain insights into how well your collaboration processes and teams are working. Surveys and other feedback mechanisms, peer reviews, and interviews can all help shed light on the effectiveness of your collaboration strategies, and help you identify performers and non-performers.

> We often do a project exercise to identify a project's most valuable players, including people, activities, resources, and technologies. It is a single question tacked onto a problem that states, "I could not have completed this project without____" and asks the person to provide a short answer on what and why.

Use data and analytics to inform your **knowledge repositories** and identify actionable insights, best practices, and ideas. Collect information on how those knowledge repositories are accessed and allow your teammates to get in there and rate and rank the ideas, solutions, and practices stored there. This performs the dual function of getting people to interact with the knowledge repository and helping you front-load the things that people are ranking as the most useful.

As you collect more information on your knowledge repositories, you can build algorithms (or use learning systems that contain this function) to **personalize knowledge delivery** to better support individual preferences and needs. If people are accessing more visual solutions for a particular type of problem, you can both front-load existing ones and put resources toward creating additional resources.

As knowledge flows through your organization, you'll want to use everything we've talked about above to create **knowledge maps.** Where are the most highly rated and effective items and practices coming from? It's helpful to know where expertise is in your organization, and identify knowledge champions who can assist in knowledge sharing across your teams.

Chapter Summary

So we're working together… both together and apart.

Yes! That's the goal, figuring out both how different types of work can and should be done, and helping align that to how the team prefers to work. This helps you better leverage motivation and strengths, as we've talked about in previous chapters, with the whole goal being getting your team to work creatively and proactively and have job satisfaction.

I want to again address the concern many folks have at this point when we discuss supporting how people prefer to work by reminding us that we are working to build the biggest and best talent bench possible for our organizations. We're attracting talented and motivated people and using measures that matter to track, improve, and incentivize performance. Preference must be part of that equation.

I'll also state that as leaders and managers, we have the responsibility to make that an informed preference. If someone wants to work a particular way and in a particular place, they should have a solid understanding of what needs to be done to make that happen. Many things that a high-performing employee wants, such as flexible work accommodations or telework opportunities or training and education resources, are possible with a little work, but they need to understand what that work is, both on their part and on the part of the organization.

Taking individual preference into account and making sure it is informed is not just a matter of employee satisfaction anymore, but a necessary approach to building a resilient, innovative, and successful organization. It creates a work environment where talented and autonomous individuals can thrive, which creates more individual satisfaction, engagement, and success. And this, in turn, attracts more top talent to your organization. It's a win win.

Notes

1 Busayo Longe (2023) "Goodhart's Law: Definitions, Implications, and Examples," Formplus, www.formpl.us/blog/goodharts-law (archived at https://perma.cc/T2YJ-MJVZ)

2 Steve Glaveski (2020) "The Five Levels of Remote Work – and Why You're Probably at Level 2," The Startup, https://medium.com/swlh/the-five-levels-of-remote-work-and-why-youre-probably-at-level-2-ccaf05a25b9c (archived at https://perma.cc/X9T8-FDPD)

3 George Orwell (1949) *1984*, Books&Coffe

4 Joss Whedon, director (2012) *The Avengers*, Marvel Studios, information at www.imdb.com/title/tt0848228/?ref_=fn_al_tt_2 (archived at https://perma.cc/TMQ6-5ZNX)

5 Alan McConchie (2020) "Pop vs. Soda," https://popvssoda.com/ (archived at https://perma.cc/3CH5-E29Y)

6 US Department of Homeland Security (2023) "U.S. Strategy on Women, Peace, and Security," www.dhs.gov/us-strategy-women-peace-and-security (archived at https://perma.cc/RH6M-DEHN)

7 Davis Winkie (2023) "Army Wants Less 'Siloed' Job Ladders and a Flexible Job 'Jungle Gym'," Army Times, www.armytimes.com/news/your-army/2023/12/13/army-wants-less-siloed-job-ladders-and-a-flexible-job-jungle-gym/ (archived at https://perma.cc/XBX9-Q2TC)

8 Janine Schindler (2018) "The Benefits of Cognitive Diversity," Forbes, www.forbes.com/sites/forbescoachescouncil/2018/11/26/the-benefits-of-cognitive-diversity/?sh=549828ff5f8b (archived at https://perma.cc/4JCU-7EZR)

9 DISCinsights (nd), "DISC Theory," https://discinsights.com/pages/disc-theory (archived at https://perma.cc/VFA6-MKDV)

10   Erin Balsa (nd) "How Does the Predictive Index Test Work?" The Predictive Index, www.predictiveindex.com/blog/how-does-the-predictive-index-test-work/ (archived at https://perma.cc/4KER-A62X)

11   Emily Cruz (2023) "How to use Design Thinking to Design an Innovation Lab," Innovation Training, www.innovationtraining.org/how-to-use-design-thinking-to-design-an-innovation-lab/ (archived at https://perma.cc/Y9UQ-LU43)

12   U.S. Army Human Resources Command (nd) "2030 Vision," www.hrc.army.mil/wcmt-api/sites/default/wcmtfiles/files/27030_0.pdf (archived at https://perma.cc/3XXN-RL63)

10

Balancing the Needs of a Diverse, Multidisciplinary Workforce

Coming together is a beginning. Keeping together is progress. Working together is success.
HENRY FORD, INDUSTRIALIST AND CHIEF DEVELOPER OF THE ASSEMBLY LINE[1]

You Can't Whistle a Symphony

There is an old saying that you can't whistle a symphony,[2] that you need a whole orchestra playing together to achieve the true power of that music. Woodwinds, brass, percussion, all of it must come together and, while playing very different functions, move along with the conductor to tell different parts of the musical story together.

This is a useful model to keep in mind as we look out at the modern workplace, which is a rich tapestry of diversity woven with varied threads of different talents, backgrounds, perspectives, training, and mindsets. These differences, while being a formidable asset for our teams, also present a complex challenge for organizations seeking to bring these different ways of working and thinking together on a cohesive team. In this chapter, we'll explore how the dynamic nature of today's workforce calls for a nuanced approach to talent management, one that effectively balances and harmonizes these varied needs through data-driven strategies.

Modern organizations can't survive any longer as monoliths with uniform workforce structures. The advent of globalization, technological advancement, and changing societal norms and expectations have contributed to a workforce that is incredibly varied. This isn't just in terms of demographics, but extends to encompass a wide range of skills, experiences, educational backgrounds, and cognitive styles. Employees bring a spectrum of perspectives and capabilities, from creative and innovative problem solvers to methodical and analytical thinkers. This shift marks a departure from traditional, homogenized work environments to more electric and dynamic ones. This is exciting from a creativity and innovation perspective but daunting from a more practical management perspective.

The power of a diverse and multi-talented workforce lies in its potential to drive that innovation and creative problem solving we want and need. Diverse teams bring together varied perspectives that can lead to more innovative solutions and a broader understanding of customer needs. For instance, a team comprising members from different cultural backgrounds can offer unique insights into global markets, while a team with diverse professional experiences might approach a problem from multiple angles, leading to more robust solutions.

The varying needs, motivations, and communication styles of this kind of team, however, can lead to misunderstandings and conflicts. Additionally, the diverse range of skills and talents means that traditional management techniques and ideas of fairness, which were typically more one-size-fits-all approaches, are unlikely to fit or be effective. The challenge for the modern organization is to find a way to capitalize on the strengths of the diverse workforce while minimizing potential friction and misalignment.

In addressing the complexities of a diverse workforce, data-driven talent management emerges as a key strategy. By leveraging data and how we identify, acquire, develop, employ, and retain our talent both individually and collectively, we can gain a deeper understanding of our employees' unique attributes and needs, where those are complementary, and where they are in conflict, so that we can come up with predictive and prescriptive mitigation and mediation strategies. We need to tailor our management approaches, developmental programs, and motivation strategies to suit the individual, both alone and in the context of the team, thereby maximizing everybody's potential.

We've discussed many of the tools involved in data-driven talent management to collect and analyze data on employee performance, skills, preferences, and behaviors (particularly in Chapters 5, 6, and 7), and how advanced analytics and artificial intelligence can further refine our understanding in these spaces. In this chapter, we'll talk a little bit about this technology but will primarily look at the strategies and best practices for identifying friction points and managing a diverse symphony of talent. We will explore how your organization can leverage data to understand and meet the unique needs of your employees, how you can foster an inclusive and collaborative work environment, and how you can align these talents with organizational goals.

As we work our way through this, remember that balancing the diverse needs of the modern workforce is not just a challenge but an opportunity to build a more dynamic, innovative, and resilient organization reminiscent of some of the most powerful teams we admire. By embracing diversity of talent, background, perspective, training, and mindset, and harnessing the power of data-driven talent management, we can turn this multifaceted and sometimes conflicting nature of our workforce into our greatest asset.

So Just What Is Workforce Diversity?

When we start talking about workforce diversity, what comes to mind first is demographic diversity—race, ethnicity, nationality, and so forth. That's just one aspect, however. The kind of workforce diversity we're seeing includes talents, backgrounds, perspectives, training, experience, and mindset. These facets play a pivotal role in shaping innovative and creative teams just for the sheer variety of skills, perspectives, and learning they bring together to solve complex problems. However, those skills, perspectives, and learning are all full of potential conflicting factors and can lead to clashes and difficulty in the workplace. But before we can talk about strategies to mitigate conflict and improve creativity, let's talk about what workforce diversity is in the context of talent management.

Workforce diversity is a multifaceted concept that transcends traditional categorization in terms of race, gender, and age.[3] It is the collective mix of various attributes and characteristics that individuals bring to an organization.

Here are some different sub-categories you should consider:

- **Talent diversity.** This encompasses the range of skills and abilities that employees possess. Talent diversity can be seen in different professional backgrounds, technical skills, and problem-solving abilities.
- **Background diversity.** This refers to the varied cultural, educational, and socioeconomic backgrounds of your employees. This diversity enriches the workplace with a wide array of experiences and perspectives.
- **Perspective diversity.** This dimension covers the different ways in which people view problems and solutions, influenced by their unique experiences and cognitive styles.

- **Training diversity.** This refers to the varied educational and professional training experiences that employees have undergone, which shapes their approach to work and problem solving.
- **Experience diversity.** This includes a range of professional and life experiences that employees bring, contributing to a richer pool of knowledge and insights.
- **Mindset diversity.** This aspect recognizes the differences in attitudes, values, and beliefs that individuals hold, influencing how they interact with others and approach their work.

There are a great number of benefits and advantages to having this kind of diversity present in your workforce. Diverse teams are more likely to generate unique ideas and creative solutions, as they bring different perspectives and problem-solving approaches. They offer a wider array of skills and experiences, which can be leveraged to tackle various challenges and opportunities. Diversity in perspectives can lead to more thorough and balanced decision-making processes, as it encourages the consideration of multiple viewpoints. This can also lead to greater market insight. A workforce that reflects a diverse customer base can provide deeper insights into market needs and preferences, enabling more effective marketing strategies.

Organizations known for their commitment to these broad ranges of experiences, skills, backgrounds, perspectives, and creativity are often viewed more favorably, which can aid in attracting top talent and customers.

But while the benefits are significant, so are the challenges. Everything you see about the different perspectives and ways of thinking that lets you better see the whole picture of a challenge or a solution also contributes a great amount of complexity. You have a lot of different factors here, and while many of them are complementary, just as many will be competing.

We mentioned the language example earlier, where English is not just English. Broadening that perspective, you can end up with language and communication barriers that can be frustrating and lead to misunderstandings. You might have issues with integration, given the wide variety of things people look for to make them feel included and valued. You might have to be creative in resolving conflict; balancing individual needs and preferences often necessitates addressing conflicts and differences in expectations, potentially resulting in interpersonal challenges.

On my last team, I encouraged discussion and debate so that people felt like they had my trust and confidence to challenge an idea or a concept that needed further review. As you can imagine, putting that proverbial genie back in the bottle is difficult, and the number of challenges that came up could be frustrating. The most useful tool to combat this is one I learned from one of my previous commanders, who also liked to encourage debate. He called it his "Phase 1/Phase 2 method." The way he explained it, when we were in "Phase 1," everyone could challenge an idea as long as we did it respectfully, and he would be open for debate. That way, he felt better about having the whole picture and not walking into a bad decision because he had found himself in a staff echo chamber. However, once we were in "Phase 2," he had either made a decision or time was of the essence, and we needed to execute. I have a lot of respect for this methodology and employ it myself, because it gives everyone a clear understanding of what needs to be done.

That's one tip that works for me, but there are lots of things you can do to manage a diverse workforce. Let's talk about implementing flexible work arrangements, promoting an inclusive culture, tailored development and training, looking at leadership a little bit differently, and figuring out how to really get outside the echo chamber.

Understanding Complexity in Diverse Workforces

I may have mentioned that I have an abiding love for complexity science, so dealing with the kind of complexity that you get from integrating all these different nuances of skill, competency, background, and personality in a data-driven talent management system is very exciting to me. And it also means we can use a lot of the principles of complexity science to get a better understanding of and develop some management principles for our multi-faceted workforce.

Complex systems, in the complexity science definition, "consist of large numbers of interacting elements or sub-systems" and "are characterized by complex behaviors growing from the numerous and often non-linear inter-actions of component sub-systems, known as emergent behaviors, which are difficult to mathematically explain and impossible to predict."[4] This system definition holds true for groups of people of all sizes, but things become especially complex when more and more of the factors, and therefore the interactions, you have are vastly different. The good news is that we can talk about using complexity science and system engineering methodologies to manage them.

So what do we understand about complex adaptive systems that can help us make sense of this very complex talent ecosystem we've created for ourselves? There are several principles that apply to the kinds of teams we're trying to create here, and by understanding and shaping those principles, we can develop some talent management guidelines. Those are:

- Self-organization
- Emergence
- Co-evolution
- Interdependence
- Self-similarity

Self-organization is when the system asserts itself through autonomous and self-reinforcing behaviors at the micro-level to create stable patterns in its behavior.[5] Create opportunities for self-organizing and autonomy by letting your teams take the initiative on ideas or solutions, seek out experts among teammates and other collaborators, and leverage their skills. This gives them a sense of ownership and responsibility, and when that emerges, people are more likely to govern their project and their collaboration rather than expecting a leader to do it for them.

Emergence is when properties and behaviors develop inside a complex system from the interaction of different entities that don't otherwise possess those properties and behaviors on their own.[6] Emergent behaviors and ideas are exactly what you want to encourage in this system, because this is where innovation and unique problem solving comes from. You create these by providing resources, training, and a permissive culture where the various factors that make your team different from each other can interact freely and safely. Communication and transparency along with trust are key components here.

Co-evolution is a concept typically used in studying biological complex adaptive systems, but it refers to how an organism and its ecosystem tend to evolve together.[7] As your people learn and adapt, your environment will adapt as well, and the converse is also true. Adapt your talent strategies as your team learns and gains new skills and provide continuing opportunities for learning and development, along with coaching and mediation as required.

Interdependence, when your team has a high degree of interconnectedness, means that what changes in one part of the team is likely to propagate and change other parts of the system.[8] This is something that you as a leader can acknowledge and leverage. Improving, messaging, and incentivizing part of the team can spread to all. Look at how people form connections (and you can grab interaction data from digital collaboration systems to study this as well) and leverage your people with the strongest connections to get messages out and impact behavior.

Self-similarity is the principle behind fractal geometry, which shows a smaller piece of an object is similar to the whole, impacting interconnectedness and behavior.[9] To apply this to leading teams, focus on the things you can do to create that similarity between the team and the whole, similarly to what we did previously with OKRs. While your team's diversity of skills and backgrounds is important, having that shared set of values and shared understanding of the mission, vision, and objectives can create the connections you need to work together.

The key with all of this is to realize that a diverse workforce, like a complex adaptive system, is dynamic and fluid. This is one of the reasons we keep talking about the need for flexibility in the workplace, managing different ways of work, and being adaptive and agile. Structured one-size-fits-all work models created enough friction when people expected conformity as a norm, but when you empower people's differences, those models really don't fit anyone.

How Can Data Help Us Lead?

Balancing the needs of a diverse and complex workforce requires a careful and thoughtful approach. You as a leader have the difficult responsibility of creating a culture that respects and leverages the diversity of the team but also ensures fair and objective management practices. Coming back to the idea that "you can't whistle a symphony," we need a means to let everyone have their unique contributing voice in that symphonic orchestra, but also guide and inspire them toward that common goal together. That guiding and inspiring is what we call leadership.

As ironic as it sounds, there is a way to create a structure around your leadership practices that allows your employees the freedom needed to complete tasks, achieve your organization's objectives, and support and align with your vision. As a leader, it involves the very careful selection of the things you need to centralize and provide direction for, and decentralizing everything else. The trade-off in this case is that the more you decentralize, the more things become complicated and less efficient. It takes longer to rally a team of autonomous operators together than it does to command a military formation, but in return, you get greater adaptability, agility, flexibility, and creativity.

General Stanley McChrystal explores this concept in his book, *Team of Teams*. "Efficiency remains important, but the ability to adapt to complexity and continual change has become an imperative."[10] Authors Ori Brafman and Rod A. Beckstrom explore how to balance between these strengths and weaknesses of centralized and decentralized organizations in *The Starfish and the Spider*, looking at the success and failure of competing organizations Onsale, eBay, and craigslist.[11] Onsale couldn't adapt to the market because it was too centralized, and craigslist couldn't own the market because operating on trust alone left it too open for people to exploit the system. eBay as a hybrid model turned more of a profit and owned more of the market than both, offering decentralized markets but identity and email validation for accountability. So how can we strike the balance between giving people enough freedom to succeed and leverage their wide varieties of talents, ways of working, and individual uniqueness, and yet still providing enough structure that we can all orient on a common goal?

Even if the U.S. Army command structure can be rigid, we developed a leadership framework under Mission Command[12] that gets after this fairly well. The whole concept hinges on empowering subordinate leadership and decentralized execution through seven key factors: Competence, mutual trust, shared understanding, commander's intent, mission orders, disciplined initiative, and risk acceptance. In short, if you build the trust and common understanding in and amongst the team, in the leadership, and in the objectives, purpose, and vision of the organization, then you can align an empowered and decentralized organization toward achieving a common purpose.

We've talked previously about being able to evaluate and measure whether your organization is able to meet its objectives through the OKR framework, and we've talked about measures of performance to help evaluate your team. These all can contribute to an understanding of how well your leader and team models are working. However, I want to incorporate some principles from the centralized/decentralized leadership model discussion to help you better evaluate your leadership methods. These can apply whether you're leading in an environment where you see and interact with your people every day, a hybrid model where you see them less frequently, or a distributed model where you might not work in person frequently at all.

Let's talk about a way to synthesize together these various principles and studies, and how to lead our organization of unique and independent individuals toward a common goal. We'll do this by discussing how to evaluate three elements: Trust, a common vision, and self-governance.

Trust

For all of this to work, you must establish and measure trust. There are a number of different factors that have to be present for trust to happen, but we'll take a look at the Trust Equation to start with.[13] According to this model, trust is composed of four elements—credibility, reliability, intimacy, and self-orientation. We'll take these factors and talk about how to measure them and measure trust.

- **Credibility:** The belief that one has the expertise and skills to perform effectively. This applies to the leader and to teammates. We can assess, as we talked about in Chapter 5, whether someone has the skills and competencies to perform their job, but it's important not just that they have those competencies, but that others perceive them.

- **Reliability:** The perception that one is dependable and consistent. Do your teammates and your leadership keep their promises and meet your expectations? Is that perceived as consistent by your team?

- **Intimacy:** The level of safety or security you feel when providing someone with confidential or sensitive information. Mike Erwin and Willys Devoll talk about the connection and closeness needed in a trusted leader model in their book, *Leadership is a Relationship*,[14] and it applies very much to this trust model.

- **Self-orientation:** The focus on oneself rather than the focus on another person. People tend to trust you more when you are perceived to have a lower self-orientation, or when they perceive you as being more concerned with the needs and interests of others rather than your own.

So how do we measure this?

Since we're measuring trust, the metrics we're going to use will largely be subjective. Still, providing the team with open and frequent opportunities to fill out peer evaluations and 360-degree surveys can help you get after this.

Collect information from teammates, stakeholders, and clients about knowledge, advice quality, expertise, consistency, and dependability. You can also collect productivity metrics to assess reliability scores and consistency. Intimacy can be scored through organizational climate surveys and comfort levels sharing information, and through personality assessments and 360 feedback scoring the individual on empathy, understanding, confidentiality, and emotional support.

Common Vision

We've spoken about how we need to align our various talents and expertise on the achievement of our organization's objectives, and we do this by communicating, understanding, and executing a shared vision. To approach this in a structured way, we need to look at two primary elements here: The effectiveness of communication and the understanding of the vision and objectives:

- **Communication effectiveness.** For this, we just need to be able to assess the degree to which our communication efforts achieve their intended purpose. Can we convey, receive, and understand the information given in the manner it was intended? This metric applies both to the leadership and to the team for intra-team information sharing. We'll want to look at metrics that address clarity, comprehensibility, and timeliness, among others. We can apply this to all forms of communication.

- **Understanding the vision and objectives.** We'll evaluate under communication effectiveness whether the message was communicated and received, but for understanding the vision and objectives, we want to know these things were both received and acted upon. Does the team have the necessary shared understanding, are they committed, and do they execute, especially in instances when they are given autonomy and the ability to show initiative?

We'll collect data on these factors through a number of metrics and instruments. A combination of surveys and observational assessments on communication effectiveness can help you understand how you and your team perceive how everyone communicates information. Include questions in these about the ease of sharing, responsiveness, and ability to get feedback. Observational assessments can also tell you who is speaking, who is being heard, and about the quality of the interactions that may impact work.

To understand how everyone has internalized the vision and objectives, you can conduct alignment surveys. These can be specifically designed to assess understanding and the alignment of tasks with your core vision and OKRs. You can evaluate performance data through an alignment lens, and look at the alignment of work with stated objectives. It's also helpful to collect feedback through focus groups and interviews, taking the time to discuss with team members how they understand and perceive the team's goals. Take in feedback, and potentially have them articulate the mission and vision in their own words.

Self-Governance

Self-governance, as a term, is a good combination of what we want our team to demonstrate in terms of autonomy, accountability, and disciplined initiative. It conveys the idea that we want people to take responsibility for their actions while acting independently and proactively. It implies that we trust them to manage their work with a high degree of freedom, and also to keep their work aligned with organizational goals. We'll want to capture data on this attribute in a number of different ways, but here are just a few:

- **Performance reviews.** Include not just what your teammates have achieved, but also how they achieved these results (approach and method). Take some time with them to conduct a self-assessment of their methods and review 360-degree feedback on how others perceive their autonomy, accountability, and initiative.

- **Goal achievement and project outcome tracking.** Tracking clear and measurable goals and project outcomes helps you evaluate a person's ability to get it done. Are they achieving their goals, prioritizing their tasks, and delivering results? These are all things you want to see them achieving.

- **Accountability metrics.** No, we're not talking about the sitting-in-seats hours metric here. Instead, we want to know how well people meet their deadlines, project milestones, and the response times you've set for them. Are they reliable?

- **KPIs.** Work with your employees to establish specific performance indicators that reflect the characteristics you're looking for in self-governance. You can measure feedback and review scores, decision-making efficiency, completion rate of self-initiated projects, self-improvement or learning objectives, and many other things that should be relevant to how they see themselves meeting their self-governance objective.

These are just a few ways you can give yourself a flexible and adaptable leader model suited to managing complex teams—or any team, for that matter. The principles of leading teams really haven't changed all that much in principle. Good leaders in structured in-person environments are still good leaders in diverse, flexible, distributed environments. However, structured environments let leaders get away with a lot of bad habits that won't survive contact in the kind of workplaces we're talking about.

New Ways of Work Need New Ways to Lead

The modern workplace is changing significantly, and it's not just because of the changing needs and expectations of the new wave of workers entering the workforce. It's because there's a greater range of ages, backgrounds, and experiences in the workforce than ever before. In 2021, almost one out of every five US workers was 55 or older, almost doubling since 2000.[15] While those older workers bring a wealth of experience to the table, the spread of ages and experiences introduces a new element of diversity altogether.

We just talked about communication effectiveness, and that's one major place where we have differences of opinions across age ranges. Older workers might prefer face-to-face meetings or phone calls, while younger workers gravitate toward instant messages and digital communication. This means that to be effective, you have to be communicating on a number of different media. The town hall or press release-style of communication is effective to only a small group, so you need to diversify your communication portfolio to be effective.

Work-life expectations will also be different. Dozens and dozens of influencers have taken to Instagram reels and TikTok to show different generational responses to activities in and around the workplace, for good reason. Younger workers tend to prioritize work-life alignment more than their older counterparts, and expect a more responsive experience model. These younger workers will seek out flexible working arrangements, while older workers might prefer the traditional in-office model and structured work schedules. As a leader you'll have to come up with systems that maybe don't provide all of these all of the time to all of the people, but have a good portfolio of options for people who want to be in the office all of the time, some of the time, or very little of the time.

These differences manifest themselves over a number of other office functions as well, including learning and development preferences—some prefer structured and synchronous, others are just fine with self-driven and asynchronous. Some value stability and predictability and others are frustrated with slower change and adoption rates, and some might be motivated by financial security while others want meaningful and impactful work, regardless of how permanent or stable it might be. All of these things will come together in your modern workplace, and as your ways of work change, you might need some new ways of leading to go along with it.

I've had the luxury of running some unusual and very talented teams in my career. Many of them have comprised subject matter experts who happen to be distributed all over the country, who are looking for a different kind of work and different types of projects, and often, a more agile and flat organization than you can find in the traditional Army hierarchy. Working with these teams has very much shaped my perspective on different things we need to be able to add to our leader models to make them more personal and adaptable to the types of teams we happen to be leading.

Here are a couple of things you might think about when you're building unique teams that you want to empower toward autonomy, initiative, and goal achievement.

Embracing Distributed Leadership

The concept of distributed leadership basically says there are a variety of leadership roles within a team and they do not all belong to one person. This seems diametrically opposed to how the U.S. Army operates, but in a way, it's how our special forces teams operate. One individual might be commanding the team and providing the vision, but each individual on the team comes to the team with a different expertise in which they are expected to be a subject matter expert and leader.

Even in a somewhat homogenous organization, no single leader can have all the answers, and we shouldn't set that expectation. Someone owns the responsibility for setting the goals and objectives, but empowering other teammates to take on leadership roles in their areas of expertise can lead to more innovative and agile decision making.

Focusing on Emotional Intelligence

Emotional intelligence is a critical skill for leaders in any setting, but especially when you have a diverse team where everyone thinks and perceives things differently. Understanding and managing your own emotions and being able to empathize with others develops trust. It's different from the stoicism you would usually picture in military leaders, which is needed in difficult combat situations, but we aren't always just providing direction. We're often providing coaching and mentorship to our teams and people and friends we've served with previously.

Encouraging Open and Transparent Communication

Open communication channels that encourage employees to share their ideas and feedback contribute to a culture that values differences. This is one area where the U.S. Army and business best practices are aligned. We conduct regular exercise reviews and feedback sessions and have open-door policies, as you would expect a leader with good communication policies in the business world to have, too. The problems we run into there are the same as in industry, though, and that's recording and using all of that feedback in a meaningful manner.

Developing People to Go Their Own Way

Instead of a one-size-fits-all approach to development, leaders should focus on personalized coaching and mentoring. This involves understanding each employee's career aspirations and working style, and providing tailored guidance and support.

We have experimented with training leaders in different roles to not just be mentors but to be coaches throughout the Army,[16] and we've found that it's helpful to train leaders to also be coaches, but if you're going to work with a coach, it's often better for our folks to have a coach who is not in their direct report line.

Facilitating Lifelong Learning

Encouraging continuous learning and upskilling is an essential part of keeping relevant skills and preparing for the future. Leaders should facilitate access to learning resources and opportunities, and create an environment where learning is part of the organizational culture.

Amazon does a great job of this. Amazon's Career Choice[17] program prepays 95 percent of tuition and fees for employees to take courses in in-demand fields, regardless of whether the skills are relevant to a career at Amazon.

Aligning Individuality With Organizational Goals

Many people talk about work-life balance and balancing the individual with the organization. I dislike the term "balance" because it forces you to think of these things as a trade-off when for you to be at your most effective, they should be in alignment as much as possible. You should work in a manner that aligns with your life goals, and work toward work values that align with your values. Similarly, your organization should look for opportunities to align the diverse talents and aspirations of your employees with the strategic objectives of your organization. This involves setting clear goals, providing the right resources, and clearly and consistently communicating your vision.

Chapter Summary

Our leadership challenges today are in orchestrating harmony between teamwork and individuality, or in prioritizing the individual and individual skills without losing sight of the needs and mission of the organization. It's a fantastic challenge, and as we consider it, let's talk about it using that phrase as a construct: Orchestrating harmony. I love the metaphor of the symphony orchestra for the task we have in front of us when it comes to managing and leading the complex adaptive system of talents and backgrounds and personalities and interactions. In an orchestra, each individual musician brings a unique sound and is often a virtuoso in their own right. However, when they come together under the conductor's guidance, all those sounds create incredible blends of sound and emotion.

In an orchestra, every instrument has a unique timbre and range. The beauty of a symphony lies in understanding these individual characteristics and integrating them to create a holistic piece of music. Similarly in the workplace, you need to find ways to recognize and value the unique skills and perspectives each employee brings, much like the conductor or composer who knows the unique capabilities of each instrument.

An orchestra's success relies on the seamless collaboration of its musicians. In the workplace, leaders should foster an environment where collaboration thrives, encouraging employees from diverse backgrounds to work together toward common goals. Just as the conductor adjusts the tempo to suit the piece, leaders must be adaptable, adjusting management styles to suit the dynamics of their team. This might involve varying communication styles, leadership approaches, and feedback mechanisms. Fortunately for us, despite their differences, each musician in an orchestra is united by the goal of a successful performance. This is where you come in, with your clear objectives and vision, aligning each instrument in your orchestra against a common goal to accomplish.

Leading and balancing the needs of a diverse, multidisciplinary workforce, you are very much the conductor. Under your guidance, when you lead with insight, competence, understanding, trust, and clear communication, you can blend that vast array of talents, backgrounds, and perspectives on your team into a cohesive and high-performing unit. The conductor's role is not to homogenize the sound but to enable each instrument to contribute its best, while ensuring alignment with the overall musical piece. By embracing the principles of harmony, unity, and nuanced leadership, organizations can not only ensure the satisfaction and development of their diverse employees but also drive innovation, adaptability, and sustained success.

And isn't that a refrain we would love to listen to?

Notes

1 Heath Hall and Brett Thompson (2012) "The Secret Sauce of Teamwork," *Harvard Business Review*, https://hbr.org/2012/03/the-secret-sauce-of-teamwork (archived at https://perma.cc/9Z3H-6UPV)

2 Halford E. Luccock (nd) "No One Can Whistle a Symphony," Pass It On, www.passiton.com/ (archived at https://perma.cc/BK6K-69QR)

3 Indeed editors (nd) "What is Workplace Diversity and How Can Employers Drive Inclusion?" Indeed.com, www.indeed.com/hire/c/info/what-is-workforce-diversity (archived at https://perma.cc/68BM-8VAS)

4 Kristin Saling and Michael Do (2020) "Leveraging People Analytics for an Adaptive Complex Talent Management System," *Procedia Computer Science*, 168, Elsevier, www.sciencedirect.com/science/article/pii/S1877050920304087 (archived at https://perma.cc/3X3F-VHEE)

5 John Skar (2003) "Introduction: Self-Organization as an Actual Theme," *Philosophical Transactions of the Royal Society*, 361, pp. 1049–56

6 Kieren Diment, Ping Yu, and Karin Garrety (2009) "Complex Adaptive Systems as a Model for Evaluating Organizational Change Caused by the Introduction of Health Information Systems," *Electronic Journal of Health Informatics*, 6 (1), www.researchgate.net/publication/30389433_Complex_Adaptive_Systems_as_a_Model_for_Evaluating_Organisational_Change_Caused_by_the_Introduction_of_Health_Information_Systems (archived at https://perma.cc/H823-64DF)

7 Richard Dawkins and John Richard Krebs (1979) "Arms Race Between and Within Species," *Proceedings of the Royal Society*, 205 (1161), https://royalsocietypublishing.org/doi/10.1098/rspb.1979.0081 (archived at https://perma.cc/PVA5-T38J)

8 Ben Ramalingam, Harry Jones, Toussaint Reba, and John Young (2019) "Exploring the Science of Complexity Series (Part 10): Concept 1 – Interconnected and Interdependent Elements and Dimensions," RealKM, https://realkm.com/2019/01/30/exploring-the-science-of-complexity-series-part-10-concept-1-interconnected-and-interdependent-elements-and-dimensions/ (archived at https://perma.cc/D3M8-QL8T)

9 Michael J. Droboniku, Heidi Kloos, Dieter Vanderelst, and Blair Eberhart (2021) "Exploring Links Between Complexity Constructs and Children's Knowledge Formation: Implications for Science Learning," in *Theory of Complexity – Definitions, Models, and Applications*, IntechOpen, www.intechopen.com/chapters/76663 (archived at https://perma.cc/JH7R-G5YS)

10 Stanley McChrystal, Tantum Collins, David Silverman, and Chris Fussell (2015) *Team of Teams: New rules of engagement for a complex world*, Portfolio Penguin

11 Ori Brafman and Rod A. Beckstrom (2006) *The Starfish and the Spider: The unstoppable power of leaderless organizations*, Portfolio Penguin

12 Army Doctrinal Publication 6-0: Mission Command (2012) www.moore.army.mil/mssp/security%20topics/Global%20and%20Regional%20Security/content/pdf/adp6_0_new.pdf (archived at https://perma.cc/LVP5-BPCM)

13 David Maister, Charles H. Green, and Robert M. Galford (2000) *The Trusted Advisor*, Free Press

14 Michael S. Erwin and Willys Devoll (2022) *Leadership is a Relationship: How to put people first in the digital world*, Wiley

15 Gretchen A. Petery, James W. Grosch, and L. Casey Chosewood (2023) "Clearing Up Myths about Older Workers While Understanding And Supporting an Aging Workforce," NIOSH Science Blog, https://blogs.cdc.gov/niosh-science-blog/2023/09/25/older-workers/ (archived at https://perma.cc/U2D7-Q4NH)

16 Army Coaching Program (2024) https://talent.army.mil/acp/ (archived at https://perma.cc/2U5U-72GZ)

17 Amazon Career Choice Program (2024) https://careerchoice.amazon/ (archived at https://perma.cc/8WQY-UVWN)

11

Rethinking Work From Individual to Team

Every form of strength covers one weakness and creates another, and therefore every form of strength is also a form of weakness and every weakness a strength.

MICHAEL LEWIS, MONEYBALL[1]

We'll Have Changed The Game

Now comes the fun part, putting it all together and thinking about how we take this data-driven talent management approach from the individual, who you've understood and whose potential you've unleashed, to how you balance the needs of diverse teams, to really creating a powerful and dynamic team. This is how we take it to the next level.

It's only natural to start thinking about *Moneyball* at this point. Much like in baseball, as famously depicted in Michael Lewis's book and the Brad Pitt movie, we've seen teams across industries shift significantly from traditional methods of managing team dynamics to more nuanced, data-driven strategies. This change reflects the same things we've been observing throughout the book, that identifying and empowering people's different talents, knowledge, skills, and abilities makes for a much more complex environment, and we need data and analytics to effectively process everything that's happening into usable information and insights.

Now we make that even more complicated by taking a look at the whole of the team, and not just the complications of the individual. We talked about balancing preferences based on different work styles, experiences, backgrounds, and preferences in Chapters 9 and 10, but let's talk about the complexity that arises when we start working together. We not only have the individual differences to look at, but interaction effects and potentially emergent behaviors, when the combination of different features in our teams produces something new that our individuals didn't have before, when the sum of the parts becomes something far more than expected.

Here, we'll explore the application of data driven talent management principles to team dynamics. And yes, we'll talk a bit about baseball and probably a lot about *Moneyball*.

The *Moneyball* philosophy, which revolutionized US baseball, countered the idea that the insights previously used to put together baseball teams were inherently subjective and flawed, and that a much better system to put together a top-performing team could be built using a different set of statistical data than previously considered. Prior to *Moneyball,* experts looked at stolen bases, runs batted in (RBI), and batting average. Instead of looking at these, Billy Beane and his team at the Oakland Athletics instead looked for undervalued players who didn't score well by the metrics of the time, but who scored well by different metrics, ones that demonstrated not just their ability to contribute as an individual player, but their ability to contribute as part of an overall team, and how they might support other players or shore up gaps.

Just as Billy Beane focused on on-base percentages and other overlooked statistics to evaluate players, modern managers must use a variety of data points to assess employee potential and fit in the context of the team. This approach involves a deeper analysis of an individual's performance with the team as a reference, including aspects like collaborative skills, adaptability, and problem-solving abilities, which might not be immediately evident through traditional evaluation methods, where the individual is evaluated solely on their own performance, not on how they contribute to the greater team or how their attributes and performance led to supporting others.

Moneyball's success was partly due to its challenge to the status quo. In the corporate world, creating a culture that encourages innovation and adaptability is equally important. Leaders must be open to new ideas, willing to challenge traditional practices, and quick to adapt to changing market dynamics and internal team landscapes. As we dig deeper into these topics, we'll explore the parallels between executing a different data-driven talent management approach and the ideas we're encouraging toward innovation and adaptability. Our goal is to derive actionable insights on how we can use data to identify and leverage the unique strengths of individuals as part of a team now and not just as individuals, how to foster a culture that values these skills both individually and collectively, and how to synthesize these elements into a cohesive, winning team.

So let's talk about how to win. Because, like Billy Beane, we hate losing.[2]

Integrating Individual Performance into Team Dynamics

Maximizing individual performance and potential has long been the focus of talent management, which isn't surprising. High performing individuals can catalyze growth and drive innovation within an organization. That's great when you're working on going from zero to one in innovation, but not when you want a sustained culture of creativity and innovation. Putting too much emphasis on individual performance can lead to silos, misaligned goals, and can reduce collaboration in favor of competition. Many businesses and organizations have completely reworked how they do performance evaluation due to that last issue.

The impact of your high-performing folks should not just be independent. You can use them to catalyze your team, and build teams around them to emphasize strengths and shore up weaknesses, and enable them to do the same. That way, ideally, everyone scores beyond their individual achievements, and becomes a team where the whole is actually greater than the sum of the parts (which is mathematically possible due to variable interaction, but that's a whole other math geek story altogether).

In this nuanced interplay, we need to track and monitor how individual attributes and behaviors can positively or adversely affect team dynamics. Performance management systems, employee engagement platforms, 360-degree feedback tools, learning management tools, workforce analytic tools, employee recognition platforms, team collaboration tools, human resource information systems (HRIS), and anything else we use to compile data on human performance, interaction, or engagement can provide us with a wealth of data we can analyze to gain these insights, and to parse out views of each of our individuals' strengths and weaknesses and the way those interact with the wealth of the team.

Here are a few examples of tools in this space that you might have already at your organization or might be able to invest in:[3]

- **Performance management systems.** These help you to set, track, and evaluate employee performance against goals. Some examples include Workday, SAP Success Factors, and ADP Workforce Now, all of which provide performance and goal management and can integrate with your other human resource functions.

- **Employee engagement platforms.** These gauge employee engagement and satisfaction through surveys and other feedback mechanisms. Some platforms in this space are Qualtrics EmployeeXM, Glint, and Culture Amp. These are survey tools but specialize in helping you develop data collection instruments to gain insights on employee experience, engagement, and culture.

- **360-degree feedback tools.** These systems are similar to survey and engagement systems but are designed to collect and aggregate feedback from an employee's manager, peers, and subordinates to offer a holistic view of their perceived performance. You can use survey instruments for this as well, but there are tools like Lattice, SurveyMonkey Engage, and Trakstar, which are specifically designed to provide 360-degree feedback platforms to your employees and aggregate the data for insights.

- **Learning management systems (LMS).** These are digital platforms that track and report employee training and development. Coursera and Udemy provide access to a large number of professional courses, and Workera helps you aggregate these and others into a dashboard and monitoring system.

- **Employee recognition platforms.** These are digital platforms to recognize and reward employee achievement. Bonusly and Kudos are two popular platforms which rely on peer-to-peer recognition, and can help you see how your teammates are supporting each other.

- **Team collaboration tools.** These are mostly digital tools which can offer insights directly into team dynamics and how people work together. Most of us are familiar with Teams and Slack as digital collaboration software, but Asana is also good for managing projects and team responsibilities.

- **Human resource information systems (HRIS).** These are comprehensive systems that manage a large variety of human resource functions and can be adjusted to collect and manage data and actions from a talent management perspective, too. Some of the most popular HRIS in use are SAP SuccessFactors, Oracle HCM Cloud, Workday Human Capital Management, Kronos Workforce Ready, and BambooHR.

So, supposing we can get and utilize data out of all of these systems to learn about individual performance and team dynamics… what are we looking for?

Here are a few things you should work to measure and gain insights about.

Complimentary Skill Sets

When forming teams, think about the balance of skills and traits you need on the team among members. Some projects might need a mix of creative thinkers, detail-oriented planners, and charismatic leaders. Think about Apple's original Macintosh team, which Steve Jobs carefully composed of diverse individuals whose skills complemented each other. They're famous for their innovative approaches and contributions to the development of personal computing due to the way their skillsets played off one another.[4]

Team Success Factors

By understanding what makes your good teams work well, you can tailor development programs to address specific areas. One of my favorite examples of targeted development is Google's Project Aristotle, which aimed to study hundreds of the company's teams and figure out just what made some teams succeed and others fail.[5] They collected data on everything from team composition and personality traits to skills and group norms. The study found that the key to successful teams was about how team members interacted, structured their work, and viewed their contributions from a lens of psychological safety, structure, clarity, and impact. They then implemented programs to help the less successful teams improve their psychological safety, communication, and sense of purpose.[6]

Predictive Analysis for Conflict Management

As we've discussed in depth, diversity in personalities and working styles, while beneficial, can sometimes lead to conflict. Here, data-driven insights become crucial in preempting and managing potential friction. Predictive analytics can help in identifying potential personality clashes or incompatible working styles. This is another area studied under Google's Project Aristotle, with recommendations for conflict management and predicting clashing team dynamics coming out of the overall analysis.[7]

Aligning Individual and Team Objectives

While individual excellence is vital, aligning it with team goals is critical for collective success. Leaders must ensure that individual goals and incentives are aligned with team objectives. This encourages collaboration rather than competition among team members. Cisco Systems redesigned its performance management systems not too long ago, focusing on emphasizing teamwork and ongoing feedback. The system, called "Connected Recognition," lets managers and peers give instant feedback, recognition, and even small monetary rewards for day-to-day achievements that align with team goals, incentivizing the employee—and incentivizing the organization to provide data![8]

Recognizing and Rewarding Team Contributions

Shifting some focus from individual achievements to team successes can promote a more collaborative culture. When team achievements are celebrated, it fosters a sense of unity and shared purpose. I'm coming back to Google again, and this time noting its gDNA initiative.[9] This was a longitudinal study to capture data on the work and life experience of Googlers. One of the key objectives was to create a more collaborative culture by recognizing and celebrating team contributions.

Facilitating Cross-Functional Interaction

Cross-functional teams bring together diverse perspectives and expertise, leading to more innovative outcomes. 3M—who we know from innovation and design thinking as much as for creative thought and the ubiquitous sticky notes—has had cross-functional teams as a core component of its business strategy for a long time.[10] The company encourages employees from different departments and areas of expertise to work together on projects, and reportedly provides amounts of unstructured time for this collaboration.

Training for Emotional Intelligence

Emotional intelligence is key in navigating the complexities of team dynamics. Training sessions focused on empathy, self-awareness, and emotional regulation can equip individuals to better understand and interact with their teammates. This is a much older example, but American Express in the early 2000s implemented an emotional intelligence training program aimed at helping its employees develop their interpersonal skills, including workshops and modules focused on self-awareness, empathy, emotional regulation, and effective communication.[11] Even though this is an older case, it's still worth reviewing. The program demonstrated a lot of positive outcomes, with employees showing improved skills in handling difficult emotional situations, both internally among teams and externally with their customers.

These are just a few of the things you can measure and evaluate to see how your teams are performing, and what factors you might be missing in individuals that might support team dynamics. Your ultimate aim is to create a team where you can effectively integrate all the pieces and parts to achieve collective success.

There are a number of studies going on currently in sports organizations, business enterprises, and the military to crack the code on optimal teaming. Looking at this from an attribute perspective, we're asking our research teams, what attributes need to be present in the team? What attributes need to be within certain work roles, and which need to just be present in someone in the team? Which ones are core competencies that everyone needs to have? If there's a good solution out there to determine that, I haven't found it yet, but I'm excited about what research might have to show us here.

Seeing the Person While Building the Team

So let's talk about what happens when we move from the personal construct to the team construct, particularly with regard to rewards and recognition. This makes me think about the symphony example we used in the last chapter, where we bring in dozens of potentially award-winning musicians and tune their capabilities into playing a beautiful collaborative piece. But how do we not lose the power of the individual in the team? How do we reward individuality but still pull our individuals into the collective dynamics of the team?

This is the balancing act that has us letting go of talent management principles and grasping for the old ecosystem. So many organizations with solid talent management programs fail to make the full transition from managing the talents of individuals to figuring out how to appreciate the talents and individuality of those folks and at the same time conduct that whole symphony. We have to figure out that balance. When individuals feel that their uniqueness is acknowledged, it instills a sense of belonging, ownership, and significance, the kind of things we need for autonomy, accountability, and disciplined initiative—the self-governance we hoped to instill in the previous chapter. It's also critical to morale and job satisfaction. Even though we need our individuals to play a part of the symphony we hope to create, we can't lose their individuality.

So how do we continue to recognize, see, and value our teammates individually but also incorporate them into the team?

There's a lot of power in the concept of **team cohesion**—the combination of individual efforts toward a shared goal. When we talk about teams, there's always a lot of focus on collective effort and shared objectives, but when we talk about a cohesive effort, we can't forget that it happens because of individuals coming together and operating together, but with their own unique roles, purposes, and skills. Striking a balance between individual achievements and team objectives is crucial. That's where we can bring in the combination of personalized talent management programs and goal-setting and start with the OKRs we talked about earlier.

Walking back organizational objectives, providing ownership of key results, and building tailored performance and development plans around achieving both individual and team goals aligned to those results are critical to making sure talent management extends from the individual to the team, and we don't lose the individual in pursuit of team goals.

A key part of all of this is just talking to our people. Providing regular and specific feedback on how the individual's performance is contributing to their goals and team goals, and providing opportunities to share expertise, collaborate, and contribute can all reinforce the value of unique contributions and convince high performers to keep participating as part of the team. Google's Project Oxygen was a good example of how to do this, and how to make managers great—not just at providing the vision but at empowering team members without micromanaging, creating an inclusive team environment, showing concern for success and well-being, being productive and results oriented, and collaborating.[12]

Following the findings from Project Oxygen, Google began to train its managers based on the qualities it discovered that made them effective leaders of high-performing teams. They also incorporated the results into hiring searches for new managers. After implementing the findings, they saw a significant improvement in team outcome, employee satisfaction, and general managerial performance.[13] This innovative, data-driven approach to understanding and improving how to manage high-performing teams has been praised, but it's also something that you can execute within your organization.[14]

So as you're going back to your talent management strategy, think about how you as a leader or manager will assess your ability to provide that strategic vision, empower your team members without micromanaging them, create trust and encourage open communication, show emotional intelligence, and still stay focused on results and productivity. It sounds like a lot, but at the same time, it should sound like it's pulling together a tapestry from common threads through all these chapters, weaving together lessons learned from all the examples we've given so far. This truly is your capstone as a leader in a data-driven talent management construct.

And making the jump from talent management at the individual level to talent management at the team level is the equivalent of breaching the Valley of Death in research.[15] Moving from prototype to scale without losing the uniqueness of the solution isn't too different from the challenge we've posed here. So how do we make sure we can actually do that and get that win? Let's talk about some things we can do to arm our individuals and teams with good skills to come together on projects and actively collaborate.

I keep making references to team sports in this section, but I really can't think of a better real-world analogy (despite my abiding love for examples from comics and Harry Potter) for how you can take the performance of incredible individuals and put it together to execute a combined collaborative mission. Whether it's the synchronized strokes of a rowing crew on a river, the tactical plays and combined stamina of a rugby team, or the coordinated efforts of a basketball squad, we see incredible groups of talented people come together again and again in contests where success hinges on the combination of skills on the field, not just individuals, and yet we don't lose the stardom held by high-performing individuals.

You would think we'd be able to take that and translate into our high-performing teams and talent management programs elsewhere, wouldn't you? So how do we do this in the corporate arena?

Perhaps part of the problem is that in sports, we see all the assists and steals and other supporting efforts that go toward the win, but in the corporate world, much of this happens outside the briefing room where the results are presented to leadership. Rarely do you see the hard work the data engineer put into wrangling a truly gnarly collection of data into something model-ready for our analysts or systems of record, nor do you hear anything about the person who built the UI/UX or workflow that improved customer satisfaction by 130 percent. It becomes a fact or a figure on a chart and the person who performed the action may or may not get recognition or any credit for the impact they made.

This isn't to say that everyone relies on recognition and accolades to get satisfaction and value from the work they're doing. However, thanking someone or rewarding them for their achievement, or at least recognizing that achievement, goes a long way.

Partnering, Pairing, and Knowledge Sharing

So, knowing that we're going to bring our team of all-stars together, what do we need to consider? How do people need to go about learning and integrating into each other's workflows and work dynamics? How can we gain enough on-the-job training (OJT) from collaborating that we can gain a solid understanding of what our teammates do to see how our skills should integrate with theirs? Let's talk about how we can partner and collaborate to share knowledge, gain common understanding, and posture our people to be able to partner and collaborate rapidly with people of differing backgrounds, skillsets, and perspectives all across the organization!

Let's start with **strategic pairing**. If you have small projects or research opportunities that you can use as training opportunities and pair team members with complementary skills, you can use these to gain experience and boost productivity. Look at your skills inventory and use analytics to find those complementary skillsets, or use them to predict what skill combinations you might need for upcoming projects, and use that to select teams. This is something that happens frequently at IBM, where they pair senior and junior engineers of different departments and specialties on projects routinely. This kind of practical mentorship has led to faster knowledge transfer and skill development across the company, and is a practice you can easily adopt in your own organization.[16]

You should develop **platforms for sharing**. Creating internal and easily accessible platforms for knowledge sharing is a critical part of being able to increase knowledge and experience across your organization. Siemens, for example, uses platforms like TechnoWeb for employees to share technical knowledge and foster conversations about the validity of certain solutions, creating an effective and informal peer review process.[17] This type of discussion increases understanding and knowledge across the organization and encourages people to add their opinions and expertise and learn.

Find times to create regular **knowledge exchange sessions**. During the time I worked for the Assistant Secretary of the Army for Manpower and Reserve Affairs (roughly 2019–2022), we conducted a large number of learning activities, from lunch and learn sessions to the Army People Seminar hosted in Louisville, Kentucky.[18] These activities were great for both broadening our perspectives and encouraging us to set aside a little bit of time for self-development. Google also ran a great program with their "TGIF" sessions, giving Googlers a forum to discuss various topics and share expertise, but they canceled the program in 2019, citing that their scale had forced them to evolve.[19] While I can understand how these meetings might have become unwieldy with the size of the company, I think this is something they could have easily powered down to directorates or departments.

Finally, lots of teams have found success bringing people together for **innovation competitions** like hackathons, innovation labs, shark tanks, and similar events. These are great for encouraging people to bring their innovative solutions to the forefront and getting both individual and team recognition for their contributions. The U.S. Army has been successfully running an innovation competition since 2020 called Dragon's Lair, encouraging soldier teams to compete for recognition and reward with innovative solutions to Army-wide problems.[20]

The more I think about all these success stories, though, the more I think about what we talked about before, looking at the individual contributions of all those who help the team achieve a goal in a sports arena and thinking about all of those who help teams achieve in the corporate arena. The biggest difference is that those corporate wins are all assisted by silent partners, by contributors who are largely out of the boardroom limelight. That makes what we do to recognize the performance of our individuals incredibly important. A skilled coach recognizes, identifies, and nurtures the distinct abilities of each athlete who comes across their field and forms them into a championship team; like that coach, we have to do the same thing with our corporate teams, recognizing the unique strengths, potentials, and contributions of every member as if they were visible on the field. Encouraging team members to express their ideas and giving them credit for those ideas is key. Let people trust that you will recognize them, and make them feel valued and heard. Even though you're aligning their work toward larger team objectives, you don't want to sublimate them, or make them feel like they are just cogs in the wheel. Celebrate their achievements and celebrate the team's achievements, and do what you can to foster a collective sense of pride and ownership.

People don't have to give up their own personal goals and achievement motivation to be part of a team if their leaders can maintain the right balance of recognition and reward for both the individual and the team; be the leader who has an eye on the goal, but also has their eyes open to see and value the contributions of the team.

Chapter Summary

People who run ball clubs, they think in terms of buying players. Your goal shouldn't be to buy players, your goal should be to buy wins.

PETER BRAND, *MONEYBALL*[21]

The team-building approach in *Moneyball* serves as a compelling framework to reflect upon after all this talk about seeing the person in the team, putting together unique skills, and how we recognize and reward the individual contribution to the whole. In that philosophy, we emphasized the value of leveraging data, and unique statistics at that, to create winning teams. The Oakland A's scouts and manager we read about didn't focus on star players, but understood deeply how each player fit into the overall team strategy. This approach to team building and management holds profound insights for our business models as we strive to balance individual talents with cohesive team dynamics.

Granted, the team in *Moneyball* was working on a budget, and we're talking about putting together a team of all-stars. However, the same principles apply. We're looking at building up individual skills and talents, but also optimizing how they work together and fit into a whole construct. We've talked about how to share knowledge and collaborate so that we can cross-pollinate skills and create better synergy between teammates. We've talked about the importance of recognizing the individual contribution to the team. And we've talked about how to look at and integrate unique skills and capabilities that might not otherwise be valued into a winning team proposition. That's pretty amazing in and of itself!

The integration of individual performance into team dynamics is a delicate yet crucial aspect of modern management. Drawing inspiration from *Moneyball*, we learn the value of data-driven decisions, the power of recognizing undervalued skills, and the importance of fostering team synergy. As organizations navigate the complexities of the modern business environment, these lessons become increasingly relevant. By valuing each individual's unique contributions while skillfully weaving them into the fabric of team objectives, leaders can create an environment where both individuals and teams can thrive and achieve their fullest potential.

Notes

1 Michael Lewis (2004) *Moneyball: The Art of Winning an Unfair Game*, W.W. Norton & Company

2 Bennett Miller, dir. (2011) *Moneyball*, Sony Pictures, information available at www.imdb.com/title/tt1210166/mediaviewer/rm330480640/?ref_=tt_ov_i (archived at https://perma.cc/K4QR-SWPH)

3 These listed tools are for information purposes and listing does not reflect an endorsement or an intent to purchase on behalf of my employer, the United States Army, or the United States Department of Defense

4 Waler Isaacson (2011) *Steve Jobs*, Simon & Schuster

5 Charles Duhigg (2016) "What Google Learned From Its Quest to Build the Perfect Team," *New York Times Magazine*, www.nytimes.com/2016/02/28/magazine/what-google-learned-from-its-quest-to-build-the-perfect-team.html (archived at https://perma.cc/WXX8-9MGS)

6 Julia Rozovsky (2015) "The Five Keys to a Successful Google Team," re:Work, https://rework.withgoogle.com/blog/five-keys-to-a-successful-google-team/ (archived at https://perma.cc/H4VT-9TCG) (Hint: Have Google Translate installed)

7 Charles Duhigg (2016) "What Google Learned from Its Quest to Build the Perfect Team," *New York Times Magazine*, www.nytimes.com/2016/02/28/magazine/what-google-learned-from-its-quest-to-build-the-perfect-team.html (archived at https://perma.cc/WXX8-9MGS)

8 Aaron Kinne (2019) "How HR Data Drives Cisco's Culture," Workhuman, www.workhuman.com/blog/how-hr-data-drives-ciscos-culture/ (archived at https://perma.cc/LSX5-D3GV)

9 Michael Schneider (2017) "Google Spent 2 Years Studying 180 Teams. The Most Successful Ones Shared These 5 Traits." Inc.com, www.inc.com/michael-schneider/google-thought-they-knew-how-to-create-the-perfect.html (archived at https://perma.cc/7FFC-C4GL)

10 Vijay Govindarajan and Srikanth Srinivas (2013) "The Innovation Mindset in Action: 3M Corporation," *Harvard Business Review*, https://hbr.org/2013/08/the-innovation-mindset-in-acti-3 (archived at https://perma.cc/P3PM-E7GS)

11 Cary Cherniss and Robert D. Caplan (2001) "A Case Study in Implementing Emotional Intelligence Programs in Organizations," *Journal of Organizational Excellence*, 21 (1), www.researchgate.net/publication/229809108_A_Case_Study_in_Implementing_Emotional_Intelligence_Programs_in_Organizations (archived at https://perma.cc/Q7PK-Q8CL)

12 Madeline Miles (2022) "Revisiting Project Oxygen: A Look At What Makes a Good Manager," BetterUp, www.betterup.com/blog/project-oxygen (archived at https://perma.cc/M6GF-FK6U)

13 David A. Garvin (2013) "How Google Sold its Engineers on Management," *Harvard Business Review*

14 Laszlo Bock (2015) *Work Rules! Insights from inside Google that will transform how you live and lead*, Twelve

15 Stephen K. Markham (2002) "Moving Technologies from Lab to Market," *Research Technology Management*, 45 (6), pp. 31–42, www.jstor.org/stable/24134651 (archived at https://perma.cc/N9VY-YN7V)

16 Lydia Logan (2022) "Everyone Needs a Mentor – Go Find Yours!" IBM, www.ibm.com/blog/everyone-needs-a-mentor/ (archived at https://perma.cc/CNS7-ENJD)

17 Susan Morl, Michael Heiss, and Alexander Richter (2019) "Siemens: Knowledge Networking with TechnoWeb 2.0," www.e20cases.org/files/fallstudien/e20cases-09-siemens_english.pdf (archived at https://perma.cc/92V6-WVNX)

18 Mark Hebert (2017) "Strategic Broadening Seminar Brings Soldiers Into the Classroom," UofL News, www.uoflnews.com/post/uofltoday/strategic-broadening-seminar-brings-soldiers-into-the-classroom/ (archived at https://perma.cc/LZ5U-KSVN)

19 Jennifer Elias (2019) "Google Will No Longer Hold Weekly All-Hands Meetings Amid Growing Workplace Tensions," CNBC, www.cnbc.com/2019/11/15/google-cancels-tgif-weekly-all-hands-meetings.html (archived at https://perma.cc/WN34-J53F)

20 Joshua Cowden (2023) "DoD Service Members Open to Submit Ideas for Dragon's Lair 8 as Part of Joint USSOCOM and XVIII Airborne Corps Innovation Venture," U.S Army, www.army.mil/article/263722/dod_service_members_open_to_submit_ideas_for_dragons_lair_8_as_part_of_joint_ussocom_and_xviii_airborne_corps_innovation_venture (archived at https://perma.cc/UY4S-H4UJ)

21 Michael Lewis (2004) *Moneyball: The art of winning an unfair game*, W.W. Norton & Company

12

Anchoring Positive Change and Thriving

Innovation is the ability to see change as an opportunity, not a threat.
STEVE JOBS, INVENTOR AND CO-FOUNDER OF APPLE[1]

When Change Becomes Positive

Let's just take a moment to think back across the amount of change we've been able to examine over the first 11 chapters of this book. We started with the driving need to design winning teams that thrive in ambiguous and uncertain environments, and that to create those teams, we needed to accept that they were composed of unique and differently talented individuals. We talked about how to create the necessary culture of creativity and innovation that would be fertile ground in which you could seed these teams. We looked at the foundations of data needed to be able to categorize, collect, analyze, and interpret all the information we needed to know about the individual superheroes that comprised our teams. We defined talent and talked about how we manage it, both individually and in teams, and how we can use data and analytics to help us derive the necessary insights we need. We talked about balancing diversity in terms of personalities, ways of working, developing the workforce, and creating a common vision and set of goals to align all our different talent against.

We've talked about a lot of different ways of doing business, and while that's all fine and good for transforming your small team or managing just your high performers, when you start wanting to scale this across an organization, it requires a lot of change management.

Change, at least initially, brings about a lot of uncertainty and discomfort. When we talk about change management, there are a lot of people who immediately assign a negative connotation to it, as if those change managers are coming in determined to force people to accept something that is wrong for them or wrong for their organization. It's hard to fight the initial resistance, because that's a natural human response to the unknown. The comfort of familiar processes and known outcomes is hard to give up! However, keeping an eye on the perception of change, whether it's negative or positive, is a good way to know whether or not your organization has turned the corner on the change.

As you go through organizational change, you have to continually work to lay the communication and trust foundations for the new process. Listen to employees' concerns and feedback while you open those channels of communication, and remember that this is not a one-time effort, but an ongoing process. As team members discuss their concerns with you, make sure you answer their questions and provide feedback about how their roles and efforts contribute to overall success of the change and the organizations, and watch to see if their attitudes start to shift. It will be slow at first, but you'll begin to see some move from a state of apprehension to one of understanding, maybe reluctantly at first, and then you'll start seeing people accept the change. But the first real win you'll achieve as a change manager is when you see people start to become advocates and be enthusiastic about the change.

What things can help you get across that gap between acceptance and advocacy? From my experience, it has been patience, creating that nurturing environment, and celebrating small victories along the way. Every change-maker is different, but I personally have adopted a philosophy of relentless positivity. I will empathize and sympathize with people whose worlds are changing dramatically as a result of the changes I've been given to effect, but I work hard to never treat the change as anything but positive. I've found that attitude, accompanied by recognizing and applauding early adopters and sympathizers to the cause, and telling their stories as success stories, creates positive momentum. Suddenly the success stories are not those of the change-maker but of people known to the rest of the organization. This makes an abstract set of objectives and ideals more concrete, and makes the benefits of change tangible.

When you start seeing this change happen as you drive toward creating your winning high-performing teams and creating that culture of innovation, when you start seeing the change be accepted as a positive thing and a good direction for the organization, then you know you've set the conditions you need for your teams and your talent management plan to truly thrive. As attitudes change, as the organization begins to reap the benefits of the change, especially if your organization functions with cohesion and embraces the interconnectedness and interdependence principles we discussed before, you'll start to see more acceptance and adoption, improved processes, innovative solutions, and a more dynamic and adaptable workforce. This is a win.

Changing How the U.S. Army Looks at Talent Through Experience

When I first started working at the Army Talent Management Task Force, we had a number of different ideas to address personnel challenges that were in various stages of maturity. Some were in early stages of ideation, some were being worked by our teams and our research partners as they designed solutions, and some had solutions ready to go for experimentation. When deciding where to start and where to prioritize, we looked at a number of different factors. Everyone was concerned with what would have impact and what involved risk, where we could invest and how much, what could be executed with speed.

However, one of our advisors warned us that sometimes what we needed was not the biggest splash or biggest risk. We needed to figure out what we might use to anchor our effort with irrevocable change. What genie could we let out of the bottle and not put back inside?

We initiated assessments, we went on speaking circuits, we began to collect data and act on it, but we still looked for what might anchor the Army psyche in the change enough for it to think differently about how we think about talent.

The answer was a surprising one.

One of our initial problems was not fully defining our sets of knowledge, skills, and behaviors, and making those accessible to our strength managers so that they could codify our positions and find the right talent. Likewise, people didn't know what kind of attributes would make them competitive for jobs and which wouldn't. So both sides listed everything… or nothing.

We worked with our various career fields to create storyboards for what attributes people needed at which grade. That helped us think about what we really expected in terms of capability for people operating at different levels of the Army, but it didn't really help us differentiate them by talent. How did we rate people against these storyboards? Was it an all or nothing decision, where they had it or they didn't? Did we use a sliding scale? Did we have our attributes synchronized across grades so that they showed an understandable progression, or did some attributes simply show up, and others appear and disappear? (Hint: It was the latter.)

If only we had a way for people to see their careers unfold, for them to figure out where they could collect the experiences needed to achieve their goals, or for them to identify places they could use their strengths effectively... like a career map.

General McConville, the Chief of Staff of the Army at the time, painted a picture for us about how he envisioned careers unfolding. As a career aviator, it looked to him like a flight plan. Some people could fly direct, others might need to take a layover or two. Some might fly first class, and some might fly in coach.

In cooperation with our research and industry partners, and with our logistics branch, we developed and tested an interactive career mapping tool. This tool, through underlying attribute data and recommendation engines, allowed us to lay out the characteristics people needed at each step of their career, differentiated by different types of assignments; it let them assess and get leader and peer assessments of their strengths, and watch their career unfold by virtue of the decisions they made about assignments. And as General McConville predicted, some decisions allowed them to gain the attributes quickly and move toward competing for those goal assignments, and others made one or two more stops necessary before they could compete.

But then something interesting happened.

Our logistics branch really started looking at their assignments, at the attributes they expected someone to have when they took that position and the ones they wanted them to develop there. They were able to use the tool to see this develop over the course of a career. And they started to think about the positions they saw as key and developmental, the milestone assignments people had to take before competing for leadership positions.

Maybe not all of those positions were created equal. Maybe different positions were critical milestones for some leadership positions, and others needed a different set. Maybe, if a person took a series of positions and collected the necessary attributes and expertise, they didn't need one of those positions we saw as key and developmental at all.

They started thinking about career paths with more flexibility and creativity until the idea of a "path" was left behind, and it became much closer to the "jungle gym" concept we discussed earlier. And at that point, there was no more interest in a single career path to rule them all, or a single pathway to leadership, but instead interest in a diverse portfolio of experiences to get people developed with the diverse talents needed for all the varied positions of leadership our logisticians took throughout the Army.

Change found an anchor, because it tied fundamentally into the officer experience.

What is Experience?

Experience, in my opinion, is the next layer of talent management that the U.S. Army (and other organizations) need to define and develop. It's a critical piece of understanding how people desire to develop, what motivates them, and how they can be incentivized, but it's also a critical piece of creating tools, policies, and processes that resonate with the people whose behavior and development you're trying to shape.

So what is experience?

We've gone back and forth in the Army about whether or not our soldiers are employees or customers (they are employees of the Army but for those of us working in human resources, they are customers of our agency functions). So we use a definition that is a bit of a blend of both. For us, **experience** is the journey a soldier, Army civilian, or family member takes with our organization, including every interaction that happens along the journey, from initial awareness to signing a contract, from joining the service to transitioning into veteran status, and beyond. It also includes the experiences that involve their role, workspace, leaders, and culture.

For the purposes of this book, we'll define your **employee experience** (**EX**) much the same way—the journey your employee takes with your organization, including every interaction that happens along their time with your company and beyond, plus the experiences that involve their role, workspace, leaders, and culture.

Positive experiences lead to improved job satisfaction, engagement, and performance. According to a study by Jacob Morgan for *The Employee Experience Advantage*,[2] organizations that invest in EX are included 11.5 times as often in Glassdoor's Best Places to Work.[3]

At its heart, EX is about creating positive and meaningful experiences for your employees. So when you're thinking about how to anchor your data-driven talent management change, or any change, think about how you're going to anchor that in improving experience for your stakeholders, and how you're going to frame that change in a way you can communicate to them that aligns with that experience.

So that's one way to create positive change. What else can we do to continue nurturing these teams that thrive in ambiguity and our culture of innovation?

Hunting the Positive in All Things: Both Failure and Winning

If you're going to get the team to fully embrace the innovation mindset, to push beyond boundaries, experiment, take risks, and achieve, you must learn how to provide a positive and safe environment for your teams to experiment in. There are a lot of negative connotations to the concept of a "safe" environment, but for my naysayers, that simply means you've decided to accept risk on behalf of your team. You've decided that failures are a part of learning and that trying things that don't work is something valuable to the overall learning part. It means you're doing your job as a leader and reminding your teams that not everything has to be a win from the start, and if it is, it means we're not actually taking enough risk!

Let's talk about how we can create that space for risk and experimentation, how we can leverage failures as stepping stones, and how we can frame challenges as opportunities for growth. Positive framing, learning from failures, celebrating successes, and constructive feedback can and should become your benchmarks for creating and supporting that culture of creativity and innovation we began to envision at the start of our journey… way back there in Chapter 2.

Can you see it back there? What a lot of ground we've covered since. Now let's turn forward and figure out how we can keep this momentum going.

The Power of Positive Framing

The concept of positive framing is just a subtle shift in perspective and language that transforms obstacles into opportunities.[4] The language and manner we use to introduce ideas can have a profound effect on how people perceive them.

One of the examples my team likes to debate is the SpaceX Starship rocket launch in April 2023. The powerful uncrewed test rocket achieved liftoff, but exploded shortly after. There have been different reports of employees cheering, but people generally agree that SpaceX tried to frame the launch as a success. The SpaceX website even stated, "With a test like this, success comes from what we learn, and we learned a tremendous amount."[5] So we wonder, was this really a success, or did they fail, or was it some combination of both?

The trick lies in when you provide this message. We all treat companies with a dose of healthy skepticism when they announce, after a failure event, that everything is fine and this was just part of learning. It feels like a slapstick comedy, like when you watch someone accidentally walk into a door and declare, "I meant to do that."

Instead, we can take a lesson from one of the most famous stories about innovators and failures, that of Thomas Edison and his attempt to create the lightbulb—or the filament within the lightbulb. Edison approached his work as an experiment from the get-go, and when asked why he kept trying and failing, he reportedly said, "I have not failed. I've just found 10,000 ways that won't work."[6] While that might still be discouraging, I've used that quote on my teammates more than a few times to remind them that a try that failed is still one worth learning from. We shouldn't toss out failures, but take them and pull them apart and figure out what we can learn from where things went sideways.[7]

If we can do that, if we can take every first version of a software release, every first analytic that doesn't return a feasible result, and keep ourselves from scrapping it as a mere failure, we can use it as a treasure trove of insights. Teach your team to delve into the shortcomings of an experiment and use it as an opportunity to learn and improve. Taking a page from Thomas Edison, who purportedly failed 10,000 times before he achieved his goal, and leveraged all the knowledge learned from all those failures to get it right… that can be pretty inspiring.

Celebrating Success to Reinforce Innovation

No matter how much you treat failures positively, not everything can be a failure. Even if you are relentlessly positive, your team can only pick themselves up from failure so many times before they start losing hope and losing momentum. Find successes to celebrate along the way. Whether these are big breakthroughs or small wins, finding things to celebrate is integral to reinforcing a culture of innovation.

There's a lot of power in small wins, and in celebrating them. It's good for your mental well-being, and has even been shown to have some physiological benefits.[8] Salesforce demonstrates a number of good examples in this space through what they term their "Ohana Culture," emphasizing the importance of acknowledging achievements no matter how big or small, both in the office and across social media. They have also leveraged their Trailhead program, a gamified learning platform where employees can earn badges and other recognition to celebrate their learning achievements.[9]

One of the small things I've tried with my team is celebrating wins of the quarter. Together, we set our OKRs for the year and typically try focusing on a couple a quarter so we know how to prioritize, and each quarter, we take a look at the progress we've made on those results and celebrate them. Sometimes it's big, and sometimes it's small. Sometimes, it's more about reminding them that, by virtue of the nature of how our various teams have worked, we're doing something new, something that doesn't have a blueprint, something that doesn't have a set version of "what right looks like," as we hear so often in the military. Progress toward defining those objectives is still progress, and it's worth celebrating.

Feedback and Appreciation: Nurturing Creative Autonomy

Any psychologist can tell you that the best way to shape behavior is through reinforcement, whether positive or negative.[10] Personally, I'm a fan of positive reinforcement, so that's what I try to incorporate first in my feedback loops. And as you think about creating your feedback loops, you need to think about how you'll deliver reinforcement in terms of feedback to your team in a way that nurtures their creativity and autonomy.

Whether it's positive or negative in nature, constructive feedback, which is both clear and actionable, is essential. This can guide your team toward excellence and innovation while giving them the latitude they need for creative freedom.

I personally love Adobe's "Check-In" Approach that they adopted back in 2012 when they disbanded their traditional annual performance system review in favor of a more flexible, continuous, and constructive feedback model. The Check-In system focused on ongoing dialogues between managers and employees that were far more frequent and timely than a once-a-year evaluation. The system focused on providing information that was clear, actionable, and aimed at promoting employee development and creativity.[11] After implementing this approach, Adobe reported a 30 percent reduction in voluntary employee turnover. On top of that, employees at Adobe reported feeling both valued and motivated because of the frequent and constructive feedback they received.

The beauty of this vignette is that it's something you can implement in your organization almost immediately. Assuming you've already gone through the work we did when we talked about OKRs and KPIs and you know what you expect of your teammates, how could you create your own bi-weekly, monthly, or quarterly check-in to provide constructive feedback on where your employees are being rock stars and where they need to redirect? And how can you record and use that data to show where people have learned, grown, and developed and what kind of engagements and incentives nudged them along the way?

Appreciation and Recognition: Fuel for Creative Endeavors

Bear with me, I just need to give you one more positive reinforcement tool to support and encourage your team toward creative endeavors! Let's give just a little more thought to appreciation and recognition of your individuals and teams, and consider it just what we say, as the fuel for their future creative endeavors.

We talked about check-in discussions and constructive feedback, and while that's great for talking about improvements, what can you do about appreciation and recognition? We want to hear our constructive criticism in a one-on-one environment, but frankly, a lot of us would like to hear our praise in public. Right? This is a tremendous reinforcing opportunity if we use it correctly, and it is the perfect complement to our check-in structure.

Let's take another trip over to Google and their award system. We already know Google has a tremendously innovative culture and has implemented a lot of different systems to recognize its employees, but let's take a moment to highlight the peer bonus system they use, where employees and nominate their peers for bonuses as a way to recognize extraordinary performance.[12] You might remember that when we talked about tools that could help us integrate our high-performing individuals into teams, we mentioned a tool called Bonusly,[13] which allows you to create a peer-to-peer reward system. That's what Google uses for their program. The bonuses typically aren't large, but it's still considered exciting to receive one.

Okay, so we've talked about how positivity rules a lot of different engagements you might have with your teams, but that's not all there is to creating teams that thrive in ambiguous environments and learn to innovate. We've talked about creating an environment where risks are encouraged, failures are seen as opportunities for learning, successes are celebrated, and feedback is given constructively, and while this is a great ideal, we still have to figure out the practical aspect. How do we really empower that innovative team beyond encouragement?

Nurturing Innovation in Your Organization

Our ultimate journey here, as we seek to create high-performing teams capable of great creativity, innovation, and adaptation in the increasingly complex and competitive global environment we find ourselves in, is walking our way through the fundamentals of data-driven talent management we've talked about, through cultivating a superior employee experience, and ultimately fostering that innovation. The concepts of talent management, employee experience, and innovation can separately bring significant improvement to how you create, develop, and utilize your talent bench, but when used together, as we spoke about with any complex system, you can get some emergent benefits that are greater than the sum of the parts.

But let's review how all of this comes together.

Starting with **data-driven talent management**, we have two separate benefits for acquiring, developing, employing, and retaining the best talent bench we can put together for our organization. Firstly, we harness the power of technology, bringing in unprecedented ability to see our people and gain insights into workforce dynamics. By collecting and analyzing data from capability assessments, employee performance, employee engagement, and preferences and aspirations, we can tailor how we manage our people at the individual level, and not just help them align their development and employment goals with our values, but significantly improve their experience at our organization. That leads us to the second benefit of a data-driven talent management plan, the philosophical plan that lets us go from counting "how many" to seeing "who," and being able to see, value, employ, and incentivize our people as powerful individuals both separately and as part of the team.

Whew! That's a lot. And it's powerful to have a personalized approach to talent management that can help us acknowledge the unique knowledge, skills, abilities, behaviors, and preferences of each of our people. If we pair that with a work environment that values creativity and innovation and cultivates growth and learning, we provide the fertile ground that lets our people grow and thrive, and the analytic power to help them figure out how to best do that.

That leads us to overall **employee experience**. How are we looking at the experiences our people have on their talent management journeys? Having that positive experience—in the case of our high-performing team, making them feel engaged, valued, supported, and in many cases challenged— provides the support and encouragement they need to take more risks, think creatively, and pursue new ideas. Add to that communication, check-ins, and feedback so that people have the opportunity to learn from failures in a supportive environment, and you reinforce trust and therefore the support needed to continue to learn and strive.[14]

We've talked about how to assess engagement and motivation, manage different thought and work styles, and balance the needs of the high-powered individual against the needs of the team, bringing all of these things together and directing them toward organizational goals. All of these things come together to form positive elements of your employee experience.

The link between positive employee experience and **organizational innovation** is undeniable. Engaged and satisfied employees are both comfortable with and challenged to break out of the status quo, drive needed changes and improvements, experiment, take risks, discover new things, and create value. They give you the ability to adapt quickly and innovate continuously, which as we've discussed, is not just an advantage, but a necessity for survival and growth.

We see these three factors—data-driven talent management, employee experience, and organizational innovation—come together powerfully in many of the most creative, adaptive, and successful companies out there. Google, Adobe, Pixar, Autodesk, and more all blend data-driven insights into talent management, progressing through the cultivation of a rich employee experience, and culminating in that culture we're striving for of creativity, curiosity, innovation, and growth. You might point out that these are all technology companies that were grown on or thrive on analytics, but that's not a reason for a less technologically mature company to not invest in data and analytics. If anything, it's a push for all of us to improve our capabilities in that space. There is no magic space where we can stop growing or innovating, because those technologically mature companies? They might have a good thing going, but you can bet they're not going to stop growing or innovating anytime soon.

So let's talk about the dual role you have as a leader in cultivating innovation in your organization.

In many circles, innovation is seen as a venture capitalist's game. Think about *Shark Tank* as an example. The popular television show was a scaled version of the venture capital process, featuring entrepreneurs who pitched their business idea to a panel of potential investors who then decided whether to invest in those ventures in exchange for equity.[15] While many people dream of being the entrepreneur who gets to bring their idea to the Shark Tank for evaluation and potential funding, as leaders, I need you to think about a different role.

As the leader, you need to be the shark—at least for half of the time. You're the one reviewing new ideas and projects and deciding whether to invest. The rest of the time? You might be less familiar with this concept, but you're the angel investor.[16]

Angel investors have been around as a concept and a name for a long time, from patron donors of the arts to supporters of various causes around the world, but in the case of entrepreneurships and start-ups, an angel investor gets involved in a company when it's just starting out, providing support when it's at its seed phase, rather than waiting for the proof of concept like most venture capital firms would.

Another critical difference between angel investors and venture capitalists? Even if they're in the arrangement for a share of equity, angel investors tend to invest their own money.

So think of yourself, with your innovative and creative team, as a cross between the shark who has to be the good steward of time and resources, and evaluate which initiatives are ready for prime time, and the angel investor. You're critical, but you're also in with your team from the start. And even if you're not investing your own money, you're investing your own time and reputation in helping that team get their ideas off the ground.

The whole conceit here is that to enable your teams to innovate and thrive, you have to balance your role. Sometimes you get to be the person providing the seed money for that new idea right from the beginning. And other times, you have to be the person evaluating whether or not the investment is going to pay.

Implementing Strategies for Success in Innovation

Okay, so now we've got a pretty good idea how to get to that culture of innovation we want. How do we make sure it's successful and how do we keep it going?

I want to dig deeply into innovation as a business process, but that could be a whole other book by itself! So for right now, let's take a look at how we take innovation and embed it into the fabric of your organization, from leadership practices and business structures to employee engagement and resourcing. Let me share a framework I'm working on as I build innovation organizations for the U.S. Army that you can use to do the same.

Step 1. Leadership commitment. Some argue that innovation is a top-down initiative, and I think that misses the mark. Innovation must be *supported* from the top if it is going to work, however, and leaders need to be committed. Without that commitment, your best idea generators—those talented teams we've been working so hard to produce—won't be able to get their ideas into prototypes that can be built, experimented with, reviewed, and scaled. From the start, get your leadership committed to fostering innovation and incorporate it into your vision.

Step 2. Diversify your risk portfolio. Think about risk like you would think about an investment portfolio. Not everything you do has to be new, innovative, and risky. An advisor would pull you back if you wanted to throw everything you had in risky futures, or if you wanted to just take it to Las Vegas and put it all on red. At the same time, that same financial advisor would probably prod you to take more risk if you have everything in safe and boring bonds or CDs that accrue a minimal amount of growth. Create a balance of steady predictable risk and experiments, and encourage your people to see it as an investment.

Step 3. Figure out your innovation structure. Isn't that a contradiction in terms? Do we want to structure something that is based on creativity? The answer to this is yes. While you want your ideas to be freeform, you need to have a business process that takes them from submission, through evaluation and experimentation, and into implementation. This helps you take creativity from ideas into tangible outcomes.

Figure 12.1 is the innovation business process my team has developed and used since 2022 with a significant amount of success. Our process begins with the submission of an idea, and immediately we value whether or not it is something **novel** (new and significantly different from other solutions we've evaluated before) or if it's something that is **process improvement.** Are we at 10 percent or are we at 10x? That starts the pipeline.

From there, if we do have a novel solution that needs to be developed and tested, we work the problem statement we're going to evaluate and, when possible, develop a portfolio of solutions that we can test. While we're at that, we figure out who is going to own the solution once we have it built,

FIGURE 12.1 Innovation as a Business Process

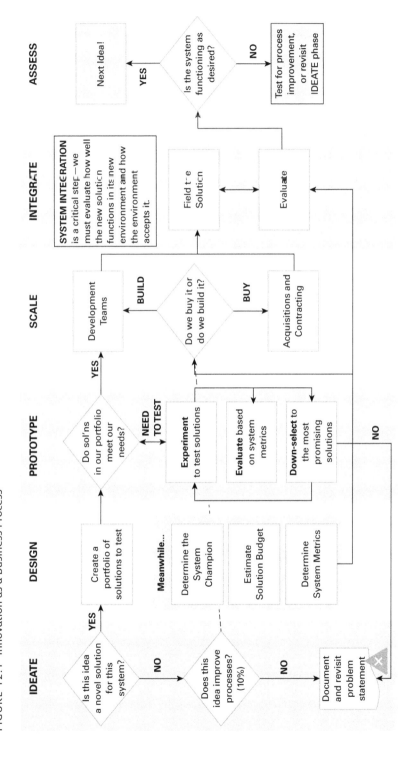

so we can start working on governance processes, budget, and how to measure its effectiveness. Then we build prototypes that we can experiment with (and sometimes we build a prototype that works well enough that we can start work immediately on scaling it), and conduct experiments. We evaluate the solution based on the metrics we developed, figure out which ones best meet our needs, down-select the others, and, sadly, sometimes go back to the drawing board because they don't work.

Fortunately, if we're successful, we can begin to plan how we scale the solution. Do we buy it or do we build it? Can we build it ourselves, or do we need to bring in outside help? How much of the solution do we want to field at a time (and how much do resources allow us to field)? From there, we work on integrating the solution into our business ecosystem, and continuously evaluate both how the solution is doing (is it performing as planned) and the business system (what kind of impact has the solution had on the system)?

Did it work? Is the system responding? Great! Then it's time for the next idea!

This particular method has worked well for us for several reasons. For one, it allows us to put the concept of executing ideas, some of them risky, into a disciplined testing process to make our leaders more comfortable with their execution. For another, it gives us a means of developing an idea well enough to really test while we simultaneously work with stakeholders to figure out who needs to evaluate it, who needs to own it, and who is going to fund it. The worst thing you can do is fund an innovative idea all the way to prototyping and testing and have it fail because no one has the resources or the people to manage it from there. Our method lets you generate buy-in and resources early on in case you achieve success with one or more of your experiments, and have a solid landing place on the other side of your experiment so that you can grow and nurture your idea into integration.

Clearly, after all my emphasis on unique understanding of capabilities in this book, I'm not going to tell you there's a one-size-fits-all strategy for success in innovation. This framework should give you enough freedom to tailor it to align with your business processes, your culture, and your specific goals. And if you need help thinking that through, that's why you're building those talented and creative teams.

It's even something you can experiment and innovate with.

Chapter Summary

This brings us full circle on our journey! We began by looking at what makes up a high-performing team and how that team is not one-size-fits-all. This led us to explore uniqueness and talent through data concepts, and propose a framework for how we can build talented teams. We then talked about what kind of an environment we need to create for those teams to thrive in, and how creativity drives innovation, and talent drives creativity. We covered the fundamentals of data and analytics, took a quick journey into how each of the types of analytics can be built and used, and touched on the applications of artificial intelligence, to build our toolkit for thinking about data-driven talent management.

From there, we delved into what talent management is, and why we need this concept to help us work with and incorporate unique people with unique abilities. We talked about the different types of talent data that can help us understand our people, the challenges inherent to collecting and using that data, and how we can help ourselves better communicate talent by creating a common language and framework. We then fit that to data, looking at how we could use data—and collect data through assessments—to understand competencies, and use data—and collect data through KPIs—on performance and motivation. Through this, we discussed how we could use this robust collection of data to start seeing ourselves and our people as unique and talented individuals.

We talked about how to develop the workforce over time and create an ecosystem of growth and learning. From there, we took a look at different thought and work styles, and started talking about how to bring these talented teams together. We challenged ourselves to think about the complex and dynamic systems we create when we bring these teams together, and how we monitor team dynamics and balance the needs of individuals while aligning everyone on a common goal, conducting all our different instruments together like a symphony.

Finally, we took a look at how to anchor positive change and create a thriving, innovative organization—and we even talked a little about how to develop innovation as a business process in your organization.

I'm hopeful that this book helps you think about how to empower and engage your talent and create that thriving culture of innovation, and that you recognize the number of different great ideas that can come from all over your organization. In this dynamic, ambiguous, and ever-changing future of ours, the organizations that thrive are the ones that are going to learn to adapt, create, and innovate, and they will do that not just through the power of data, but by understanding that data fuels a deep understanding of people, of their unique capabilities, what motivates them, and how they work and learn and grow. The organization that harnesses that power is the one that can not only adapt to change, but drive it, shaping the future of our various industries, and setting new benchmarks for what is possible.

That's an exciting future for us, and an exciting future for talent.

Notes

1   Steve Jobs, "Innovation," Pass It On, www.passiton.com/inspirational-quotes/8196-innovation-is-the-ability-to-see-change-as-an (archived at https://perma.cc/JWM6-M6NX)

2   Jacob Morgan (2017) *The Employee Experience Advantage: How to win the war for talent by giving employees the workspaces they want, the tools they need, and a culture they can celebrate*, Wiley

3   Anne Marie Lee (2024) "Glassdoor Unveils the Best Places to Work in 2024," CBS News, www.cbsnews.com/news/glassdoor-best-places-to-work-2024-top-10-employers/ (archived at https://perma.cc/Y823-P6EZ)

4   Gail T. Fairhurst (2010) *The Power of Framing: Creating the language of leadership*, 2d ed., Wiley

5   Jackie Wattles (2023) "Was the SpaceX Launch Really a Success?" CNN, https://edition.cnn.com/2023/04/21/world/spacex-starship-explosion-success-failure-scn/index.html (archived at https://perma.cc/C2YX-UT82)

6   Thomas Edison Quotes (nd) Edison Innovation Foundation, www.thomasedison.org/edison-quotes (archived at https://perma.cc/X9DA-VFZN)

7   Chris Coldwell (2022) "Why Failure Is a Necessary Part of the Innovation Process," Forbes, www.forbes.com/sites/forbesbusinesscouncil/2022/11/04/why-failure-is-a-necessary-part-of-the-innovation-process/?sh=27a1d0103ff7 (archived at https://perma.cc/FLV8-XMR8)

8   Meg Selig (2012) "The Amazing Power of 'Small Wins,'" Psychology Today, www.psychologytoday.com/us/blog/changepower/201207/the-amazing-power-small-wins (archived at https://perma.cc/ZU58-XNDD)

9   Marc Benioff (2019) *Trailblazer: The power of business as the greatest platform for change*, Crown Currency

10 Charlotte Nickerson (2023) "Positive Reinforcement: What Is it and How Does it Work?" Simply Psychology, www.simplypsychology.org/positive-reinforcement.html (archived at https://perma.cc/8DFS-KYNT)

11 David Burkus (2016) "How Adobe Scrapped Its Performance Review System and Why It Worked," Forbes, www.forbes.com/sites/davidburkus/2016/06/01/ how-adobe-scrapped-its-performance-review-system-and-why-it-worked/? sh=6962bfa155e8 (archived at https://perma.cc/C94J-8FU2)

12 Laszlo Bock (2015) *Work Rules! Insights from inside Google that will transform how you live and lead*, Twelve

13 John Quinn (2023) "A Look at Google's Peer-to-Peer Bonus System," Bonusly, https://bonusly.com/post/a-look-at-googles-peer-to-peer-bonus-system (archived at https://perma.cc/HH5L-P6W6)

14 Ed Catmull and Amy Wallace (2014) *Creativity, Inc.: Overcoming the unseen forces that stand in the way of true inspiration*, Random House

15 E. Molick (2016) "The Dynamics of Crowdfunding: An Exploratory Study," *Journal of Business Venturing*, 29 (1)

16 Brian O'Connell and Benjamin Curry (2022) "What Are Angel Investors?" Forbes, www.forbes.com/advisor/investing/what-are-angel-investors/ (archived at https://perma.cc/B8Z6-UEG9)

13

The Future of Talent Management

There was an idea, Stark knows this, called the Avenger Initiative. The idea was to bring together a group of remarkable people, to see if they could become something more. See if they could work together when we needed them to fight the battles that we never could.

NICK FURY, *THE AVENGERS*[1]

Trends in Data-Driven Talent Management

Depending on where your organization is in your data and analytics maturity journey, some of the things I've put in this book might seem like a far-off future. The exciting and terrifying thing is, though, that in some organizations, these are commonplace. I'm a practitioner and not a researcher. This book came together from piles and piles of research and reading I've done since I first entered the U.S. Army's people enterprise in 2016 to figure out better ways of doing business. I haven't been doing cutting-edge research or analytic development during this time; I've simply been trying to find people and companies with best practices and new tools that I can experiment with and bring back as solutions to help my commands solve problems.

So let's spend a little bit of time talking about the future, and where all this is headed! Again, I warn you, I'm a practitioner, not a researcher, so I'm not working in the technology space bringing all of these things to fruition. I am, however, a data analyst, so I want to identify some top trends I'm seeing in this space as I continue to dig into it, and pose a few ideas about where these might go.

If you're willing to come with me on a journey into the potential not-so-far-off future of talent management and human resources, let's go!

Trend #1. An Explosion of Artificial Intelligence and Machine Learning

AI and machine learning are already becoming standard tools for use in human resources. However, as we're able to feed intelligent models with more and more data and get more people fine-tuning them through intelligent interfaces, they will only keep growing in use and importance, and continue to transform how we manage and develop our talent.

Recruiting and hiring. We're already using AI to automate tasks like resumé screening (although a lot of these algorithms could use improvement) and initial candidate evaluation. Organizations are deploying interactive chatbots to help talk prospective employees through the hiring process and help them fill out and adjust forms. Companies are also taking in data to predict candidate success and goodness of fit within the company.

Personalized development. AI-driven platforms are already deployed to develop personalized learning and adaptive learning programs. These platforms look at individual performance data and create appropriately leveled training programs, improving the employee's learning experience.

Employee experience. AI will process and interpret vast amounts of EX data, enabling more nuanced insights and more actionable recommendations for how to engage with our employees and shape their experience.

Predicting retention and turnover. Machine learning algorithms are much more accurate at predicting employee turnover, down to the individual level. These algorithms help companies create targeted retention strategies. We are using our algorithms to test the effectiveness of retention incentives based on seeing if we can change the behavior of those who are likely to leave with different incentives to a statistically significant degree.

Performance management and feedback. AI systems can provide continuous feedback and insights about employee performance. We can use this to move emphasis away from annual performance reviews and instead hold ongoing performance conversations. Through check-ins and goal tracking, we can make our performance management processes more dynamic and effective.

Trend #2. Enhanced Metrics and Collection Processes for Employee Experience

Over the next decade, as we continue to observe and leverage the impact of EX on business performance, we are only going to see the importance of experience grow. Methods of collection and shaping will become more sophisticated.

Comprehensive EX metrics. The more we learn about the employee journey, the more we're able to learn where we can collect data. Future EX metrics may go well beyond surveys and feedback, and pull sentiment from anywhere a person engages, including social media. We may see warnings that we are being recorded for quality assurance in many more new and surprising places, which may in turn lead to privacy concerns and controls.

Predictive EX. Predictive analytics will become more prevalent in how we interpret and use EX data. Well-constructed models in this space will allow our organizations to anticipate and address potential issues before they escalate, and we will need to think through the tools and training we want to give our managers on how to effectively use that data.

Personalization. Enhanced EX metrics will naturally facilitate more personalized talent management experiences, allowing us to better understand the experiences, preferences, and motivations of each of our people. These will shape how we offer career development opportunities, learning and training opportunities, and wellness initiatives.

Focus on well-being. We're seeing increasing emphasis on employee well-being metrics, and the more we're able to monitor the impact of well-being on experience, we will increase our focus accordingly. Work-life alignment, mental health, and culture are already being measured more broadly, and this will continue to grow. We will see more human performance centers of excellence developing and leveraged to explore this data and make recommendations.

Ethical considerations. Whenever we bring together large amounts of personal data, ethical considerations regarding privacy and sensitivity of data use will increase. As we must in any organization where we collect and use large amounts of personal data, we will need to develop and employ ethical review bodies to ensure we balance our need for detailed insights against employee privacy rights, and that we commit to transparency and consent.

Trend #3. More Software, Less Hardware

We have already seen a significant shift from standard on-premises systems to the use of the cloud, and the digital sharing economy is booming—almost anything you can imagine is offered in the X-as-a-service frame. This is impacting and will continue to impact our data-driven talent management processes. With a move toward software-dominant infrastructure, we'll increasingly look for systems that are flexible, scalable, and easy to integrate. Software-as-a-service (SaaS) platforms will become commonplace and dramatically reduce the need for investment in hardware. As we run analytics less on our own machines and more in the cloud, computers as we know it will change dramatically, and we will invest much less in hardware and more in network bandwidth, cyber security, and zero trust protocols. Here's a little of what we'll see.

Increased accessibility and adaptability. Software-centric systems facilitate access regardless of location, and will support organizations looking to become more distributed and support global talent management. This allows organizations to fish in broader talent pools and effectively support teams distributed widely across geographic regions.

Data security and privacy. With the increased reliance on software and cloud, and less on on-prem systems, organizations will have to invest more time, talent, and resources into understanding and protecting these systems. We'll have to devote significant effort to cyber-protection efforts and to data governance and protection to ensure we comply with regulations. Regulations themselves will have to adapt significantly. Many laws and statutes for the protection of personal information have not been updated, and the processes they require are no longer suitable for the types of systems we must protect.

More integration and less customization. Organizations will no longer have the luxury of taking time to create personalized and customized management systems. SaaS solutions will push updates and create integrations, and in order to shape those, we will need to push data on system performance, requirements, and requests for improvement to the provider, creating new concerns for data security and data governance.

Trend #4. Virtual Teammates

Over the next decade, we can expect to see the number of virtual agents providing assistance increase dramatically. This will include virtual agent "teammates," and require an increase in human-machine teaming in the workplace. As we see the continued digitization and automation of manual work processes, it will fundamentally change the way we work in the office.

Virtual agents. Virtual agents will continue to grow more and more sophisticated, and be able to handle a wide variety of tasks for their human partners. Some organizations are already able to use them to schedule meetings, take questions, and answer calls, and this will only increase. We will need to shift our focus and training to see machines not just as tools but as supporting team members, working alongside us.

Workforce skill shift. The integration of human-machine teaming will force us to relook at how our workforce works. What kinds of skills do we need to effectively collaborate and communicate with machines? We've seen the advent of "prompt engineers" rising to help people better interact with generative AI systems, so there may be equivalent skillsets emerging to help people better understand and work with their synthetic teammates.

Redefined job roles. As routine tasks become automated, employees will be freed up to focus on different types of work. This is likely to happen faster over time, so workforce development plans accounting for this are essential. Because we are likely to have work roles and areas of expertise shifting so quickly, we need to think about the foundational value of education programs, how quickly skills either decay or become obsolete, and how we inject new knowledge and skills into our population.

Bias mitigation. An unfortunate number of people assume that when you bring a machine into the mix, you will mitigate bias. Not so: Machines are programmed by humans who have biases, and they may also learn them from the information they are fed. Quality control systems and methods to ensure biases are removed or adjusted from our AI tools will become increasingly important, and we may see full-time "ethics engineers" employed.

Trend #5. Soft Skills and "People" People

Somewhat paradoxically, as we see technological advancement continue, we will also see a growing emphasis on soft skills in the talent management and human resources space. While technical skills are crucial, emotional intelligence, adaptability, collaboration, and creativity are essential for the modern workplace—perhaps more than ever because these are things machines don't know how to duplicate. As automation and AI handle more routine tasks, those with the necessary soft skills are freed up to navigate complex team dynamics, drive innovation, and lead.

Redefining recruitment criteria. Organizations will increasingly develop and field tests for soft skills in their hiring process. AI and analytic tools to identify and assess these characteristics will continue to develop, and with more candidates than human hiring managers can handle, we'll rely on these to conduct detailed pre-interview screening.

Leadership development focus. Leadership training programs will focus on leaders' ability to inspire, motivate, and connect with their teams, as these skills will become increasingly important in driving engagement and success. Data and analytics can be used to gauge their effectiveness, and the health of workplace dynamics.

Trend #6. Intelligent Learning and Development

The next decade should be truly transformative in how we look at learning and development systems and how we augment them with data, analytics, and AI. Intelligent learning systems are already offering customized learning experiences to employees, and these systems will only grow in sophistication. They will learn to analyze and respond to individual learning styles, performance data, and career goals.

Continuous skill development. As fast as technology is changing things and as quickly as skills become obsolete, organizations must consider how to prioritize and field continuous skill development strategies and programs. Intelligent learning programs can provide ongoing learning opportunities while externally focused analytic systems report emerging trends from the field. Learning and development professionals will have to have robust analytic teams to monitor and conduct quality control on these systems.

Integrating learning and development with talent acquisition. The insights we gain from intelligent learning systems can inform our recruitment strategies. Understanding the skills available and the learning potential of the individual at the time of hire can help us understand the full potential of the employee and where development can be applied or hiring is needed.

Measuring ROI of learning and development initiatives. With more advanced applied analytics, organizations will be better able to measure the ROI of their development initiatives in terms of performance, productivity, innovation, retention, experience, and job satisfaction.

Trend #7. More Things Become Smarter

The past two decades have seen a proliferation of smart devices in our lives. We will continue to see that increase and see more smart devices integrated into the workplace, leading to an increased presence of connection, which comes with a host of different perks, challenges, and ethical concerns. From smart wearables tracking wellness to virtual agents, these can have significant implications for how you manage and engage your workforce.

Enhanced wellness programs. Smart wearables already monitor vital health metrics, and we will just see the use of these increasing. If individuals share those, you can use them to tailor wellness programs, reduce stress in the workplace, and provide incentives and motivation to promote healthier lifestyles. This can lead to increased productivity and better experience, but it can also feel invasive if not done properly.

Data-driven workplace optimization. How are the lights and the sound level? Should that window shade be open or closed? Smart sensors in the workplace can collect data on how we use and enjoy different spaces. This can help with everything from optimizing office layouts for utilization and productivity to automatically adjusting the work environment to preference.

Smart learning and development tools. The use of smart devices in learning and training can lead to more immersive experiences. Virtual reality, augmented reality, and extended reality are already terms used frequently in this space, and we will just see the ability and sophistication of training applications in these environments increase.

Challenges in data privacy, security, and safety. The more connected we are, the more information we share, the more we have to think about who's using it, for what purpose, and demonstrate transparency to foster trust. Protecting employee data will become ever more critical and important.

Trend #8. Quantum Leaps

Over the next decade, we're going to witness groundbreaking advances in quantum computing. Even in a fairly nascent stage, quantum computing is fundamentally changing the way we think about optimization and encryption. With its ability to both produce and crack complex datasets at incredible speed, it will bring changes across dozens of fields, including human resources and talent management.

Advanced predictive analytics. Quantum computing will revolutionize how we can look at patterns of health, behavior, productivity, and workforce needs with much larger datasets than ever before.

Complex scenario modeling. Strategic workforce planning, demand forecasting, succession planning, and talent mobility could all be revolutionized by this kind of computing power.

Real-time HR decision making. Real-time data processing could allow for immediate adjustments to strategies, policies, platforms, and processes in response to emerging trends or issues, with the ability to overlay those with scenario modeling.

Technical and ethical challenges. The integration of quantum computing comes with a lot of challenges, not least the talent needed to understand it, operate it, run it, and run quality control and ethics checks. Data integration and system compatibility are other significant challenges.

I Still Believe in Heroes

We've talked a lot about the future of technology and its contributions to transforming talent management from a routine human resource function into a mission to assemble teams as extraordinary as the Avengers, or James Bond's support team in Q's lab, or the X-Men, or the heroic crew that led the charge in every story that ever inspired you. Don't pull back from that dream of leading a story-worthy team, because we've talked about all the means and methods to create, develop, and employ that team. And we've talked about how we can use data and data analytics techniques to guide our quest.

There's a lot of technology in this story, but fundamentally, this story is still about people. For us, technology is the vehicle to get us closer to harnessing the extraordinary potential within each individual. The core essence of innovation and adaptation, of learning and growth, of surviving and thriving, is the human element. Our process here is about elevating, not replacing, the human experience at work.

As we continue to work toward a future of incredible technological advances and new ideas, I want to remember Nick Fury's unwavering faith in the Avengers, that despite everything he'd seen, he still believed in heroes. It should remind us that at the heart of every dataset, analytics tool, and algorithm, you find people—the people made of all the bits and pieces of data that feed them and the people that create those amazing tools for us to use. Even as we advance, the future of our organizations will still be driven by the human spirit, augmented by data, aided by AI, supported by leadership and culture.

And it won't be how many of them, but who.

Note

1 Joss Whedon, dir. (2012) *The Avengers*, Marvel Studios, information available at www.imdb.com/title/tt0848228/ (archived at https://perma.cc/ZUQ8-LN4X)

INDEX

Page numbers in *italic* denote figures or tables.

Looking for another book?

Explore our award-winning books from global business experts in Human Resources, Learning and Development

Scan the code to browse

www.koganpage.com/hr-learning-development

More data titles from Kogan Page

ISBN: 9781398614567

ISBN: 9781398610828

ISBN: 9781398610040

www.koganpage.com